Epworth (

General Editor
Ivor H. Jones

The Apocrypha

THE APOCRYPHA

IVOR H. JONES

EPWORTH PRESS

British Library Cataloguing in Publication data

A catalogue record for this book is available
from the British Library

0 7162 0572 6

First published in 2003
by Epworth Press
4 John Wesley Road
Werrington
Peterborough PE4 6ZP

Typeset by Regent Typesetting, London
Printed and bound in Great Britain by
Biddles Ltd, www.biddles.co.uk

CONTENTS

v

GENERAL INTRODUCTION

The *Epworth Preacher's Commentaries* that Greville P. Lewis edited so successfully in the 1950s and 1960s having now served their turn, the Epworth Press has commissioned a team of distinguished academics who are also preachers and teachers to create a new series of commentaries that will serve readers into the twenty-first century. We have taken the opportunity offered by the publication in 1989 of the Revised English Bible to use this very readable and scholarly version as the basis of our commentaries, and we are grateful to the Oxford and Cambridge University Presses for the requisite licence and for granting our authors generous access. They will nevertheless be free to cite and discuss other translations wherever they think that these will illuminate the original text.

Just as the books that make up the Bible differ in their provenance and purpose, so our authors will necessarily differ in the structure and bearing of their commentaries. But they will all strive to get as close as possible to the intention of the original writers, expounding their texts in the light of the place, time, circumstances, and culture that gave them birth, and showing why each work was received by Jews and Christians into their respective Canons of Holy Scripture. They will seek to make full use of the dramatic advance in biblical scholarship world-wide but at the same time to explain technical terms in the language of the common reader, and to suggest ways in which Scripture can help towards the living of a Christian life today. They will endeavour to produce commentaries that can be used with confidence in ecumenical, multiracial and multifaith situations, and not by scholars only but by preachers, teachers, students, church members, and anyone who wants to improve his or her understanding of the Bible.

Ivor H. Jones

PREFACE

This commentary began its life as a set of popular notes on the Apocrypha written at the invitation of *The Methodist Recorder*. The interest aroused by that series suggested that the possibility of a more extended commentary should be explored. The Epworth Press Editorial Committee took up the idea and commissioned an Apocrypha volume for the *Epworth Commentaries* series additional to those already planned.

Such an addition is appropriate in that the Revised English Bible, which has served as a basis for the commentary series, contains a form of the Apocrypha, and both the presence of the Apocrypha in the Revised English Bible and the new translation of the Apocryphal books there deserve attention and comment. The Introduction to this commentary and the commentary itself provide a brief exploration of reasons for the inclusion of the Apocrypha in a modern Bible, and of the texts chosen and the translations offered.

It was a particular delight to take up the discussion of the Apocrypha, since the first Principal of Wesley House, Cambridge, made a substantial contribution to the study of the ethics of the Apocryphal books, and wrote a number of significant articles devoted to that area. That particular period in the history of Cambridge biblical studies proved to be a significant one in the translation and study of the Apocryphal books, and it is impossible to overestimate the importance of the work which was done then. As one who owes that tradition of scholarly work, both in Wesley House and in the Cambridge Faculty of Divinity, an incalculable debt, the opportunity to contribute a commentary on the whole Apocrypha comes as a singular honour and a major challenge. Since every single book of the Apocrypha and the history of the Apocrypha itself have been covered by many monographs and commentaries, it would seem almost an impertinence to attempt a single-volume commentary on what amounts to a library of books, particularly when this series has on the whole devoted a whole volume to each of the other biblical books in turn. The massive work which has been done on the Apocrypha in the past and the present mounting interest in that literature constitute a powerful argument for attempting the task, although important decisions have had to be made to complete the task. A volume of this size could hardly contain just a short bibliography for the Apocrypha, let alone a verse by verse commentary on so many chapters. Indeed, the fact that two hundred pages of the text of the Apocrypha have to be covered has made it necessary to choose between an adequate commentary without a bibliography and a considerably curtailed commentary with an appropriate and balanced bibliography. In view of the purpose of this commentary series I have chosen the former alternative. But that means that I must apologise to all the scholars with whose work I have engaged, and express my deep indebtedness to them for their work, without which my own reading of the texts would have been immeasurably poorer.

The commentary could also be seen as a small tribute to the work of all the various scholars and students who lived and worked in Wesley House, Roman Catholic, Orthodox and especially the Jewish–Christian Centre which began its life at Wesley House and has already done so much to stimulate the study of Jewish literature. My admiration for their energy and enthusiasm is unbounded. Out of courtesy to them, since this is a commentary on Jewish literature, there is one feature of the commentary which may initially cause surprise. Instead of BC (Before Christ) and AD (Anno Domini, in the year of our Lord) the reader will find that years and centuries are registered using BCE (Before the Common Era) and CE (Common Era). That feature is a mark of courtesy; it also underlines the important fact that, if literature is best regarded as a communicative text, then the Apocrypha should primarily be read in terms of its original setting in Jewish history wherever that is relevant. Since one of the arguments of this book is that to read the Apocrypha in terms of its Jewish history is to release it from some of the polemics of more recent years, that single small feature may be a reminder of the commentary's basic perspective. A communicative text is of course open to any reader's interpretation, and that will enable the Christian reader to suggest other contexts for the text's exploration. But the source of a communicative text can itself be a refreshing area of research. So, although it is never easy to decide between the two alternatives BC/AD or BCE/CE, in the case of this particular commentary to use the latter seems right and in keeping with the general purpose of the volume.

Many individuals, libraries and conferences have helped me on my way. I must express particular thanks to all who contributed to the

Second East–West Conference, 'The Old Testament as a Christian Bible', which was sponsored by the Theological Faculty of the University of Sophia 'St Kliment Ochridski' and held in the Monastery of Rila in 2001, and also to the Oxford/Bonn Symposium on 'The Unity of Scripture and the Diversity of the Canon'. To the Revd Dr Cyril Rodd I must express my personal thanks for reading through the entire text, for his scholarly detailed comments which have caused me to go back to the text and to my own work on the text with fresh eyes, and for his friendship and encouragement over many years. To all these, and to all who have taught me so much about the Apocrypha I wish to express my personal appreciation.

Finally any gratitude is due to the SCM editorial manager Alex Knights and all his colleagues for their expert work in the preparation of the text for printing and to all who have seen the book through to its publication.

Ivor H. Jones
Lent, 2003

INTRODUCTION

This introduction deals with what the Apocrypha is (Section A), what the word Apocrypha means (Section B), and ways of approaching the Apocrypha (Section C).

A. The Apocrypha: what is it?

At the time of the German Reformation issues concerning certain Jewish books were brought to a crucial point of decision: they were gathered together and given the name Apocrypha. Although the word Apocrypha had been used many centuries earlier, from that moment Apocrypha became a Protestant term, over against Roman Catholic and Eastern Orthodox usage. So the presence or absence of the Apocrypha is one way in which Bibles today may differ.

In 1967, the anniversary of Luther's posting of his 95 Theses (and 1967 belonged to the days when ministerial training had time to explore church history!), those of us who were working in the Bishop's Hostel, Lincoln, staged a dramatic, unscripted reconstruction of that Reformation event. Such unscripted drama can be an exciting learning experience, and that occasion certainly was. Among the illuminating moments in that reconstruction was one particular confrontation between Martin Luther and an interrogator (representing Johann Eck). The question concerned the evidence for justification by faith: what, asked Luther's interrogator, had Luther to say about 2 Maccabees 12 on purgatory and 2 Esdras 8.33 and its stress on salvation by good works? As we shall see, a modern response to that challenge will be very different from the response given in that historical reconstruction; but Luther's answer in that drama, as no doubt in real life, followed a particular line of argument; and that line of argument required the existence of the Apocrypha. 2 Maccabees, the actor said (on Luther's behalf), was not to be found in the Hebrew Bible – it was only to be found in the Greek Version of the Old Testament; and portions of the Greek Version of the Old Testament such as 2 Maccabees had not been wholeheartedly endorsed by all the Church Fathers. So 2 Maccabees could only be regarded as 'useful and good to read'; it could not be made a basis for doctrine.

A modern response to the interrogator's challenge would be very different from the response given in that historical reconstruction. A modern response would probably run as follows: the interrogator's questions take the passage from 2 Maccabees out of its original context; they submit the ancient text to terminology which the author would not have recognized. Whether a modern response would have invoked the status of the Apocrypha at all is very doubtful.

Nevertheless, none of us who participated in that drama will ever forget the genuinely historical point that was made. Luther, at the time of the posting of the 95 Theses, was working towards the creation of an Apocrypha. He had available to him (in addition to the Latin translation – the Vulgate) two forms of the Old Testament, the Hebrew form and the Greek form (the Greek translation we can refer to for the moment in general terms as the Septuagint, which Luther had available to him in its 1519 Aldine edition). Those two forms of the Old Testament differed in three ways: *textually* (sometimes the Septuagint was not a translation of the original Hebrew), in *content* (some books or parts of books were found in the Septuagint and not in the Hebrew). and in *order* (the two forms of the text differed in the way they were organized). Luther took the view (which some Fathers of the Church had taken before him) that the Hebrew Bible was the older and therefore should be followed in text and in content. The contents which were special to the Greek translation of the Old Testament should, he decided after careful study of them, be separated off from the main body of the Old Testament and made into a separate unit; and he planned to publish those portions, the portions not found in the Hebrew Bible, as a separate part of the Bible, as the Apocrypha.

Luther was by no means uninterested in these books. In no way did he neglect them, even though he gave them a lower status and placed them in a section by themselves. In 1529 he completed his translation of the Wisdom of Solomon. In 1532 he was working with Philip Melanchthon and Caspar Cruciger on a German version of the book of Sirach. In 1533, despite his own poor health, he made sure that the translation of 1 and 2 Maccabees was done by Melanchthon, and that of Tobit by Justus Jonas. By 1534 he had ensured, step by step, that the entire Bible, the so-called Wittenberg Bible – Apocrypha and all – had been translated. There had been a parallel venture in Zurich led by a little-known German translator called Leo Jud, who in a 1530 reprint used the title 'Apocryphi'; so actually the honour of being the first of the German translators to use the name should go to Jud. It was, however, the first edition of Luther's complete German Bible, published in Wittenberg in the autumn of 1534, which was the one that had the lasting impact. The Wittenberg Bible had six parts, and the fifth part bore the following text:

> Apocrypha, that is, books which are not held as equal to holy Scripture, yet which are useful and good to read:
> 1. Judith.
> 2. Wisdom.
> 3. Tobit.
> 4. Sirach.
> 5. Baruch.
> 6. Maccabees.
> 7. Parts of Esther.
> Parts of Daniel.

Four points about the Apocrypha in the Wittenberg Bible:

1. Luther's judgement that these books were *useful and good to read* can be illustrated from his comments on the Wisdom of Solomon. This book, he maintained, should be read by the rulers of the world; the author shows well that worldly authorities have their power from God and that those who fill such a divinely appointed office should not do so tyrannically. Moreover, Luther argued, that book is a good exposition of the first commandment, that God is One, the Creator and Deliverer, and we must love the Lord our God with all our heart and with all our soul and with all our strength. That second argument remains powerful today; it remains, as it was for Paul the Apostle himself, a key for Jew and Christian alike.

2. Luther's list of books is different from the one we shall be using. Ours is the list chosen by the editors of the Revised English Bible (REB). It is different because (i) some of the books have alternative titles (Luther chose one title; the REB editors another); and (ii) Luther came to different conclusions from the REB editors: there were books which he did not like or thought to be dangerous, so he left them out, whereas the REB editors kept them in.

3. Luther's Apocrypha was therefore the result of a *series of important decisions* which he made personally as a Reformer: (i) to separate certain books out because they were 'Greek' and not 'Hebrew'; (ii) to

include some because he valued them or had made earlier use of them; (iii) to take up the ancient word 'Apocrypha'; (iv) to place them in a particular order.

4. The books which we have been mentioning so far – Wisdom, Sirach, Maccabees, Tobit, Judith etc. – had been known by Luther from a source other than the Septuagint. He knew them from the Vulgate, the Latin translation; but in the Vulgate they were not grouped together as a separate section, they were interspersed through different parts of the Vulgate Old Testament. It was Luther, as we have seen, who took that particular step of separating them out. In the Vulgate these books were a part of the Old Testament.

Books such as these had been the subject of much debate over many centuries, but they had usually been discussed under different titles. Protestants called them Apocryphal, Roman Catholics called them Deuterocanonical (i.e. later canonical books), and Eastern Orthodox called them Anaginoskomena (i.e. books that are being read).

Sometimes the books were a matter of debate because they were thought to be originally written in Greek. Various early Fathers of the Church had taken the view that the Hebrew Bible, being earlier, had a greater authority; Luther had followed them in this. One of the early Fathers of the Church, *Origen* (the third century CE), illustrates the complexity of the debate. He worked in Caesarea, a city with a large Jewish population where rabbis were skilled in the interpretation of the scripture. Origen took a particular interest in the biblical list of books, treating Jewish testimony on the subject with great seriousness, but also taking seriously, perhaps regarding as of divine origin, books that were used in the Christian community but were not accepted by contemporary Jewish scholars. *Jerome*, a Latin Church Father (the late fourth century CE) expressed a preference for the Hebrew Bible over against the Greek Septuagint; but he was chosen by Pope Damasus in 382 CE to make an authoritative translation of the Bible into Latin (the Vulgate), and that translation has the books known only from Greek texts distributed among all the other books of the Old Testament. *Augustine*, writing a century after Jerome, supported that longer list, inclusive of books known from both Hebrew and Greek texts, and as a result of his influence a majority of Church Fathers, both Greek and Latin, preferred the longer, inclusive list; they stressed the authoritative status of the wider collection.

So when Luther developed his Apocrypha the debate concerning the contents of the Old Testament canon (or list of books) was already many centuries old. It was only to be expected therefore that the

Catholic (or Counter) Reformation would also dedicate a major session of the Council of Trent to the subject of the scriptural canon. The result of that session was that in 1546, just fourteen years after Luther published his German Bible and in the very year that he died, the Council of Trent listed the books of the Old Testament canon, making the distinction formalized later in Roman Catholic discussion under the terms 'Protocanonical' and 'Deuterocanonical'. The earlier Hebrew books were called 'Proto-canonical books' (*proto* = first or former); the later books were called 'Deutero-canonical' (*deutero* = second or secondary). The Council of Trent followed their listing of canonical books with the decree: 'If anyone does not accept as sacred and canonical the aforesaid books in their entirety and with all their parts, as they have been accustomed to be read in the Catholic Church . . . let him be anathema.'

The consequence of that sixteenth-century decree is that the list of the Old Testament books and their order in the Bible used by Roman Catholics still follows today that of the Vulgate. Even modern translations such as the New Jerusalem Bible use that list; they include the Deuterocanonical books as part of Old Testament scripture and intersperse them among the other books of the Old Testament. Just as Apocrypha became a Protestant term, Deuterocanonical became the Roman Catholic term.

The Eastern Orthodox canon is less easily defined. Some agreements were reached in the Synod of 691 CE in Troullos and the Seventh Ecumenical Council of 787 CE. But differences within the Orthodox tradition remained, and remained even in the more recent Pan-Orthodox Conferences of 1961 and 1968; they continue unresolved today. In the Orthodox tradition the decision concerns the Anaginoskomena (literally Anaginoskomena means: those books which are read). These include, among others, books called by the Roman Catholic Church Deuterocanonical: Tobit, Judith, Wisdom, Sirach, 1 and 2 Maccabees, the Greek version of Esther, the additions to Daniel, Baruch, the Letter of Jeremiah; they also include books found among the Protestant Apocryphal books: e.g. 1 Esdras (for the precise reference for this book see the commentary on 1 Esdras); they also include books accorded value in the Orthodox tradition such as Psalm 151 (now known to us in a Hebrew text from Qumran and in translated form in the NRSV), Psalm 153, the Odes of Solomon, and the Prayer of Manasseh. The appendices include the Greek of IV Maccabees and the Slavonic version of 2 Esdras. The lists are diverse. The Armenian, Coptic, Syrian and Ethiopic canons are still more so.

In both East and West the doctrine of the Church is not based on these books, whether they are called Apocryphal, Deuterocanonical or Anaginoskomena. But in the Orthodox tradition they play an important role which deserves attention. In the West the reasons or explanations for the canon have been basically fourfold: the *rule of faith*, the *consensus of the faithful*, (in the case of the New Testament writings) *apostolicity*, and the *processes by which they were established* (e.g. decisions of the Councils of the Church such as the Council of Trent). Historically these four were mutually interconnected, mutually dependent and reflected a prior usage of the texts as much as judgements concerning them. But in the Orthodox tradition the idea of the canon is expounded differently from this Western position: the place of *koinonia* (fellowship, communion, community), the place of Tradition (the capital T indicating that it includes faith, life, doctrine and worship), the lex orandi (that the context of Christian life is known primarily in eucharistic worship as the reliable guardianship of the faith), and *theoria* (tracing, in a similar manner to that used by Wesley, the activities of the Spirit in the work of the Antiochene Fathers and their successors, in their sense of the unity of Old and New Testaments, and in the search for a place for literal meaning of the text within the context of interpretation).

This discussion of Apocrypha, Deuterocanonical and Anaginoskomena has practical consequences. It poses a major problem faced by any publisher of the Bible text. Which canon should be used? The British and Foreign Bible Society, when it was founded in 1804, found itself under pressure from 'evangelical' and 'non-conformist groups' to reject Bibles with the Apocrypha; the German Bible societies on the other hand published Bibles with the Apocrypha. The United Bible Societies have had to exercise the greatest care in their publishing policies, and it is only as recently as 1987 that guiding principles were agreed for interconfessional co-operation in this area.

It is worth bringing the subject a little more up the date. So far we have mentioned the Lutheran Reformation and the Roman Catholic response to the Reformation at the Council of Trent. We have not mentioned the Reformed Churches, those which followed the work of Zwingli and Calvin and the Confessions of the sixteenth and seventeenth centuries. These are important, not least because they offer interesting reasons for questioning the use or status of the Apocrypha, reasons which are often repeated today. Zwingli, the Swiss Reformer, comments in the 1531 Zurich Bible that there is much in books such as Wisdom, Ecclesiasticus and Judith, for they tend to piety of life and edification, although *not everything is so excellent and clear as in other biblical books*. Indeed there is much that corresponds to *invented fable* rather than to *genuine truth*. Nevertheless they should be printed so that each may find what is to the particular taste of each; and, as Paul said, we are to 'test everything'. Calvin's views can be divided between his comments before and after the Council of Trent. Before 1546 his concern was primarily with how faith can be certain: how it can be legitimated on the one hand by the public nature of scriptural books (as against the 'private' status of the Apocrypha) and on the other hand by the Spirit's internal testimony. After 1546, as a response to the Council of Trent, Calvin argues differently; he lists his theological objections to the Apocrypha: 2 Maccabees had been used to prove purgatory and the mediation of the saints, Tobit to prove satisfaction for sins and exorcisms, ben Sirach to prove the freedom of the human will. Calvin's main challenge to the Council of Trent was this: he contended that the Councils of the Early Church, from which the Council of Trent drew its authority, had not agreed on the precise content of scripture, and, in any case, scripture *should not be made subject to the judgement of the Church*. Calvin was happy to consider what individual books of the Apocrypha had to say when he was seeking support on matters otherwise attested, matters such as the resurrection of dead and the eternity of the Word. There was little mention of these in the Old Testament, so he was happy to see what the Apocryphal books had to say on them. There was, however, a major problem. In the Preface to the Apocrypha which Calvin provided for the Geneva Bible in 1546 he commented on how difficult to translate the texts of the Apocrypha often prove to be, and he judged that they had been left in a poor state because they had not been treated as fully authoritative books.

When we come to the seventeenth-century decisions of the Reformed Churches we find a much less accepting approach to the Apocrypha. The Congregational Points of Difference in 1603 decreed that the Apocryphal books should not be used in church. The Westminster Confession of 1647 taught that the Apocryphal writings had no more authority than other human writings. The stage had been set for forms of the Bible to be printed which omitted the Apocrypha; and that remains the preference for some churches today.

As far as England was concerned, there was an immediate sequel to Luther's decision on the Apocrypha. Coverdale's translation of the whole Bible drew on several sources, on Luther's German Bible, on the Latin Vulgate, on the Zurich Bible and on Tyndale's work (interrupted by the latter's execution in 1536). In Coverdale's 1535 Preface to the Apocrypha he comments:

> These books (good reader) which be called Apocrypha, are not judged among the doctors to be of like reputation with the other Scripture . . . And the chief cause thereof is this: there be many places in them that seem to be *repugnant unto the open and manifest truth in the other books of the bible.*

But even the phrase 'of like reputation with the other Scripture' could be an implicit admission that the Apocrypha is in some sense scripture. Coverdale had, however, put his finger on the chief problem for his readers: they did not find throughout the Apocryphal books 'the biblical truth' expressed with the clarity they required. Just what 'the biblical truth' might be we must consider later.

A reasonably positive view of the Apocrypha was sustained by the Church of England. According to some of its official documents, the Apocrypha contained examples for Christian living. *The Book of Homilies* (authorized addresses to be read by those not licensed to preach) and *The Book of Common Prayer* confirm that positive view. So, despite the popularity of those forms of the Bible in England which lacked the Apocrypha, the official position as set out in the Thirty-Nine Articles (1562 and 1571) was that the church reads the Apocrypha among its set lessons but does not 'apply them to establish any doctrine'. According to that official position, the King James' Bible of 1611, in every edition for use in parish churches, had to contain the Apocrypha. As set out in the Thirty-Nine Articles that still remains the official position today, despite the many qualifications and criticisms introduced in the intervening years.

The attempts to overturn that official position were many. There were the powerful political events associated with the parliamentary and republican periods of English history; there were the protests of many of the Puritan divines, and of scholars such as John Lightfoot, who preached against the printing of the Apocrypha between the Two Testaments on the grounds that it divided 'two sweet singers'; and they included various specific proposals for the revision of *The Book of Common Prayer*.

John Wesley's decision in 1784 to fix the legal position of his Conference and determine its status and future included just such a revision. His *Sunday Service of the Methodists* arose from the needs of Methodism in England, but also from the needs of the Methodists in the then 'new' United States of America. It 'abridged' *The Book of Common Prayer* and among these abridgements was the exclusion from the lectionary of lessons from the Apocrypha and the exclusion of the section from Article VI of the Thirty-Nine Articles concerning the commendation and listing of the Apocryphal books. A useful context in which to understand that omission is offered by Frank Baker: John Wesley 'succeeded in retaining the core of the Protestant Trinitarian faith, much more concisely expressed and almost freed from its splendid but dangerous ambiguities, so that it was nothing like so liable to antagonize critics of various colours' (*John Wesley and the Church of England*, p. 251). In this case, however, as in so many other parts of John Wesley's work, the firmness of his official pronouncements was not altogether consistent with the generosity of his practice. Both John and Charles retained the use of the Apocrypha, not least in their preaching and their hymnody, so that whereas the 1784 change to Article VI was intended to provide a clearer, more concise presentation of the Christian faith, their hymnody retained the richness and imagery of the Wisdom of Solomon, ben Sirach (or Ecclesiasticus), 1 and 2 Esdras, and even 2 Maccabees 15.

To bring the subject right up to date, *Common Worship* (the Services and Prayers of the Church of England) includes among the Canticles parts of Tobit 13, Judith 16, Wisdom 3 and 9, ben Sirach 51, Baruch 5, Manasseh , and two forms of The Song of the Three. *The Methodist Worship Book* includes Canticles from Wisdom 6, 7–8, 10 and lections from ben Sirach 4, 10, 15, 18, 24, 27, 35, 38, 42, 43, 44, Baruch 4, Wisdom 1, 2, 3, 7, 8, 11, 12, Manasseh 1, 1 Maccabees 2, in each case with an added alternative.

The current theological debate regarding the canon is also important for a contemporary assessment of the Apocryphal books. For Christians, if the witness to their faith is to be drawn from both the Old Testament and the New, then the authority of the canon has to be explained widely enough to encompass many forms of discipleship and ecclesiality. In such circumstances criteria such as 'the clarity of scripture', 'the truth of the gospel', and 'the justification of the unrighteous' are insufficiently sharp to allow clear distinctions to be made between Old Testament and Apocryphal books. While we can affirm the usage of the Church across the ages, which has found wisdom in distinguishing between books which may be regarded as decisive for doctrine and those which are useful to read, to use that affirmation as the sole determinant of what constitutes a canon goes against the history of Christian usage which we have described and is contrary to the contemporary need to make sense of Christian life as well as Christian faith in terms of the witness of Old and New Testaments. Section B will help to confirm that judgement.

B. The name Apocrypha: what does it mean?

The name Apocrypha can be understood against two distinct but related backgrounds: the Hebrew scriptures, where for various reasons a document might be 'hidden away'; and the Christian scriptures, as the idea of a canon emerged or was restated and the form and text of the canon was edited.

Literally, on the basis of its background in the Greek language, the word Apocrypha means 'things hidden away'. But the reasons for things being 'hidden away' can be many and varied. They may not be suitable for public circulation; they may not be suitable for circulation at the present; they may need specialist knowledge if they are not to be misunderstood; they may be contagious; they may be especially valuable or holy; they may valuable or holy but no longer usable; or they may need to be safeguarded for the future. Those different reasons for 'things being hidden away' help us to observe the way in which biblical books were treated in the history of Judaism and the way in which they were treated in the history of the Christian Church.

The development of the body of Hebrew scriptures is not easily traced; it includes language about lists, holiness, what is hidden and, in the rabbinic period, the notion of what is excluded. At various historical points, from what was becoming a vast volume of material, a core of material emerged as distinctive of Jewish identity, piety and faith.

One of the Apocryphal books is ben Sirach (Ecclesiasticus). In its Prologue (dated 117 BCE) ben Sirach refers to 'the Law, the Prophets and the others who followed in their steps', and a little later to, 'the rest of the books of our ancestors'. The implication of the Prologue's comments is that written material had been brought to Egypt, that the material was in Hebrew, and that translation of the teaching about the Law into Greek was for ben Sirach a relatively new procedure. The term 'the Law' in ben Sirach's Prologue presumably refers to the first five books of our Old Testament (the Pentateuch or Torah). We cannot be sure precisely what is meant by 'the Prophets'; it could refer to Joshua, Judges, Samuel, Kings, Isaiah, Jeremiah, Ezekiel and the Twelve Minor Prophets. These books, the Law and the Prophets, provided a pattern and other writers followed them ('the rest of the books of our ancestors'). This third group might of course be 'The Writings' (Ketubim), a Hebrew title later used of Psalms, Job, Proverbs, the five Festival scrolls, Daniel, Ezra, Nehemiah and Chronicles. But the two expressions in ben Sirach's Prologue are loose and slightly different; they may well point to an early stage when there was a third group but the group was not yet clearly defined. In fact some of the Writings had not been written by the time of ben Sirach. All the books of the Hebrew Bible must have been written by 70 CE, since fragments of them all (except Esther) appear in the Qumran material and the Romans destroyed Qumran in 70 CE after they had destroyed the Jerusalem Temple. It is by no mean clear that Qumran recognized a tripartite canon (see the recent discussions of 4QMMT).

A core collection probably existed by 100 CE. The Jewish historian Josephus reported that by 100 CE there was a collection of 22 books (Josephus: *Against Apion* 1.37–42; perhaps this was a relatively new development since it does not harmonize with the information in his *Antiquities*). 2 Esdras 14.45, one of the Apocryphal books probably written after 70 CE, refers to 24 available books; in numerical terms the Babylonian Talmud *Baba Bathra* 14–15 agrees with 2 Esdras, and the Midrash on *Koheleth*, i.e. Ecclesiastes 12.4, comments that 'whoever allows more than 24 books into his house brings confusion into his house'(!). Several of these 22 or 24 books received substantial additions (as in the case of the Psalms), or were substantially rewritten (as we shall see in the case of Esther), or (as we shall see in the case of Daniel) were extant in more than one Hebrew or Aramaic form and in more than one textual form. The collection was certainly not sacrosanct letter by letter.

So far we have referred to the tradition of Hebrew scriptures. By the time of ben Sirach many of them had been translated into Greek. A striking account of how this is supposed to have happened is to be found in *The Letter of Aristeas* (about 160 BCE), and a celebration of the translation into Greek of an early collection of Hebrew books was witnessed by the Jewish writer Philo in about 10 BCE. The corpus of Jewish books was growing and some Jewish books were being composed in Greek (an example is 2 Maccabees). A Greek corpus was developing.

The gathering of a collection of books from this growing Jewish tradition did not follow the pattern that we found in the development of the Christian canon. The terminology used in relation to this gathering process illustrates some of the differences. First, some books were 'kept back' as only suitable for the wise to read. 2 Esdras distinguishes the 24 available books, important for Israel's salvation, from 70 others which contain the mysteries of the future. Of the 70 books which are to remain hidden 2 Esdras 14.46–47 says: 'the last seventy books are to be kept back, and given to none but the wise among your people; they contain a stream of understanding, a fountain of wisdom, a flood of knowledge'. In a later period, the period of the rabbis, some books were recorded as holy. But what constituted a holy book is not clear from the judgements the rabbis record. *Mishnah Yadaim* 3.5 in the second century CE questions if the Song of Songs and Koheleth (Ecclesiastes) are holy. In the same period *Tosefta Yadaim* 2.14 denies that Koheleth is holy and makes this oft-quoted comment: 'The books of ben Sirach and all the books since his time are not holy scripture' (2.34). There is also discussion in the rabbinic period of the 'exclusion' of books. In a discussion of Rabbi Akiba's statement that 'Whoever reads the "excluded books" has no share in the world to come' *Talmud Sanhedrin* 100[b] presents the following comments of Rab Joseph: 'It is forbidden to read the book of ben Sirach, although we may teach the good things it contains.' (Some texts there read, 'If the rabbis had not hidden this book away, we should be able to teach the good things it contains'!) So although the collecting of Jewish books seems similar to the forming of the Christian canon of scripture, the language used of the Jewish corpus suggests that it would be unwise to read back a Christian view of the canon into those earlier stages of the Jewish scriptures.

The development of a collection of writings within a growing corpus of Jewish writings can be related to periods in Jewish history. Certain periods were definitive for Jewish identity, piety and faith. Four such formative moments were: the Maccabean/Hasmonean period (about 168 BCE onwards), the arrival of Pompey in Jerusalem and the birth of the Roman Empire (60 BCE onwards), the Fall of Jerusalem (70 CE onwards) and the defeat of Bar Kosiba (Kochba) (125 CE onwards; see 'Dates relating to the Apocrypha'). It has to be remembered that many Jews were dispersed across the Mediterranean world (the so-called Diaspora). Certain forms of piety became characteristic of groups in different geographical areas or in isolated situations. This might explain why books such as *The Book of Jubilees* did not become part of the core material. The Psalms of Solomon (composed in the style of the Psalms and probably written down at the time of Pompey's entry into Jerusalem) similarly did not always find acceptance. They were perhaps considered to be too overtly political. Across the three or four centuries during which the main collection emerged, definitive periods gave particular expressions to Jewish piety and faith. But continuity too was greatly valued. So documents which extended the Pentateuch and Prophets were valued among the Writings, and additions were made to the core books.

There are many unanswered questions about when and how a core of Jewish material emerged. Particularly difficult is the question how, alongside the scriptures in Hebrew, writings in Greek such as we have already mentioned were gathered together – ben Sirach, 2 Maccabees, the Wisdom of Solomon, 2 Esdras etc. Some of the possible answers will be looked at in the commentaries on those books, and the role of Greek-speaking areas such as Egypt will be particularly evident. The four formative periods in Jewish life referred to above were important both for a collection of writings in Greek as well as for those in Hebrew, but another factor, to which we now turn, was of even greater significance: it was the emergence of the Christian canon.

As we saw in Section A the title Apocrypha takes its present meaning from the Reformation period of the Christian Church. But it was chosen by the Reformers because of its use during the development of the Christian canon, particularly its use at the point when Melito of Sardis and then Jerome took up the distinction between the originally Hebrew texts and the originally Greek texts: the Hebrew were regarded as the older and those only in Greek as later – texts which Jerome named 'apocrypha'.

Within the Christian canon the core Jewish documents we have been considering take on a different title: they become the Old Testament. Since the early Christian Church was mainly Greek speaking it tended to accept those books available in Greek. The Old Testament in Greek became foundational, alongside the newly emerging Christian literature, for worship, theology, pastoral care and practice. Historically, however, the word 'canon' also reminds the churches how an early church leader called Marcion tried to limit the books in Christian usage to Luke and the ten Pauline letters, and to exclude the Old Testament altogether, a move which Irenaeus countered by insisting on the continued use of all four gospels, the thirteen Pauline letters and the Old Testament.

The core documents in Greek not only take on a new title; they also in some cases take on a new form. Among our important sources for the Old Testament as it was used in the Early Church are three great uncial (i.e. written in capital letters) manuscripts from the fourth to the sixth centuries. The three great uncial manuscripts contain what is known as the Septuagint, a classic form of the Old Testament in Greek: Codex Vaticanus (B), Codex Sinaiticus (S) and Codex Alexandrinus (A) have the Octateuch (i.e. the first five books followed by Joshua, Judges and Ruth); they also have the historical books, providing a historical grounding for Israel's life and faith (except that A lacks Esdras at this point). Codex Vaticanus ends with the Prophets; the other two codices S and A end with the group associated with the name of Solomon (except that A adds at the end, with an indicator of lesser authority, the Psalms of Solomon). According to these ancient uncial manuscripts, the Septuagint contains the wider canon; they include the books we have come to associate with the Apocrypha and, in general terms, it is the Septuagint text which the REB translates.

But what of the order of the books? Have the books been reordered in this Christian testimony to the Septuagint? Did the Christian version of the Septuagint have a special ending? Did the Septuagint (as distinct from the later Hebrew order) conclude with the Prophets, providing an important link between the Old Testament and the New? The Christian version of the Septuagint is the result of some important editorial work by Christian scholars on both the text and its ordering. So it is useful to see how some of the other early Christian testimonies to the Septuagint look. Did the Christian Septuagint end with the Prophets? The minuscule (i.e. not written in capital letters) manuscripts which date from the eighth to the twelfth centuries give a less than positive answer to that question; and the quotations from the Eastern Fathers, which provide much earlier evidence than even the uncials, do not give a unanimous judgement either. In some of the Fathers the outline ends with the Prophets; but that is not true of other Fathers of the Church, notably Epiphanius, Theodoret, Rufinus, Leontius and Junilius. The Early Church evidently had different forms and orderings of the Septuagint.

We begin to see that the text which the REB translates, the Old Testament in Greek, the Septuagint, has a long and complicated history, and so has its order. We can see also that, although the Septuagint represents Jewish writings, it does so in a form which Christian traditions have influenced. Although the history of the Septuagint goes back to the time of the Qumran material and earlier, the form in which the Early Church used it has developed significantly.

The Old Testament scripture in Eastern Orthodoxy today uses a particular tradition of the Septuagint. It too has the Octateuch (i.e. the first five books followed by Joshua, Judges and Ruth). There is the extension of the historical books to include 1 and 2 Esdras, and the variations of order, sometimes following the 1928 edition of the Septuagint, between Tobit, Judith and Esther; there is the central pivot of history in 1–3 Maccabees, the important group of writings associated with the name of Solomon, and, preceded by or framing the book of the Job, the Twelve Minor Prophets; then the major prophets Isaiah, Jeremiah (with Baruch, Lamentations and the Letter of Jeremiah), Ezekiel and, finally, Daniel with its three additions and 4 Maccabees as an appendix.

The term Apocrypha, then, can be understood against two distinct settings: the Hebrew contexts, where for various reasons a document was 'hidden away'; and the Christian contexts, where in the history of the biblical tradition the idea of a canon emerged or was restated and the form and text of the canon was edited. Jerome took up the term Apocrypha, using it in his own Christian context to set apart the writings known only in Greek, and it was this usage which the German Reformers adopted.

C. How should we interpret the Apocrypha?

The history of the Apocrypha is one of disputes and polemics, and it was in those troubled contexts that the criteria for assessing the Apocrypha were worked out. Today we could rehearse ancient debates, or attempt a contemporary assessment within our present multifaith, multicultural society.

We offer six different answers, each one contributing a facet to our total project.

(i) We can interpret the Apocrypha as part of the Christian canon

The wealth of worship material in the Apocrypha (see both *Common Worship* and *The Methodist Worship Book*) helps us to recognize that we operate with a twofold canon, one narrower and the other broader.

(ii) We can interpret the Apocrypha via a comparison of patterns of religion

Many of the polemics regarding the Apocrypha have been based on selective terminology. Too little attention has been given to the patterns of religion represented in the Apocryphal texts. So the criticism that the Apocrypha represents salvation by works of the Law needs to be judged by reference to the patterns of religion presented by each of the books. The commentaries demonstrate that this is what the Apocryphal Wisdom material requires. Wisdom relates Law to the total experience of living within a religion where grace provides a foundation for community to flourish.

(iii) We can interpret the Apocrypha as part of a continuum of tradition

Scholars and preachers often make a direct link between the Old Testament and the New Testament, leaping across the temporal gap between them. A good example of this is how Messiahship is discussed. The Apocryphal books tell a great deal about the ways messianic hopes developed and changed between the two Testaments. We can link the Old and New Testaments by means of the literature which spans the time-gap between them and shows the development of messianic hopes from Old Testament prototypes, through the power structures of a kingdom, towards a spirituality of messiahship, and to that dependence on God essential for the richness of the worship of Christ in the New Testament and the Early Church.

(iv) We can interpret the Apocrypha as imaginative literature

Several books in the Apocrypha could be called historical novels. These can be compared and contrasted with ancient novels outside the biblical area, and compared and contrasted with how modern novelists work. The ancient novel differs from many modern novels (such as, for example, Iris Murdoch's *A Word Child*) in moving from descent into chaos toward ascent into deliverance. But old and modern novels, and detective stories (which also have their parallels in the Apocrypha), have in common that they can use narrative to promote particular attitudes or policies, or celebrate particular events; and recent approaches to narrative criticism are particularly helpful in highlighting how both ancient and modern narratives make their mark through the use of the extraordinary, as J. K. Rowling's Harry Potter series does.

The relationship between narrative and theology deserves particular attention. Stories from the Apocrypha have often been the cause of disputes, arguments and battles. If we are to get beyond those disputes we need to operate as theologians, and for theologians stories are not just communicative tools, nor are they the only communicative tools. Theologians work with statements, affirmations, concepts, questions which enable judgements and comparisons to be made among the materials offered. The materials offered in the Apocrypha are of course not only stories but also prayers, psalms, discourses and proverbs. It was perhaps one of the factors which led the Reformers to reject the Apocrypha that they took Paul's style of argumentation as exclusively determinative of theology. They did not balance those judgements with all the other kinds of material of which they were fully aware, of which Paul himself was aware and of which the Apocrypha was a particularly rich source.

(v) We can interpret the Apocrypha as a collection of communicative actions

In the Apocrypha we are often confronted with the problem of which text to choose, and our choice of which text to translate can change how we read the text as a whole. We need, however, to distinguish between the inevitability of variations in the retelling of stories and the communication which a specific form of the story can carry. Just because stories are open-ended does not mean that they may not be shaped to carry a particular communication.

One of the central questions in biblical study today is whether the newer critical techniques such as narrative criticism and rhetorical criticism have made the old critical techniques of historical criticism out of date. Do we need to explore the historical setting or the historical person behind the text, or can we simply concentrate on the text itself and the techniques appropriate to the text? This Epworth series of commentaries affirms the importance of both; and an argument can be presented that the communicative action expressed in the text can only adequately be understood and its meaning defined when both historical and literary skills of analysis are used.

One of our tasks, therefore, is to take each part of the Apocrypha and explore its meaning using those interlocking skills of analysis. Some parts of the Apocrypha particularly lend themselves to this kind of interlocking analysis of communication, organization, reception, narrative and rhetoric. The Wisdom of Solomon is an excellent example of this.

(vi) We can interpret the Apocrypha as part of the whole project of biblical exploration

It is clear that the attitude to the Jewish Law in the New Testament is by no means a simple rejection or a simple affirmation. In Paul's writings both rejection and affirmation are to be found; aspects of the Law which are nationalistic, literalistic, idolatrous and fail to recognize the changing times are rejected, but aspects of moral discipline, corporate responsibility and divine purpose are affirmed, and affirmed for those who seek as Christians to become obedient children of God.

In Paul's writings other aspects of Jewish faith are also strongly affirmed. One of these is the affirmation that God is one, the one Creator and Redeemer. Few more central and normative affirmations can be found than this. It is presented powerfully in the Wisdom of Solomon, in a form which Paul himself seems to have approved. This is not, either in Wisdom or Paul, a verbal or intellectual affirmation only. It is an affirmation of heart and soul and mind and strength. Scripture, in directing us to this end, constantly questions the ways we attempt to evade this challenge, ways which the Old Testament, Apocrypha and the New Testament all call 'idolatry'.

It is also important that central moments in the New Testament record are affirmed through reference to scripture (the Nativity, the Passion, Easter, Pentecost), and affirmed not as records which deny the value of what provides the affirmation, but as that which gives it an abiding significance. The work of commentary on the Apocrypha will amplify that important way of relating Jewish and Christian texts, with particular references to literature and the arts.

DATES RELATING TO THE APOCRYPHA

In the first column this list of dates follows our present calendar reckoning. In the second column are some of the historical events or significant persons relevant to the material of the Apocrypha and the commentary. The third column suggests where the various texts may fit into the historical outline. A glance at the columns indicates several general points.

First, it is interesting to see how many of the texts from the Apocrypha are allocated a date between 199 BCE and 103 BCE. This seems to have been a most productive period in terms of Jewish literature, and the association of this literature with Egypt is also worth noting.

Second, the outline illustrates the four major periods during which Jewish literature provided a focus for Jewish faith and piety, and gives examples of literature at those periods.

Third, the outline indicates some of the interesting moments in the history of the Christian canon, and the place of some Hebrew and Greek texts within that development.

The outline will be particularly useful for the study of the text of 1 and 2 Maccabees.

561 BCE	The Babylonian Empire. Israel in exile. The beginning of the Jewish Diaspora (the Dispersion) to the East and the South (including Egypt).	Later work on the Pentateuch, and the Deuteronomic history.
520 BCE	The Persian Empire. Israel rebuilds. The beginning of the Second Temple period.	Prophetic collections. Haggai and Zechariah 1–8.

Dates relating to the Apocrypha

336 BCE	Philip of Macedon dies. Alexander the Great, his son, begins his conquest of the Persian Empire, introducing Greek culture (= Hellenism) everywhere in the Mediterranean area.	
323 BCE	Alexander dies. His kingdom is divided among his generals.	
301 BCE	Two dynasties develop in the Mediterranean area: the Seleucids in the North; the Ptolemies in the South. Jerusalem under the rule of one then the other.	
260 BCE	Ptolemy Philadelphus rules Egypt.	The legend of the translation of Jewish Law into Greek at Ptolemy's initiative.
219 BCE	Simon II High Priest in Jerusalem.	
199/8 BCE	A Seleucid ruler Antiochus III takes over Jerusalem.	A form of 1 Esdras?
180 BCE		The Hebrew work behind ben Sirach.
170 BCE	The murder of Onias III.	
168 BCE	Antiochus IV works with high-priestly groups to turn Jerusalem into a Greek city.	The development of the Daniel traditions. A version of Judith? The book of Tobit?
167 BCE	Death of Mattathias; a guerrilla war with Judas Maccabaeus as leader results in the rededication	The war is recorded in 1 Maccabees.

of the Temple (the
Festival of Hanukkah
celebrates this). The
Maccabeans rule as
vassals of the Seleucids.

153 BCE	Jonathan vested as high priest. A dispute separates the Maccabeans and the predecessors of Qumran.	*The Book of Jubilees.*
143 BCE	Simon's first year.	
*c.*117 BCE	Ben Sirach moves to Egypt in 132 and translates the Hebrew text into Greek. The Hasmonean John Hyrcanus expands the Judaean empire. A new festival is inaugurated in Judaea to celebrate the purification of the Temple.	Ecclesiasticus written. Part of 1 Baruch? A Greek version of Esther? The Greek of 1 Esdras? 1 Maccabees written? 2 Maccabees written?
103 BCE	The Hasmonean Jannaeus rules in the pattern of Hellenistic rulers.	The Prayer of Azariah, Bel and the Snake and the Story of Susanna are incorporated into the Greek of Daniel.
63 BCE	Pompey, the Roman general, besieges Jerusalem. Rome proclaims Herod King of Judaea. Augustus becomes Roman Emperor. Judaea under direct Roman control (6 CE onwards).	The Psalms of Solomon. Wisdom of Solomon? The Jewish philosopher Philo writes in Alexandria.
*c.*40 CE	The beginning of Christian literature.	Paul's letters.

Dates relating to the Apocrypha

66–70 CE	Jewish revolt against Rome results in fall of Jerusalem, destruction of the Temple, end of the high priesthood and end of Qumran and Masada.	
70–100 CE	Attempts to reformulate Judaism. Jewish communities spread through Western Mediterranean. The development of Christian literature: the Gospels, the Acts of the Apostles, the Pastoral epistles.	4 Ezra = 2 Esdras 3–14. Jewish historian Josephus settles in Rome, writes *The Jewish War*, *The Jewish Antiquities* and *Against Apion*, a response to ancient antisemitism. Syriac Apocalypse of Baruch = 2 Baruch.
95–132 CE	The writings of the early Church Fathers.	1 Clement, Ignatius, the *Didache* (quoting ben Sirach), the Epistle of Barnabas.
132–135 CE	The Bar Kosiba (Kochba) revolt.	
140 CE	Pius I bishop of the Christian Church in Rome.	Marcion (about 144 CE) asserts negative aspects of Judaism and attempts to excise from Christianity the Old Testament view of the Creator God. Irenaeus writes of him 'mutilating' the Gospel of Luke and 'dismembering' the epistles of Paul.
c.160 CE		Justin Martyr (a Christian apologist) writes his *Dialogue with Trypho* (a Jewish apologist). Justin Martyr knows the Greek Septuagint, the Jewish copies and their interpretative methods.

*c.*190 CE	In response to teachers such as Marcion a document was produced discussing what scriptures were acknowledged, read or just received (although rejected by some) in the church in Rome.	Muratorian Fragment: includes the Wisdom of Solomon after Jude and the letters of John in a Christian list of books.
200 CE	The Mishnah becomes a foundation document for rabbinic Judaism.	
203–254 CE	Origen works in Alexandria and Caesarea.	Origen's 'Old Testament' texts.
312–324 CE	The Emperor Constantine extends religious toleration to West and East.	The period of the great uncial texts: Sinaiticus, Vaticanus.
312–325 CE	Eusebius of Caesarea.	Eusebius's *Ecclesiastical History*.
295?-373 CE	Athanasius of Alexandria.	
347–420? CE	Jerome.	The Vulgate (382–405 CE).
354–430 CE	Augustine of Hippo.	

The First Book of Esdras

Nations and national groups during a time of change retell their histories in the search for identity and purpose. Sometimes this requires heart-searching honesty as questions of truth and fact are exposed. The exhibitions in Berlin during 2000 and 2001 regarding responsibilities in the Second World War illustrated how painful and courageous that can prove to be. During the present century, when massive changes are taking place in so many countries across the world, no doubt that process may be required of all of us. Sometimes the retelling of the story requires an imaginative, creative touch, fantasy even. Fantasy about the past can of course be dangerous, but the imaginative, truth-seeking retelling of the past can point forward to new options and hopes. 1 Esdras is in all probability that kind of book. It picks up the great themes of the continuity of Israel's life in Temple, King, Priest, and in the story of exile and restoration.

Chapter 1

1 Esdras begins with King *Josiah* celebrating *the Passover to his Lord at Jerusalem . . . He installed the priests, duly robed in their vestments* (v. 1). *No Passover like it had been celebrated in Israel since the time of the prophet Samuel* (vv. 20–21a). It followed *the manner prescribed by King David of Israel and provided for so magnificently by his son Solomon* (v. 5). The source of 1 Esdras here is 2 Chron. 35.1–27, except that 1 Esdras does not provide a full explanation for the celebration, whereas 2 Chronicles does. According to 2 Chronicles the reasons for the celebration are Josiah's early reforms, the purification of the land, the reinstatement of the Law, the confirmation of the Covenant and, the one reason which is noted by 1 Esdras, the fulfilment of David and Solomon's purpose for the Temple (1 Chron. 29). Seen in that light 1 Esdras has either lost its beginning, or begins with a key example of Josiah's piety and the historic role of King, Temple and Priest (v. 21). Probably the second is the more likely (see the parallel in 2 Macc. 1.1–2.18).

The ending of 1 Esdras is much shorter too than its source would lead you to expect. 1 Esdras ends with a festival day (again see 2 Maccabees): *So they held their assembly* (9.55c); its source, in this case Neh. 8.12, records a festival day which is the first in the seven-day sequence of reading and teaching the Law. Nevertheless, the final chapter of 1 Esdras has a genuine climax; its climax is the bringing and formal opening of the book of the Law *and when he* (Ezra) *opened it they all stood. Ezra praised the Lord God, the Most High God of Hosts, the Almighty, and all the people cried 'Amen, Amen'* (9.46–47). So the reading of the Law, by Ezra, *priest and doctor of the Law* (9.39–42), omitted from the beginning of 1 Esdras, becomes a central point at the book's conclusion.

Alongside the themes of King, Temple and Priest is the story of exile and restoration: Israel has been consigned to exile in Babylon, its Jerusalem Temple and religious and social patterns in Jerusalem destroyed, because, so the story goes, Israel had been unfaithful and her kings unjust; she had, however, been given a new opportunity. 1 Esdras is picking up the story of exile and restoration, and handling it with a view to what the people need to be and do in the present and for the future. 1 Esd. 1.24 reads: *The events of his* (Josiah's) *reign are to be found among earlier records, records of sin and rebellion against the Lord.* That the people's sin brought down divine judgement is a central pivot of Israel's thought, set out in its stark realities by Deut. 8.11–20. It is reinforced in the tradition which 1 Esdras used here: the writer is using both 2 Chron. 35 and 2 Chron. 36, except that 1 Esdras recalls *the earlier records* which contrast the king's piety with the people's *sin and rebellion against the Lord.* Even Josiah's fine example could not turn God's judgement away. He fails to heed God's warning given via the king of Egypt and Jeremiah (vv. 25–28; contrast 2 Chron. 35.20–25), and as a consequence dies, not on the battlefield as earlier traditions recorded, but *back in Jerusalem* (v. 31). Josiah's untimely death heralds the beginning of a time of desolation, when even the king (Joakim) did *wrong in the sight of the Lord* (v. 39). The Babylonian ruler Nebuchadnezzar takes the sacred vessels from the Temple to Babylon. Joakim's depravity is matched by his son Joakim II, whom Nebuchnezzar replaces with Zedekiah. (Zedekiah is not linked in 1 Esd. 1.34–58 with the direct royal line as he is in 2 Chron. 36.10 and 2 Kgs. 24.17; in 1 Esdras the royal line is Josiah, Jeconiah, Joakim I, Joakim II=Jehoiakim. The change is probably intentional.) However, it is not only the kings who are to blame. *The leaders of both people and priests committed many impious and lawless acts* (vv. 49–51a, 53). Not that

God was unaware that this would happen, so the story ran. Through the prophet Jeremiah God not only prophesied it would happen but had already set a limit to the exile. The people would be in exile *until the land should have run the full term of its sabbaths, it should keep sabbath all the time of its desolation till the end of the seventy years* (v. 58; see 2 Chron. 36.21). The exile would end with the intervention of King Cyrus of Persia (1 Esd. 2.1; 2 Chron. 36.22–23). Exile and restoration provide a key to the opening section of 1 Esdras; and it is a key to its ending also. The Temple vessels have by then been restored to Jerusalem; Artaxerxes king of Persia has given Ezra authority to administer justice (8.23). But Ezra discovers that things are no better than they were: *Our sins tower above us and our offences have reached high heaven* (8.75). In this predicament Ezra recalls the mercifulness of God: *he secured for us the favour of the kings of Persia* (8.80a). The pattern of exile and restoration carries with it hope for the future – if Jerusalem can be purified from its polluted style of life.

1 Esdras is a rewriting of a selected portion of the material from our Old Testament. The parallels with 2 Chronicles already quoted illustrate how the writer is working. He is using well-known material which he redrafts with deft touches, some more, some less important. Having begun with 2 Chron. 25–26, he moves on to Ezra 1.1–10.44 (with Ezra 4.6–24 introduced very early), and then to Neh. 7.73–8.12. So part of our task is to note the changes 1 Esdras makes and to recognize why such a well-known story needs to be retold.

The story of Israel's exile and restoration is of course found elsewhere in our Old Testament (see Isa. 40–55 and 56–66). The prophets Haggai and Zechariah 1–8 belong to the period of the restoration and have their own visions of how that restoration might be understood, with the governor Zerubbabel and the high priest Joshua both exercising a role in the process of restoration.

The reuse of Old Testament material in 1 Esdras can be illustrated by a particular problem which is bound up with the title '1 Esdras'. First, we are studying the book of that name as it is found in the REB; but the name 1 Esdras was also used for a very different book. The name 1 Esdras has been used (and in the 1956 Bible of the Russian Patriarchate is still used) for the Old Testament Book of Ezra, that is, the book in the Old Testament translated by the REB translators from a Hebrew and Aramaic text. But those Old Testament texts had been translated into Greek, at least by the end of the first century BCE, a translation which became known as the Septuagint. So there exists in the Septuagint a Greek version of Ezra and Nehemiah, headed in some versions of the Septuagint by the title 2 Esdras. There are then two books in the Greek Septuagint based on Ezra/Nehemiah: we have the straightforward translation, 2 Esdras; and we have the book we are studying here, called in the REB 1 Esdras. (Incidentally 1 Esdras appears in the Vulgate under yet another name, 3 Ezra.)

Second, when we use the title 1 Esdras and suggest that it is a rewriting of a selected portion of the material known to us from 2 Chronicles, we are probably talking, initially, about a piece of editing which took place at the Hebrew and Aramaic stage, in the priesthood of Simon II or earlier. Only later was it translated into Greek (our 1 Esdras), perhaps at the same time as the writing of 1–2 Maccabees: that is a date suggested by the use of the geographical term Coele-Syria and Phoenicia to translate the original 'Abar Nahra – a translation found six times in 1 Esdras, also in Maccabees and in an inscription of that same period. The earlier administrative Ptolemaic term, Syria and Phoenicia (known from an inscription of 195 BCE), is also found seven times in 1 Esdras. So the mixture of uses suggests a Greek linguistic tradition in the first half of the second century BCE. The title 1 Esdras is therefore ambiguous; it could be used of the original version in Hebrew and Aramaic (which we do not have), or of the translation of that version into Greek (which we do have and are at present reading).

Why should such a well-known story have been retold? The concentration on the Temple, its restoration as a building and an organization, the assistance of foreign rulers in that enterprise and the rewriting of Israel's history point to the time of the conquest of Jerusalem by Antiochus III in 198 BCE and to his co-operation with Simon II (219–196 BCE), the last of the priest-kings of Israel. Josephus, the Jewish historian, describes how the aristocratic council (the predecessor of the Sanhedrin), the priests, the scribes of the Temple and the temple singers gained exemption from tax as gratitude for the support of Antiochus III (see 2 Macc. 4.11). Perhaps such a political situation gave rise to a Hebrew and Aramaic revision of the Chronicles–Ezra–Nehemiah traditions (the original 1 Esdras). The council, along with Simon II who was one of the great teachers of the Law, succeeded in obtaining from Antiochus III a regulation (later withdrawn under Antiochus IV) to secure the purity of the people and the sanctity of the Temple, restricting the dealings of aliens in the city, together with the right to an internal ordering of the people on divinely given principles. That, as we shall see, chimes with another of the emphases of 1 Esdras concerning Ezra, his reading of the Law, the new role of the Levites and the instruction of all the people in the

Law. The later translation into Greek, our 1 Esdras, can be dated from the style in which it was written. We shall meet the style again in 1 Maccabees (see 'Dates relating to the Apocrypha').

Behind that reference to Antiochus III's proclamation and the tax benefits enjoyed by some of the aristocratic leaders, and so behind the Hebrew or Aramaic 1 Esdras, hide the remnants of an ancient power struggle in Jerusalem and the source of a forthcoming enmity, in which some priests and their scribal followers unsuccessfully (at this stage) competed for influence and authority over against the high-priestly group and their political and economic power. We shall meet this latent conflict again, both in the writings of ben Sirach and in its more open expression in 1 Maccabees.

Chapter 2

Just as ch. 1 concentrates on the period of desolation, ch. 2 concentrates on the period of the restoration. *In the first year of King Cyrus of Persia the Lord, to fulfil his word spoken through Jeremiah, moved the heart of the king* (vv. 1–2a). The motif of God instructing foreign rulers concerning his will and using them to execute his purposes of judgement and mercy is a feature of 1 Esdras. The writer, at this point in the narrative, turns to the book of Ezra (see Ezra 1.1–3), neatly picking up the ending of 2 Chronicles (2 Chron. 36.20–23). That ending of 2 Chronicles brings together the prophecy made by Jeremiah and the transforming of the heart of King Cyrus so that he becomes the agent of the prophecy's fulfilment.

Nearly three hundred years later than our 1 Esdras, after the Second Temple had once more been destroyed, the Jewish historian Josephus, describing the religion of the Second Temple period and setting out a case for the Jewish belief in divine providence, chose the texts of Ezra, 1 Esdras and 2 Esdras as the basis for his record of the Jewish restoration. His *Jewish Antiquities* Book XI begins with the effect upon Cyrus of Israelite prophecy; Cyrus, according to Josephus, was impressed by the fact that he, Cyrus, had been named by an Israelite prophet (Isa. 44.28) as the one who would rebuild the Jerusalem Temple – 140 years before it was ever destroyed! That might not impress us as modern readers; we know that the prophecy was made, not by a contemporary of King Hezekiah in the eighth century BCE but by a later prophet in the time of Cyrus (see the reference to Isa. 40–55 above). But it impressed Josephus. Moreover, the calculation to which

Josephus refers depends on yet another prophecy, a prophecy of Jeremiah which, as Josephus himself recognized, was to have a profound effect on subsequent history. The Jeremiah prophecy concerned 70 years: 70 years between Jerusalem's desolation and her restoration (Jer. 25.11–12; 29.10; see 1 Esdr. 1.58; Josephus, *Antiquities* XI.1). Perhaps it was on the grounds that the 70 years was not quite up that Haggai and Zechariah met opposition to restoring the Temple; we do not know whether such a figure would have been understood literally in 520 BCE. (Would it have meant '70 years' or simply 'a generation'?) What is beyond question is that at a still later date the figure was treated both literally and figuratively: yes, it did mean years; but no, it meant that the 70 years were sabbatical, a sabbath of desolation; and a sabbath is a seventh of the week; hence if a week equals a year, the 70 years would have to be a whole week of 70s, i.e. 7 x 70 years = 490 years. This interpretation of Jeremiah's prophecy is what is implied in 1 Esdras 1.58: *until the land should have run the full term of its sabbaths, it should keep sabbath all the time of its desolation till the end of seventy years*. The sabbath of its desolation would be 70 years, making a total of 490 years. That is an interpretation which appears also in the book of Daniel, a book written at the time of Antiochus IV's threat to the Temple (see Dan. 9.22–27). Various similar applications of that timetable are found in the writings of Josephus in his description of Israel's history (see Josephus, *Antiquities* X.267–80), including its final application to the Fall of Jerusalem in 70 CE at the hands of the Romans. For Josephus it was the prophecy of Jeremiah which showed how God's providence was at work in Jewish history.

Christian discussion of this prophecy has taken many forms. Some scholars find examples of it in the gospels of Mark and Luke. One rather later but classic example is in the early Christian historian Eusebius's *Ecclesiastical History*. Another illuminating example comes from the time of Jerome, the translator of the Vulgate. Apollinarius, whose name is associated with a famous heresy of the Early Church, worked out that, beginning from the birth of Christ, 490 years would mean that the Temple would be rebuilt again in 482 CE. Jerome replies that this amounts to transforming 'interpreters' into 'foretellers',

> by breaking away from the stream of the past and directing one's longing toward the future . . . If by any chance those of future generations should not see these predictions of his fulfilled at the time he set, they will be forced to seek for some other solution and to convict the teacher himself of erroneous interpretation.

A moral tale for the present!

The modern understanding of divine providence requires much greater care. It is part of a modern debate which considers the nature of time and the relationship of God to time. One way of approaching the issue is this: while God may be eternally aware of every moment in time, that does not mean that God must dictate at every moment what occurs or where those moments will lead. Prophecy cannot be a matter simply of what God has decided and will do. Our responsibilities in time and how we fulfil them are part of the divine purpose, and as such are enfolded within divine providence. In that sense God is contemporary with past, present and future, whatever those modes of time are; but God has not foreclosed on the future. The prophetic voices of the past have their place in divine providence; but their testimony to that providence is to specific moments by which God in that eternal purpose is constantly helping us to flourish, not to any timetable by which that will be achieved.

One of the characteristics of 1 Esdras, and especially of ch. 2, is the gracious way the writer handles official correspondence. Not that this makes the work any more reliable historically; rather, it belongs with the other features of administrative awareness which characterize the writings of this period, in their Hebrew, Aramaic and Greek stages. Specific to the Greek translator, however, is the way the decree of King Cyrus begins: *The Lord of Israel, the Most High Lord, has made me king of the world* (v. 3). The terms are intentionally reverential. This is not the language of flattery or definition, but of worship (see also 6.14). It associates Cyrus with Israel's faith. Moreover, it retains, as in Daniel 2.18–20 (where the Septuagint uses the same ascription to God), the sense of unworthiness before that fearful divine presence which cannot be named but only worshipped. This contrasts with the opposition to the rebuilding of the Temple of the Lord registered by the letter in 2.17–24, an opposition which, as events illustrate, cannot thwart Cyrus' initial perception of the divine purpose. The rebuilding was only held up temporarily (see v. 30c; Ezra 4.24).

1 Esdras 2.30c and Ezra 4.24 may agree that the rebuilding could only begin in Darius' second year, but the stories which follow immediately in each of them, in 1 Esdras 3.1 and Ezra 5.1, provide very different accounts. The reason for the difference seems to be that 1 Esdras wishes to set Zerubbabel centre stage. To do this 1 Esdras has to change the order of events from those in the biblical book of Ezra. According to 1 Esd. 3.1–5.73 Zerubbabel is the key figure; and he is so because he wins a crucial contest in Darius' court. According to Ezra

5.1–6.22 Zerubbabel has a subsidiary role; it is Haggai and Zechariah who rebuke the people and Tattenai and Shetharbonezai who prevent the work from continuing until Darius has been consulted. 1 Esdras does have the account from Ezra 5.1–6.22 but it is to be found (with different names) later on, as late as 1 Esd. 6.1–7.15; and the leadership role of Zerubbabel is to be found in Ezra, but much earlier on, almost at the beginning of Ezra, in Ezra 2.1–4.5. In comparison with the biblical book of Ezra, 1 Esdras wants to make a particular point about Zerubbabel, even though in doing so the writer has to offer a different sequence of events; a less likely sequence of events, some would even say an impossible sequence of events.

Why then is Zerubbabel so important for 1 Esdras? In Haggai and Zechariah Zerubbabel is important as the governor of Judah who operates alongside the high priest Joshua (Hag. 2.2; Zech. 4.3–14; see 1 Esd. 6.28). In 1 Esdras Zerubbabel has the wisdom to gain Darius' confidence, to sit beside him, be called his 'Kinsman' (4.42) and be sent as the royal emissary to secure fulfilment of the king's will (4.47–48; he seems to be a replacement for Nehemiah); he is also the one who affirms God as the source of wisdom and as deserving of all praise and glory (4.59–60). He becomes a focus of attention for another reason too: according to 1 Esdras *he stands in David's line* (5.5, see 1 Chron. 3.19). The role of Zerubbabel, reminiscent of figures such as Solomon, is underlined by 1 Esdras above all by the debate at the Persian court. 1 Esdras, written in the second century BCE, presents Zerubbabel (who lived in about 520 BCE) as a surviving royal contender (see Zech. 6.9–14).

Chapters 3 and 4

The debate is set in the aftermath of a great feast. *Three young men* (3.3) establish a competition and nominate Darius as donor of substantial prizes. From the beginning the criterion is Wisdom (3.7). The three set down in writing their view on 'What is the strongest?' and are invited to speak to their theme in turn. The speeches are interrelated but do not move logically or systematically. The first – 'Wine is strongest' – is briefest and undermines the second – 'The king is strongest' (see 3.19). The second is arguing that the king is always obeyed but does not avoid the impression that such obedience is irrational. The third, the longest, argues from the beginning that 'Women are strongest but truth conquers all'. Zerubbabel is the third speaker. He undermines both the first and the second in that women bear both kings and vine-growers. Two aspects of the power of women are presented, both in part irrational: there is the power of their beauty and their skill in coaxing a husband, even if that husband is Darius himself. Zerubbabel then trumps his own argument by praising divine truth as sovereign for ever, as judge and destroyer of all injustice whether in wine, kings or women. The people acclaim his speech: *Great is truth: truth is strongest* (4.41). Whereupon Zerubbabel reminds Darius of a vow (of which we have no other evidence: 4.43), Cyrus' vow to destroy Babylon (4.44) and to rebuild the Temple destroyed by the Edomites (4.45). In this way he becomes Darius' emissary to put into operation not only the building of the Temple and the return of the holy vessels but also the inauguration of a vast bill of rights. Turning heavenward Zerubbabel prays: *From you come victory and wisdom; yours is the glory* (4.59–60)

The section is probably Aramaic or Hebrew in origin, translated into the same quality of Greek which we met earlier in the book. It resembles in style some of the other material we shall study later, in the additions to Daniel. But in one respect it is unusual. It used to be said that the Apocrypha is largely non-messianic. That certainly cannot be said of 1 Esdras. Its central figure is Davidic, is heir to the wisdom of Solomon, and the wisdom he inherits is that which is rooted in divine justice and truth. It is a wisdom which sets the pattern of living, spiritual courage and prophetic candour which establishes an understanding of messiahship that the later centuries were to value and espouse.

Chapter 5

Darius authorized Zerubbabel to take charge of the restoration. One naturally assumes that it was in the second year of Darius' reign that those chosen to return were escorted to Jerusalem to lay the foundation of the Temple (vv. 1–6). However, the end of ch. 5 reads: The people of the land *prevented its completion during the lifetime of King Cyrus* (v. 73). The writer of 1 Esdras has, to put it mildly, taken liberties with his source material. The writer has created a new section, vv. 1–6, and this makes a link with the Darius–Zerubbabel story, using, for example, details picked out from Nehemiah's time and from the book of Ezra. 1 Esdras then takes up the story at 5.7, from Ezra 2.2, of what happened in Cyrus' reign (see Ezra 1.2; 1 Esd. 5.55), leaving the impression that all this happened in Darius' reign. As a story all this is problematic. Historically too it is problematic: between Cyrus' reign and Darius' reign there was an eight-year reign by Cyrus' son, Cambyses, of which 1 Esdras makes no mention.

So what is the value of 1 Esdras 5? It continues Zerubbabel's success story; it records the names of those chosen to take part in the restoration; it describes the restoration as a great festival (a Tabernacles or Harvest festival according to v. 51); but it also points to social factors (like those mentioned earlier) which begin to emerge in the chapter, which hold the key to the remainder of the book and have strong resonance with some of our contemporary issues. *Other peoples of the land* joined them (v. 50), *who were hostile and too strong for them. Sidonians and Tyrians* brought cedar trees from Lebanon (v. 54). Above all, those who had been settled in the land by *King Asbasareth of Assyria* (that is, by Esar-hadon of Assyria, 681–669 BCE; see v. 69, Tobit 1.21) and *the enemies of Judah and Benjamin* interrupt the building (v. 66). Social, geographical, tribal, political and religious groupings, some clearly defined, some only becoming evident as events unfold, complicate the project of restoration, throwing doubt on its viability and significance, and resulting in serious social instability (v. 73). Zerubbabel's project is threatened by instability.

Chapter 6

The story continues along its confusing route. *In the second year of the reign of Darius* (v. 1) *Sisinnes, the governor-general* (v. 3; he is called Tattenai in Ezra 5.3) initiates an enquiry concerning the authority for the rebuilding programme. According to 1 Esd. 4.47–49 this would have been quite unnecessary. The governor-general's letter to Darius making this enquiry does, however, give fresh support to Zerubbabel's position. It is to Zerubbabel that Cyrus hands over the Temple vessels.

Thanks to the Lord (v. 5) the intervention of Sisinnes does not cause the project to be discontinued (v. 6). Darius orders the search for the Cyrus scroll, and on the basis of its contents issues instructions that no-one is to hold up any longer the work on the house of the Lord. A comparison of Darius' instructions in 1 Esd. 6.24–34 with Darius' letter in Ezra 6.6–12 shows that what is envisaged in both accounts is a royal temple (1 Esd. 6.31). And whereas in Ezra the governor of the Jews is not named, in 1 Esd. 6.27, 29 he is specifically called Zerubbabel.

Chapter 7

A motif of the book that foreign rulers are agents of the divine purpose is underlined in 1 Esd. 7.4 (see 7.15). In comparison with the celebrations recorded at the beginning of the book in 1 Esdras 1, the celebrations which follow the completion of the Temple are low key. They follow the same basic requirements as Josiah's: all is done *according to the book of Moses* (v. 9; see v. 6). Notably, it is the priests and Levites who celebrate the Passover *for all the returned exiles, for their kinsmen the priests, and for themselves* (v. 12). In comparison with Ezra 6.16–22 too, the celebration in 1 Esdras is not merely low key but, according to 7.12, restricted to a specific group: the returned exiles (contrast Ezra 6.21; and see 1 Esd. 1.21). The issue of an exclusive group, only those who had returned from the exile, unpurified (who had, however, *held aloof from the abominations of the peoples of the land*, v. 13), means that the issue which we saw earlier reappears (5.73). There was a cause of serious social unrest. The resulting problems have to be dealt with by Ezra in the following chapters.

Chapter 8

We cannot be certain what precise historical interval separated the restoration by Zerubbabel from the restoration led by Ezra. The reference to *Artaxerxes . . . king of Persia* (v. 1) might suggest somewhat less than or somewhat more than a century. The chapter begins with various kinds of information concerning Ezra. His genealogy, known to us in various progressively abbreviated forms (see the REB footnote on v. 2), links him with the priesthood of Solomon's Temple. He is both priest or high priest and scribe or reader of the Law. Traditionally, Ezra was known as Ezra the scribe (Ezra 7.6–10), with the responsibilities of studying the Law, doing it, and teaching its statutes and ordinances in Israel. Traditionally he shared those responsibilities with the Levites (Neh. 8.7–9). 1 Esdras moves away from the term 'scribe'; the writer only uses it once (v. 3) and prefers 'reader of the Law of the Lord'. The REB translates this with the less literal *doctor of the law of the Lord* (v. 8). The translation is justified in so far as the term appears in several cases as an official form of address (8.8–9, 19; 9.39, 42, 49), and *Ezra's knowledge of the law of the Lord and the commandments was full and exact* (v. 7). So 1 Esdras sets Ezra apart from the traditional roles of those recognized by the name 'scribe'. Ezra's special position is underlined by his high-priestly office in 1 Esdras (9.39–40, 49). He is responsible not only for the administration of justice, but also for worship in the Temple, which, as in 1 and 2 Chronicles, involves temple singers and many other temple functionaries (vv. 5, 22, 42, 54–60). These various roles come together in ch. 8. The people are organized (v. 28) and registered (v. 30); they include the priestly and royal families; and they are made complete through the addition of descendants of priests and Levites (vv. 42–49). The preparations for the long journey include a vow *that the young men should fast before our Lord* (v. 50) and financial safeguards for the money and vessels (vv. 58–64). The conclusion of the journey includes the safe handing over of the silver and gold, and the offering of sacrifices in multiples of 12 for the 12 tribes of Israel. Then, in vv. 68–96, leaders of the people inform Ezra that *The people of Israel, including even the rulers, priests, and Levites, have not kept themselves apart from the alien population of the land . . . so that the holy race has become mixed with the alien population of the land* (vv. 69–70ab). Holiness has been defined as a matter of race and so defined within a mixed population – a definition which will cause problems for the centuries to come. Ezra's response is an act of contrition and a prayer of penitence for this corporate 'act of sinfulness'(see the Prayer of Manasseh). The centre of his response is confession, recognition, affirmation and worship of the rightness of God's responses to Israel. Ezra recalls the exile (v. 77) and God's mercy in the restoration of Jerusalem: *Yet even now, Lord, how great is your mercy!* (v. 78). But there is the sin of mixed marriages (v. 82, of which the prophets gave warning) and the evidence of a *root that is left* (v. 89b). The response to Ezra's prayer is a response of the people; it is an oath to *get rid of our wives of foreign race together with their children* (vv. 93–96).

Chapter 9

1 Esdras 9.1–36 takes up the story from Ezra 10.1–44: the returned exiles enquire about men who had taken foreign wives, and the foreign wives and their children are dismissed. But at several points in this chapter the use of the biblical book of Nehemiah shows through the text as we have it. At v. 1 the priestly grandson of Eliasib appears; in Neh. 13 Eliasib's relative of foreign extraction was expelled by Nehemiah from the Temple courts after the public reading of the Law. Then at v. 37 there is a parallel to Neh. 7.73, and from that point to the

end of the chapter Neh. 8 takes over, except that in Neh. 8 Nehemiah is the governor, whereas in 1 Esd. 9 Nehemiah is never mentioned. Finally, a very abbreviated form of Neh. 8.13 ends the book.

All these facts produce quite a puzzle. First, the reading of the Law in 1 Esd. 9 takes place after the dismissing of the foreign wives, whereas in Neh. 13 there is a reading of the Law that precedes the separation of foreigners and the dismissal of the foreign wives. Second, Neh. 7.73 belongs to Nehemiah's early attempt to repopulate Jerusalem and Neh. 8.1 introduces the (seven months later) reading of the Law by Ezra. The corresponding verse in 1 Esdras (9.37) introduces the reading of the Law after the dismissal of the foreign wives. The most likely solution to the puzzle is that 1 Esdras has deliberately simplified the story by linking the narrative of the biblical book of Ezra (Ezra 1–5, 10) with Ezra's reading of the Law (Neh. 8).

So 1 Esdras revises Ezra's role and gives him the priority in the reading of the Law, with the Levites to assist him in teaching the Law. The foreign women have been dismissed. The leaders three times affirm that the day is a day for festivities.

The dismissing of the women and their children raises a host of questions for the contemporary reader. There is the form of the dismissal, not so violent, apparently, as in Neh. 13.25, but nevertheless they are 'got rid of' (v. 93) by male decision. There is the question of how such women would be able to sustain themselves and their children if, as seems to be the case, no provision is made for them. There is the question of who the women are: are some of them Moabites? If they are, the writer of the book of Ruth would appear to take a very different attitude from that of 1 Esdras. Perhaps the women were 'foreign' in the sense that they did not belong to those 'returning from the exile' (v. 65), although vv. 69–70 suggests a longer-term problem. The reading of the Law as classifying foreign wives as a 'flagrant violation' (8.70; 9.2) deserves some explanation. Certainly some Jewish communities did not read the Law in that way; the non-biblical book *Joseph and Asenath* recognizes the possibility of the conversion of a 'foreign wife'. The prophets are quoted as evidence for the dismissal of foreign wives (vv. 82ff.), but that may well have been an appropriate warning, as Israel established itself in the context of various local cults; on the other hand, at the end of the exile the protection of legal rights for foreigners is a feature of Ezekiel's prophecy (Ezek 47.21–23). Perhaps Ezra–Nehemiah and 1 Esdras in its first context recognized a similar need, but there is no evidence that such action was ever taken.

We are quite clear regarding the rights of women in such a situation. But we are all too unaware of the kind of boundaries we insist on, and the effects of such boundaries on the liberties of others. 1 Esd. 9 is unacceptable, but we are hardly the people to make that judgement.

The Second Book of Esdras

These chapters shift between divine judgement at the historical level and mythological patterns of defeat and victory. At one level they describe historical events such as the destruction of Jerusalem and events on the battlefield, and at another they move to a deeper level than description, as the Battle Hymn of the Republic does: 'He is trampling out the vintage where the grapes of wrath are stored'. When that hymn was sung at the funeral of Winston Churchill, those then alive recalled through that hymn how Churchill had lived through days which were decisive for the future of humankind, when God's requirements of justice were indeed being demanded of all humankind. All of 2 Esdras moves between those two levels: historical realities and fundamental realities.

2 Esdras in fact comprises three separate books: 2 Esdras 3–14 (which is usually called 4 Ezra, a long work including visions and their interpretation), 2 Esdras 1–2 (usually called 5 Ezra), and 2 Esdras 15–16 (usually called 6 Ezra).

1 Esdras illustrated the importance of the Law and was written long after Ezra's death. That is true also of 2 Esdras 3–14 (= 4 Ezra). 4 Ezra was written in the desperate period after the destruction of Jerusalem by the Romans in 70 CE, rather as the book of Revelation was written in the time of the Roman Emperor Domitian (81–96 CE).

A useful approach to 4 Ezra is to read it as we have learnt to read the biblical book of Job: as a long series of dialogues and monologues raising the fundamental question of whether God can be both good and just. Like Job, but much more fiercely, Ezra speaks the truth about God as he finds it. The result seems a mass of sometimes contradictory claims, but read as the reflections of a grief-stricken wise and holy scribe seeking the truth for his own and others' enlightenment, it assumes the quality of a devotional classic. Overwhelmed by the possibility of God's reclaiming the world through his Messiah and, in the light of that possibility, concluding that the fulfilment of God's Law might yet be feasible, the writer of 2 Esdras 3–14 offers an astonishingly powerful approach to the problems of his day.

The Hebrew original of 4 Ezra is lost, and so is its Greek translation. Clement of Alexandria (writing at some point before 190 CE) quotes 2 Esd. 5.35 in Greek, adding the phrase 'Ezra the prophet says', an indication that he viewed the book as authoritative. 4 Ezra is only known to us through translations into Latin, Syriac, Ethiopic, Georgian, two Arabic forms, Armenian and a fragment in Coptic. 2 Esdras 1–2, 3–14 and 15–16 are treated separately because they differ in content and dating; the earliest quotations of 4 Ezra do *not* include quotations from chs 1–2, 15–16; when 5 Ezra is quoted in reasonably early sources, 4 Ezra is not; the earliest full manuscripts copy them sometimes in the order 5 Ezra, 4 Ezra, 6 Ezra, sometimes in the order 4, 5, 6; one Greek fragment of 6 Ezra does not appear to have been preceded by 4 Ezra; and there is one partial manuscript of 5 Ezra alone. So the likelihood is that 2 Esdras is three documents in one.

How did three documents come together? The evidence available suggests that 4 Ezra and 6 Ezra were linked by the time of Gildas (a writer of British history who died about 570 CE), and were probably linked as early as 400 CE; 5 Ezra was associated with 4 Ezra and 6 Ezra as early as 450 CE. There is some evidence that one of the influential characters in the story of their association may have been the Spanish scholar Priscillian of Avila (about 380 CE), who mounted a spirited defence of both 4 Ezra and 1 Enoch.

5 Ezra

We have no very early texts of 5 Ezra. The earliest copies of these two chapters are in Latin and fall into two main types: one is represented by a French tradition, the other by a Spanish tradition. Modern editors have tended to choose one or the other. The REB chose the text published by Bensly in 1895. In this commentary we shall consider that version in relation to the Spanish tradition of the Latin text as published and translated by Bergren in 1990, since it may be that the latter is closer to the original.

If we ask whether this text is Jewish or Christian we have to take into account the possibility that a Christian hand may have been responsible for a particular manuscript or manuscript tradition. We have also to reckon with the difficulty of distinguishing a Jewish from a Christian text. At the present moment a number of suggestions are being made as criteria for making such a judgement, but there is no clear consensus among scholars as to their consistency as criteria. In simple terms we might look in a Christian work for christological terms; but many christological terms have a previous Jewish background. Apparent references to the book of Revelation might be considered decisive; but in many sections of the book of Revelation Jewish traditions predominate.

Did the author of 5 Ezra know 4 Ezra? The two share many themes and images: the portrayal of Jerusalem or Israel as a 'mother', a similar emphasis on the resurrection and the use of similar language to describe the pre-resurrection state, the depiction of Ezra as a prophet and visionary seer, the reference to people coming from the east, a vision of a multitude surrounding a son or servant of God on Mount Zion, and Ezra's conversation with an angelic interpreter. If 5 Ezra did know 4 Ezra, and 4 Ezra was written after the fall of Jerusalem in 70 CE, then 5 Ezra could have been a rewriting of 4 Ezra for a similar catastrophe; this could have been the failure of the Bar Kosiba (Kochba) revolt and the destruction of Jerusalem in 135 CE.

In 5 Ezra (2 Esdras) 1.1–14 the REB introduces Ezra as a prophet with nineteen ancestors; this is the French tradition, which picks up this information from Ezra 7.1–7. The Spanish tradition begins more succinctly: 'The word of the Lord came to Ezra, the son of Chusi, in the days of Nebuchadnezzar, saying' (i.e. the document is set in the Babylonian exile of 587 BCE). The two traditions, the French and the Spanish, represent different approaches to Ezra and two different settings.

The message of the book is summarized as follows: *Go to my people and proclaim their crimes* (1.5) . . . *for they have forgotten me and sacrificed to alien gods* (1.6b). This warning is linked to a prophecy that God will 'go over' to another nation or other nations. At the end of the book God's people are to be *a throng too vast to count* (2.42, 48). Some see this as an example of Supersessionism: the Christian Church taking over the place of Judaism. Almost certainly the text is too early to be described in that way and, as we shall see, the contents of the document do not really fit Supersessionism.

Jerusalem plays an important role in 5 Ezra. Sometimes the references are allusive: *your house is forsaken* (1.33); *The mother who bore them says: 'Go, my children; I am widowed and forsaken'* (2.2). Sometimes the name 'Jerusalem' or 'Zion' is used: *Tell my people that I shall give to them the kingdom of Jerusalem* (2.10), *Take your full number, O Zion* (2.40, see also v. 42).

If the fate of Jerusalem is once more an issue (in 135 CE as it was in 70 CE) and 5 Ezra is a response to the failure of Bar Kosiba's revolt, this could explain why in the Spanish tradition one of the cities said to be destroyed, along with Tyre and Sidon, is Bethsaida (1.11; see Matt. 11.21 and Luke 10.13). In the same context, another useful approach to 5 Ezra is via the chronicling of Jewish and Christian responses to the Bar Kosiba revolt in the *Dialogue with Trypho*, the work of Justin, a second-century Christian apologist in a dialogue held with a Jewish scholar.

In the *Dialogue with Trypho* and in 5 Ezra the issue of sacrifice *to alien Gods* (1.6) arises. In Justin's work, idolatry appears as an important area of debate between Christians and Jews: Christians could point to Jewish practices in Exodus and 1 Kings; and Jewish scholars could point to evidence (going back to Paul's time) of Christians who ate food offered to idols. Certainly Christians were prepared for martyrdom rather than risk idolatry; on the other hand some Jews felt that Christians had not stood by them when the Roman Emperor Hadrian precipitated the Bar Kosiba revolt. In terms of the debate on idolatry 5 Ezra could be either Jewish or Christian.

Yet they have aroused my anger (1.7c) belongs within the traditional Jewish pattern of historical reviews. Such a review is found in Psalm 78, which could be regarded as an outline for this section of 5 Ezra. Despite all God's mercifulness on Israel's behalf, Israel provoked and defied God; the result is the 'utter rejection' of Israel (Ps. 78.59). However, God strikes back at his enemies to protect his own name; he rejects the clan of Joseph and Ephraim, 'but chose the tribe of Judah, Mount Zion which he loved' (Ps. 78.65–68). This pattern is found in another Psalm, the Psalm of Solomon 2, which dates from that other disastrous desecration of Jerusalem, the attack on the city by the Roman commander Pompey (60 BCE): Pompey's attack will be punished and God will distinguish the righteous from the unrighteous. Another similar passage will be considered later from Baruch 1–5; in that case Jerusalem, a widow forsaken by many (Bar. 4.12), will be restored (Bar. 5.1). The important question in 5 Ezra is what we make of 1.8, *my people are beyond correction*. That particular phrase does not appear in the Spanish tradition; but even in the REB's French tradition it is not clear that this is a *final* judgement.

In 1.30–33, according to both French and Spanish traditions, Ezra presents a series of divine intentions. *I gathered you as a hen gathers her brood under her wings. But now, what am I to do with you? I shall cast you out from my presence. When you offer me sacrifice, I shall turn from you . . . I sent my servants the prophets to you, but you took them and killed them . . .* Anyone conversant with the gospel account of Jesus' lament over

Jerusalem can recognize the similar language and direction of thought in 1.30–33a (see Matt. 23.37–38; Luke 13.34–35). Because of a similarity in the context of 2 Esd. 1.30–33 and Matt. 23.37–38, concentration has centred on the Matthean parallels, especially as the similarity extends to the Old Latin Itala Gospels version (that is, the early pre–320 CE, pre-Vulgate translation of the gospels, represented in the case of this passage by Irenaeus, Zeno of Verona, Hilary and Pseudo-Cyprian). But in what is often claimed as the older tradition, the Spanish tradition, there are significant similarities with another gospel context too, that of Luke 11.49. The Spanish tradition reads in 2 Esd. 1.32, 'and tore to pieces the bodies of the apostles (or emissaries)' and 'I shall require their souls and blood of them'. There is no reference to 'apostles' or 'emissaries' in the Matthean parallel, nor is there a reference to their blood being required of them, whereas references to both appear in the Luke passage: Luke 11.50 and 51. Between 1.32 and 33, three manuscripts add what seems to be a specifically Christian comment, part of which reads: 'Thus says the Lord Almighty: "Most recently you even laid hands on me, crying out before the tribunal of the judge for him to hand me over to you".' With regard to the killing of the prophets, this belongs to an ancient Jewish tradition (1 Kgs. 19.10), offered as an explanation of the people's suffering and as a basis for the call to repentance. It was taken up in the New Testament (see Acts 7.52) and is also featured in Justin's *Dialogue with Trypho*. In the *Dialogue*, however, discussion concentrated upon Jesus as the one sent by God in the line of the prophets.

I shall hand over your homes to a people yet to come: a people who will trust me, . . . who will do my bidding, though I gave them no signs; who never saw the prophets. (1.35–36). Was this a case of Supersessionism? The following points deserve consideration:

(1) Extreme circumstances (such as revolt and failure) require extreme rhetoric

(See Ps. 78.59b, God 'utterly rejected Israel', whereas that threat was later modified in the Psalm by a decisive act of God for the sake of his own name.) It would be a major development in Israel's tradition to move from utter rejection to complete replacement by another race. 2 Esd. 1.37 (REB), *I vow that this people yet to come shall have my favour*, could, but does not necessarily, refer to those of a different ethnicity (and the phrase does not appear in the Spanish tradition; see also 2.34, which is only found in the French tradition). A place allowed to the patriarchs and prophets in 1.38 appears to support a modification of the initial judgement. That God would finally bring his people to a divinely-made heavenly sanctuary (2.42) is found in Jewish reinterpretations of the Exodus (see Odes 1.17). The possibility of extreme Jewish rhetoric in the original document is not disproved.

(2) Care must be taken not to determine the original purpose of the document by a theory of dependence on Matthew's gospel.

There is evidence of use of the Matthean tradition in the association between 1.30a,1.32 and 1.33; but, as we have seen, there is a link between 5 Ezra and Luke's material where Matthew has no parallel. The parallels with Matthew's gospel can be misunderstood: in the case of 2 Esd. 2.20–21, quoted as a parallel to Matt. 25.31–46, the material in Matt. 25.31ff is deliberately shaped to correspond with well-established Jewish standards. The fulfilment of these standards is what is required of the new people of God in 5 Ezra. The theory of dependence on Matthew's Gospel is open to question.

(3) 5 Ezra may be a later commentary on 4 Ezra.

The later commentary seems to assume that the righteous may yet be set apart as God's own (see 2 Esd. 2.41). There is also the possibility of God reclaiming the world through his Messiah (see 2 Esd. 2.46–47: *I asked again, 'Who is the young man setting the crowns on their heads and giving them the palms?' The angel replied, 'He is the Son of God.'*

It is difficult to read 5 Ezra 2.42–45 without hearing resonances with the Christian book of Revelation: *I . . . saw . . . a throng too vast to count, all singing hymns of praise to the Lord . . . I asked the angel, 'My lord, who are these?'* (see Rev. 7.9–15). The resonances are a reminder that the problem faced by Jews concerning the justice and goodness of God was now being answered by expectations of a life after death, and that Jewish martyrs were presented as occupying an honoured place in visions of the final victory of God (see 2 Macc. 12). Such visions were shaped in the book of Revelation through an emphasis on Christ the slaughtered Lamb.

5 Ezra is something of a mystery. It is possible that it began as a Jewish document, but certainly by the time of the early scribes it had been adjusted to an acquaintance with early Christian traditions.

4 Ezra

The writer reflects in the period after the Fall of Jerusalem in 70 CE on the biblical traditions of election, creation, judgement, retribution and reward. Like the book of Job this is a process of exploration. He finds most difficulty in the attempt to relate Israel's election to God's purpose in creation; he struggles with retribution and reward, seeking some comfort in the knowledge of God's covenant loyalty and freedom to deliver, and in the distinction traditionally made between the unrepentant nation and those who genuinely seek, if falteringly, to be obedient. The power of evil, present from the beginning but increasing with every generation, initially provides for him an almost insoluble problem. As in Job, there is a moment of conversion, at the point when, as often in scripture, the writer's problems are transferred into the relationship of prayer.

In the thirtieth year after the fall of Jerusalem (3.1–2). The date could be part of the fiction: the fall of Jerusalem might be the one in 587 BCE; see the reference to Babylon (3.28). Alternatively or additionally, it could refer to the writer's living situation after the fall of Jerusalem in 70 CE. In either case the perplexity is real enough; the fall of Jerusalem produced a genuine crisis of faith. The name Salathiel may be a misreading of 1 Chron. 3.17 (in the Hebrew text of 1 Chronicles the name Salathiel is linked with the word for 'prisoner', which somewhat resembles the name Ezra), but it is certainly appropriate for such a Job-like character; the name means in Hebrew 'I asked God'. There are many forms of Jewish literature which deplore the tragedies which Israel experienced. Some look to the past for explanations as 1 Esdras does, or to the opportunities of the present as in 1 Maccabees. Not even a future perspective can help, as in the Psalms of Solomon. A different solution has to be sought.

First vision

Ezra addresses God directly. Like the writers of Wisdom literature, 4 Ezra finds the prosperity of the nations (e.g. Babylon) inexplicable when Israel, who has shouldered the responsibility of God's Law, has to endure God's Temple in ruins (3.27, see Ps. 73; Job 12–14). He finds it utterly perplexing that an *evil heart*, which was given a place in Adam's constitution (3.21), should have been allowed to make that original weakness inveterate (3.22), causing even Israel to persist in evil. There are similarities with the apostle Paul's attitude to Adam (see Rom. 5.12–14). Adam's disobedience led God to make *both him and his descendants subject to death* (3.4–7; see 3.21). It was a fate shared by the nations (3.8–11). Clearly, with increasing sinfulness God's purpose must have relied upon election: *But one man, Noah, you spared* (3.11; ben Sirach 44.17; Wisd. 10.4). And it depended on a future disclosed only to certain elect: *You chose for yourself one of them; Abraham* (3.13) . . . *secretly at dead of night, you disclosed how the world would end* (3.14; see *The Apocalypse of Abraham*, also probably written after the Fall of Jerusalem in 70 CE). In such circumstances even the Law was ineffective (3.20–2; see 4.30–31; 7.62–92). The thought of David's Temple raises a hint of sarcasm (3.24), and what depresses Ezra most is the contrast with Babylon's preservation (3.30). This is unintelligible, unjust, inconsistent, and unfair to Israel's sustaining of the Law (3.31–36).

This review of history is a characteristic way of presenting the upheaval experienced by the Jewish writer. What is happening in his day is no random event. It is a final phase in a pattern of events. Our writer, however, is concerned by elements of inconsistency and unintelligibility in the pattern. So an alternative way of understanding a contemporary crisis presents itself: by recording a vision of, or visit to, the other world where secrets of what will happen could be revealed. Jewish sages had employed that way (not always appreciated, as we shall see in ben Sirach), and Christian editors and writers of this period tended to use this also.

For the moment the response to Ezra is left, rather unsatisfactorily, with the (arch)angel Uriel: God's ways are unintelligible to humanity's limited and corrupted mind (4.2–11; ben Sirach is equally realistic). But, like Job (Job 3.23), Ezra finds that response not altogether acceptable: *Better never to have come into existence than be born into a world of evil and suffering we cannot explain!* (4.12). Ezra presses the question of why he has been given a faculty of understanding (4.22) and of what he had seen with his own eyes (4.23). So Uriel switches to the future (4.26–32): sight belongs not to this present age with its massive evil harvest but to the future (see the metaphor of *the field where the good is sown*: 4.29). Ezra's misery is treated by Uriel as self-centred, although the *righteous in the storehouse of souls* have asked the same question (4.34–37). In 4 Ezra, as in 5 Ezra, there are various forms of afterlife and various kinds of entry into the afterlife. Uriel describes the storehouse of souls as like a womb (4.40–43). But Ezra sees his misery extending indefinitely (4.48–51). Uriel's answers assume, as all the following chapters do, that there is very little time left and the time left is characterized by a catalogue of signs, expounded in more detail in later chapters: social chaos, the end of the Roman Empire, universal disorder, weird events, an unwelcome ruler (Who? A demonic counterpart of Antiochus Epiphanes? See 1 and 2 Maccabees), unnatural happenings; friends become enemies, unreason, wickedness and vice rule, justice is lost (5.1–12). Ezra gives himself to prayer and fasting.

Between the visions, the people's leader intervenes. Phaltiel is a reminder to the reader that what is written is for the sake of the people as they suffer the distress, vulnerability and ignominy of the Roman destruction of Jerusalem.

Second vision

According to the traditions of the Psalms Israel can be described as one vine, plot, lily, river, city, dove, sheep; they are one nation, to whom a law was given, and *approved above all others* (5.27). If that is so, says Ezra, and if they have offended, it should be God's hand that punishes (5.28–30). The dialogue begins with the paradox of human ignorance and the promise of divine love (5.38–40). Humanity is ignorant; it cannot answer the fundamental questions of life. (The Armenian version of 4 Ezra has an addition which sounds like 1 Cor. 2.9.) The dialogue now turns on the question of who will be alive at the end (5.41; see 1 Thess. 4.13–18.). God's answer (at this point, thankfully, Uriel disappears for a time) introduces a riddle: *I shall compare my judgement to a circle: the latest will not be too late, nor the earliest too early* (5.42). One solution to the riddle is that all will appear at the end (5.45). Another is that creation needs time to allow for the many to exist (5.44). Ezra picks up both solutions: If all are to be restored to life, the same problem of sheer space would apply then as now. If God's answer interprets creation via the intervals and stages of human reproduction, then what stage are we at? God's answer draws on a theory of time common to biblical and non-biblical tradition: humanity grows weaker, therefore the world is growing old (5.50–55).

How 5.56–6.6 fits into 4 Ezra is unclear, mainly because the textual history of those verses suggests Christian editorial work. Through whom will you judge your creation? The context in ch. 6 looks for a transfer of power. If Esau represents the power of the Roman Empire and Jacob represents Israel's messianic kingdom, then the final signs (6.12a) would include an immediate transfer of power from one to the other, although how that would fit with the heavenly climax in 6.12–26 is unclear. When judgement, unnatural events and signs of war follow (6.20b–25), the issue becomes that of survival and salvation: *They will see the men who were taken up into heaven without ever tasting death* (6.26; see Ezra's translation to heaven, promised in 14.9). Thereafter repentance and truth will flourish (6.26–28). The section ends with a divine statement of approval for Ezra's integrity.

Third vision

Ezra asks again why the nations trample Israel down; but this time he asks how this can be when the seven days of creation were for the benefit of God's chosen people (6.54–59; see Isa. 40.15). This is a powerful and ancient plea; but Ezra appears here to be preparing the way for an even more fundamental question. If God's creation reflects his purpose and was for Israel's sake, why then create humanity only in the end to destroy it (7.18; 8.14)?

2 Esd. 7.1 reverts to an angelic partner in the dialogue, although the angel speaks with divine authority. Israel has to pass through the narrow entrance of this world to the greater world and its immortality (7.1–10). *Such is the lot of Israel. It was for Israel that I made the world, and when Adam transgressed my decrees the creation came under judgement* (7.11); hence the grinding hardship and subsequent death (see Gen. 3.16–19). But in Ezra's view this does not explain the suffering of the rest of humanity (7.18). What follows suggests that, in the divine view, it would better that many should die than the Law be despised (7.21–24; see Ps. 14.1–4). The pattern of justice and covenant must remain sacrosanct.

A further revelation concerning the future is given (7.26–44): the unseen city and country will appear, the survivors will see the wonders (7.27), the Messiah will come and die (7.28–30), with all humankind. Seven days of silence follow, then the ages will change (7.31), the dead will be given up and the storehouses will give souls back for judgement; the works of each will come forward and the nations will be told the consequences of denial (7.35–38). The radiance of the Most High's glory will reveal all that lies before them (7.42).

The section 7.36–105 seems to have been removed from the St Germain manuscript, presumably because it seems to suggest that prayers for the dead are not efficacious. The missing section was discovered in 1875 by R. L. Bensly and is translated in the REB text (see the marginal note and the brackets around the verse numbers). The key elements of this dialogue are: Ezra contrasts the few who will enjoy the next world with the many who will not (7.45–48), to which the answer comes: so it is with the most valuable elements, gold over against silver etc. (7.49–61). Ezra maintains that it would have been better if the human mind had not been made, simply to grow up and know that its fate is to be judged (7.62–69). The response is that it is precisely *despite* the human mind that sin follows and therefore judgement. And how patient God has been – *for the sake of the destined age to be* (7.70–74). Ezra asks if torment begins at once; the answer offers personal comfort to Ezra: because of his good works he should not count himself among those to be tormented (7.75–77). A picture is given of death (7.78): all spirits return to render adoration to God (7.78); those rejecting God's ways wander in endless grief (7.79–87). Those who have kept God's ways rejoice to see God's glory and enter rest through victory here and now over evil (7.88–99) and as they see the Lord (7.91, 99). It is fascinating to compare and contrast this passage with Newman's *Dream of Gerontius*, especially in view of the time span described in 7.100–101.

Ezra's concern for the wicked still remains: can the just plead for the wicked? The day of judgement is decisive, comes the answer (7.102–105). What then, asks Ezra, of the intercession spoken of in scripture (7.106–111)? That applies because the end is not yet, he is told; judgement ends this world and begins an eternal world where the wicked have lost their case (7.112–115). All of which brings Ezra to the point he has been seeking to make throughout: *But this is my point, my first point and my last: how much better it would have been if the earth had never produced Adam at all, or, once it had done so, if he had been restrained from sinning!* (7.116). What good is the hope of eternity when we are part of Adam's fallen race and, thoughtless of what follows after death, have *made depravity our home* (7.117–126). It is a matter of victory or defeat, replies the angel, of the responsibility each must assume; as Moses said, *Choose life and live!* (7.127–131). Then all depends on God's mercy, concludes Ezra (7.132–140), but 'recall the argument for the rarity of gold and the plentiful supply of other elements', comes the response. *Many have been created, but only a few will be saved* (8.1–3).

Here Ezra resorts to prayer, which proves to be the turning point in the dialogue, as it does in Ps. 73.17: 'O Lord, implant a seed that fallen man may obtain life. You preside over every stage of human life; so you can put it to death or give it life' (cf. 8.6). *But if you should lightly destroy what was fashioned by your command with so much labour, to what purpose was it created?* (8.14). Concerning mankind you know best; but it is for Israel that I grieve and pray, recognizing how far we have fallen and how quickly your judgement will follow. Your glory is beyond conceiving, yet *while I have understanding, I must respond* (8.25). Look on those who serve faithfully, not on the offences of your people (8.26–28). *We and our fathers have lived evil lives, yet it is on account of us sinners that you are called merciful* . . . Otherwise, when rewards are given to the just it will be no more than they deserved (8.31–33; the point is not, as so many have assumed, that the just will be rewarded according to their deeds, but that, like Noah and Abraham, the just may plead for humanity's salvation, since it is possible for mercy to be shown to sinners). The affirmation of justice and mercy now begins: your justice and kindness are made known to those with no fund of good deeds (8.34–36). To the angel's recapitulation that 'like plants, not all men will be saved' (8.37–41; see Mark 4.17), Ezra questions the comparison (8.42–45) and pleads for *pity*. He receives the reminder that Ezra's love for creation cannnot rival God's own love, and never again should Ezra *rank* himself, for all his humility, *among the unjust* (8.46–48, 53). Ezra requests indications of the time of the last things, and with a listing of the end signs the angel adds that God saw a spoilt world and could save but little; so a cluster of grapes, one tree from the forest, was all God's labour could bring to perfection (9.17–22).

Fourth vision

Ezra follows the instructions to go where no house was built (9.24), and reflects on the survival of the Law despite the failure of Israel's ancestors (9.28–37). Now a vision of the *woman in great distress* reflects back to Ezra his former attitudes, as she grieves and wishes to be alone, *for great is my bitterness of heart and great my affliction* (9.41). In the same way he feeds back to her Uriel's advice to him, especially the advice to trust in God's justice (10.5–17). With Ezra's emphasis on Zion's misfortunes, that Zion has *forfeited its glory* (10.23), a transformation occurs which terrifies Ezra, leaving him unconscious and in need of angelic help (10. 25–34): the woman is transformed into Zion; her distress is interpreted as Zion's sufferings; and, at her transformation, she brings hope to Ezra of God's future purposes; the revelation is given to him of her *radiant glory and her surpassing beauty* (10.50).

Fifth vision

Further confirmation of God's victorious justice comes for Ezra in the vision of the eagle rising out of the sea. The strange imagery of 11.1–35 would probably have been recognized as representing various historical events in a hidden form. We can recognize that the eagle represents the Roman Empire and that the three heads are the three emperors, Vespasian, Titus and Domitian (11.1; 12.23). Many of the other details escape us. Details of the vision recall Dan. 7 (see Dan. 7.3, Rev. 11.7 and the reference to the sea in 2 Esd. 11.1), although, of course, in Dan. 7 the background historical events concerned the *Greek* Empire. Here the subject is the Roman Empire. In 11.37 a lion, a messianic beast (12.32), dismisses the eagle (11.45). God speaks his word of judgement on the nation that destroyed Jerusalem, and the Messiah is promised, who will tax the Roman leaders *openly with their sins, their crimes, and their defiance* (12.32).

The people have felt abandoned by Ezra (12.40–45), but he is equipped now to encourage them (12.46), and instructs them to return home until his intercession and the seven further days are completed (12.46–51).

Sixth vision

Again the mysterious sea (13.2,52), in its turmoil, yields up a figure, this time like a man (see Dan. 7.13–14; Mark 13.26) who *flew with the clouds of heaven*, one who is identified later as God's *son* (13.32, 37, 52; see 2.47). The forces of the world gather to defeat him (13.5; the ancient Armageddon), but they become *dust and ashes* (13.11) before him. According to one interpretation. he will destroy them *by means of the law* (13.38). But in their place he summons to himself those who are *a different, peaceful company* (13.12, 39), interpreted as *the ten tribes that were taken into exile* and who are now waiting to return, led through *the narrow passages of the Euphrates* just as the people of Israel were brought out of Egypt (13.40–47; see Isa. 66.18–20). Ezra is concerned

27

about those who survive this ordeal, but he cannot forget the rest (13.17–18). He is assured that the one from whom the danger comes will protect the faithful, and those who survive will be *more blessed than those who have died* (13.24). This revelation is given to Ezra because he has laid aside his own affairs and devoted himself entirely to God's affairs and to the study of the Law (13.53–54). Ezra glorifies God for God's *providential control of the passing ages* (13.57–58).

Seventh vision

The third day (14.1a) completes the forty days covered by all Ezra's experiences, the precise period during which God appeared to Moses on Mt Sinai. In a direct call from God, like that of Moses before the burning bush (14.1b; see Exod. 3), Ezra is told that, just as Moses was given revelations, some of which were to be made public and others to be kept hidden, so Ezra too must store up in his mind all that he has seen and their interpretations (14.5–8). In that way he can reprove and comfort the people and gather them together around the Torah. As Moses was instructed what to do before he left the people (Deut. 31.14ff.), so you will be instructed what to do because *You are about to be taken away from the world of men* (14.9). In view of the desperate times drawing near (14.17), Ezra pleads that, if he is to leave the people, God will send his *holy spirit* so that he can *put in writing the whole story of the world from the very beginning, everything that was contained in* the *Law* (14.22ab). The assumption is made that the Law has been destroyed by (Babylonian) fire and therefore needs replacement; and at this juncture Ezra appears to have no reservations about the people's ability to hear, understand and obey the Law. So everything is organized for the forty days of inspiration and writing – by *five men all trained to write quickly* (14.24). The divine instructions are fulfilled and the forty days of dictating and writing begin and are completed. At the end of this period the divine command is: *Make public the twenty-four books you wrote first; they are to be read by everyone, whether worthy to do so or not. But the last seventy books are to be kept back, and given to none but the wise among your people; they contain a stream of understanding* (14.45b–47). This is the passage mentioned earlier in our discussion of the size and character of the collection of Hebrew writings. The message conveyed here is that the possession of the hidden books would grant access to a secret store of wisdom that will surpass the publicly accessible knowledge represented by the 24 books of the traditional

Hebrew collection. The figure 70 in Hebrew letters spells out the word for 'secret', and this suggests that the significance of the books which Ezra dictates is that they contain the secrets of all the ages, past, present and future. The Law is given to all to enable them to find and live out the divine way, and Ezra's first task is to ensure that this can be done (Deut. 29.29). But to understand the desperate times in which people are living, to explain the Fall of Jerusalem and the destruction of the Temple, that requires access to a hidden knowledge. Only the sage can know the answer to those mysteries.

6 Ezra

Chs 15–16 form an anonymous work preserved only in Latin, although it existed once in a Greek form, as is confirmed by the discovery of a small fourth-century Greek vellum fragment at Oxyrhynchus. The earliest witness to the Latin text is Gildas. Like 4 Ezra the two chapters are known to us from two clearly distinct Latin traditions, the 'French' and the 'Spanish'. But unlike 4 Ezra the 'French' in Ezra 6 is probably nearer the original, and the 'Spanish' secondary.

It is a prophetic writing: *Proclaim to my people the words of prophecy which I give to you to speak, says the Lord* (15.1). Its purpose is to quieten the fears of God 's people: *Do not be afraid* (see 16.74–75). Opponents who plot against the readers will die (15.2–4). Threats against the opponents are given a formal shape using what appear to be geographical terms: Egypt (15.10), Assyria (15.33), Babylon (15.43 = Rome?) and Asia (Asia Minor, 15.46; see 16.1 for similar terms but in a different order). The threats against opponents sound like those in 2 Esdras 6 and are a response to evil human beings who *have spread their wickedness the whole world over*, surpassing all limits (15.6). Divine tolerance is past; the incessant pleas of the innocent will at last be answered (15.8). God's cosmic response for his exiled people is depicted using terms drawn from the Exodus tradition (15.10–13: see Wisd. 9–16) and from the famine, misery, pitilessness and chaos of war (15.14–19). The nations are drawn together by God (the geographical picture varies from one manuscript to another: *kings of the earth* suggests they come in fact from all points of the compass); and they will be repaid *in their own coin* (a translation in 15.21 which suggests violence repaying violence done to God's people. 15.20, however, suggests a historical setting for this: that God provokes the nations to turn on each other and answer each other blow with blow: see 15.35).

The pouring out of *innocent blood* (15.22–27) is a reminder that grace, love and charity need to be balanced by justice, firm resolve, clear judgement, and acceptable punishment. Yet that balance itself stands under divine judgement. The novel *The Reader* by Bernhardt Schlink (son of the great ecumenical theologian Edmund Schlink) attempts to reflect on the bewildering consequences when international law is invoked and applied to complex situations. In the biblical texts the innocent are never forgotten; when their blood is spilt, responsibility cannot be avoided before one another and before the Holy God, but that responsibility is itself horrendous and costly (15.25–27).

15.28–33 is prophecy, but it is not clear what level is addressed: historical realities or fundamental realities. It could be read as a reference to precise historical events. If it is, this passage becomes one of the most important keys to the dating of 6 Ezra. *Hordes of dragons from Arabia will sally forth . . . The Carmanians, beside themselves with fury, will rush like wild boars out of a thicket* (15.29–30). The period 262–272 CE is a difficult one in which to try to distinguish fact from fiction. A distinction can, however, be drawn between the reign of Emperor Valerian (257–260), when threats from barbarians, recession and civil war coincided with the persecution of Christians, and the reign of the next Emperor, Gallienus, when for the Roman Empire it was a relatively peaceful time. There was, however, during Gallienus' emperorship a unique series of battles on the eastern boundary of the Roman Empire, between a group which might be called 'Arabs', led by an Odaethanus of Palmyra, on the side of the Roman Emperor, and forces from the Sassanian Empire (within the Persian area). These latter forces included Carmanians and were led by Shapur, son of the founder of that empire. Are these the battles to which 6 Ezra refers? The text itself presents many difficulties to the theory. Probably 15.28–35 moves not at the level of historical realities but at the level of fundamental realities. Its picturesque language distinguishes this section from earlier parts of 2 Esdras 15. *Dragons from Arabia* whose *hissing is borne across the land* recalls the mythological imagery used by the Greek historian Herodotus of the famous winged serpents in Arabia; the name Carmonia/Carmania (15.30) would have evoked notions of an exotic, mysterious people, as Roman writers like Pliny indicate; the picture of *a lurking enemy from Assyria* (15.33), inappropriate in the context of the Palymere–Persian wars, would be entirely appropriate as a reference to crisis and calamity.

How to give a name to such prophetic visions is unclear. Some use the word 'eschatological': it is eschatological prophecy because it invokes hopes of a imminent divinely initiated end (*eschaton*: Greek for 'end'); some use the word 'apocalyptic' because it purports to be a revealed vision of the future (*apocalypsis*: Greek for 'revelation'). These technical terms can suggest important features of the text, but they have gathered to themselves complicated histories which are sometimes unhelpful; for example, does 'end' mean what we might mean by the 'end of history' and does 'revelation' mean what we mean by 'revelation'? What we have here is probably a visionary prophecy expressed in language to indicate the fearsomeness of experience and its divine context. If the fearsome events are associated with persecutions, the reference could be to the reign of the Emperor Diocletian (see the book of Revelation) or to the Emperors Decius or Valerius.

15.34–63 has its focus in yet another fearsome set of events, those surrounding the fall of Babylon, a favourite way of describing Rome: *They will force their way to Babylon, and destroy her* (15.43). Here the language is even more picturesque and violent. It resembles the images of *The Lord of the Rings* and, even more, the film version of Tolkien's trilogy. Human forces and powers of the world coalesce to cause havoc and enslave. Issues of power are seen in all their destructive and enslaving fury, as instruments and expressions of arrogance, pride and ruthlessness; but these bring their own ultimate recompense (see Isa. 13.11 for the Oracle on Babylon, and also Isa. 21.9). The descriptions of Babylon and Asia, Babylon's imitator, sound a note of judgement. Asia, like Babylon, and like Rome in the book of Revelation (Rev. 17.1), is a *vile harlot* (15.48, 55), and she, like Babylon, is to be pitied because she will become *a poor, weak woman, bruised, beaten, and wounded* (15.51; see Isa. 23.16). Rev. 17.1–18.24 has the same imagery and, like 6 Ezra, regards the harlotry as infectious and universally corrupting. Revelation also makes the same connection between Babylon's persecution of God's people and Babylon's fate (Rev. 17.6, 16; 18.7). This is a key to 6 Ezra, as is evident from 15.53–57: *I should not be so fierce with you . . . if you had not always killed my chosen ones*, and that ferocity seems to be more central to 2 Esdras 15 than to Rev. 17.1–18.21. The fate of both Babylon and Asia also has parallels in Revelation, not least because it can be said of them, as of Rome in Rev. 18, *not a trace will be left of your splendid beauty* (15.63; see Rev. 18.14).

This is a remarkable series of parallels between 6 Ezra and the book of Revelation. How are they to be understood? It could be argued that 6 Ezra must have known the book of Revelation, and could have adapted the latter's prophecies of Babylon's downfall to a later, geographically different situation. Alternatively, we could repeat the argument that Revelation (certainly earlier than 6 Ezra) is in many ways a book dependent on Jewish traditions, idioms and language; they could both represent common traditions, and each could have adapted those traditions to their particular circumstances.

2 Esdras 16 begins by shifting the emphasis in two ways. First, the emphasis moves from the afflictions of Babylon and Asia to the one who afflicts them, from the arrows directed at Egypt and Syria towards the archer who directs them: *when the Lord God sends calamities, who can avert them?* (16.8). Because it is the Lord who threatens them, the disasters are like a lion which cannot be driven away, or a fire that cannot be put out, or an arrow which once launched by a powerful archer cannot be diverted (16.3–16). Second, the writer turns to his own fate and that of his contemporaries *in those days* (16.17). Famine, plague, suffering and hardship should *teach them better ways;* but people will still be caught unawares (16.18–21). In similar language and pictures to those of the Hebrew prophets (e.g.Isa. 6.11–13; 7.18–25; 9.20; 13.4–22; 18.4–6; 24.1–23; 27.11–12; 32.9–14), devastation is promised (16.22–34) and these *calamities are close at hand, and will not be delayed* (16.37–39; on the divine power to decide the time see Isa. 56.1).

The divine purpose is that *in a very short time she* (i.e. wickedness and her deeds) *will be swept away from the earth, and the reign of justice over us will begin* (16.52). With that in view the writer addresses his readers as *My people,* and advises them to *behave as though* they *were strangers on earth* (16.40). Pressing times call for fresh patterns of behaviour (16.47–48; see 1 Cor. 7.29–31).

The reign of justice will be prefaced by indignation (16.49), *when the champion arrives to expose every sin on earth* (16.50). In the original texts the function of the 'champion' is not clear; probably it designates 'the one who comes to defend such indignation against all wickedness' rather than, as the REB translation suggests, an individual, 'one who exposes every sin on earth'. The REB translation suggests a parallel with some Jewish messianic hopes or with some Christian parousia expectations. Perhaps neither of those particular parallels is implied; rather, the text here suggests that the ultimate defender of justice is God himself. The following verses, 16.53–67, concern God who scrutinizes all, made everything and knows the universe, especially the full nature of humanity (see 1 Cor. 2.10). He is the one who comes as judge when *your wicked deeds stand up to accuse you on that day* (16.65–67), and as your deliverer (16.67).

2 Esd. 16.68–73 adds further imagery about the days that are coming. They depict the coming time of testing in terms reminiscent of the Maccabean period: *they will seize some of you and compel you to eat food sacrificed to idols* (16.68b; see 1 Maccabees, especially 1.62–64). It has been argued that 16.68–73 appear to represent a mob attack rather than an official edict such as characterized the Maccabean persecution. But 16.68 could well imply such official compulsion, and many of the features of 2 Esdras – taunting, humiliation, plundering, maniacal destruction, ejection – appear as a typical context for the testing of God's chosen ones rather than descriptions of discrete and datable mob actions (16.73). It has also been argued that this section of 2 Esdras describes a period which knew Christian rather than Jewish experiences of persecution. But it is not easy to distinguish actual times of persecution from a mental world where persecution and conflict were the norm, and Judaism developed its own imagery, language and literature in relation to such circumstances, which Christians adopted and adapted. 16.68–73 still leaves the possibility open of a Jewish origin for 6 Ezra.

6 Ezra concludes with a repetition of the warning to God's chosen people not to become involved in evil ways (16.77b–78). But there is also a promise: *Listen, you whom I have chosen, says the Lord: the days of harsh suffering are close at hand, but I shall rescue you from them* (16.74). This verse could well summarize the purpose of 6 Ezra: God will deal fiercely with those who humiliate and kill his chosen people. They in turn must recognize the seriousness of God's demand for justice, and the dependence of the fulfilment of God's promise of deliverance on that obedient response.

Tobit

As a text for today the book of Tobit found a contemporary commendation in Salley Vickers' novel *Miss Garnet's Angel*. Miss Garnet is a middle-aged Englishwoman who finds a fresh stimulus in a haunting experience of Venice. Via her discovery of the Guardis of Tobias and the Angel in the church of Angelo Raffaele and her consequent study of the Apocrypha and the book of Tobit, Miss Garnet discovers resonances in her own life which open up for her possibilities of new beginnings and perspectives. The author of the novel, Salley Vickers, digs deeply into recent studies of the book of Tobit as the background for her book, and this enables her to provide a novelistic interpretation of the text which she prints in italics as a parallel to Miss Garnet's story. This results in not merely a moving novel but also an engaging reconstruction which makes good sense of many features of the text of the book of Tobit (in its King James Version), even if it fails to explain the whole book of Tobit as we have it. The strengths of her interpretation lie in her reconstruction of the lives of Jewish families in different parts of the Diaspora, her determination to understand the role in the story of the archangel Raphael, and her concern to explore the significance of the marriage of Tobias and Sarah. Its weaknesses are in its omission of the parallel between Tobias and Sarah with which the book of Tobit begins, in her over-zealous Zoroastrian expansion of the dog reference (the dog motif is stronger in the Vulgate and the Syriac than in the Greek: see 11.9), and in her failure to be honest about the paternalistic assumptions behind the text.

The plot of Tobit concerns two righteous people, Tobit and Sarah, both of whom suffer undeservedly. Thanks to Tobit's son, Tobias (with, of course the help of the angel Raphael), all turns out well for them both and the righteous live happily ever after. Several of the books of the Apocrypha deal with this issue of vindication for the righteous. Some look for the vindication beyond this human existence. The writer of the book of Tobit is happy to find vindication in this life – despite the troubles that have to be endured here, and despite the considerable evidence that the good die young. But before we are too critical of Tobit's apparent naivety, we might recollect with the Psalmist that righteousness and true happiness are closely related (Ps. 73.1); they do belong together, and they belong together because this is God's world.

As an ancient novel the book of Tobit strikes us as somewhat lacking in dramatic sense. Rather like the Prologue to Piramus and Thisbe in Shakespeare's *A Midsummer Night's Dream*, the book of Tobit spills all the beans before the story ever begins. The level of humour is different too (Tobit excels in irony) but both Tobit and Shakespeare's Prologue are concerned that what is to happen should in no way be misunderstood. God's intended purpose is openly declared and completely fulfilled in Tobit, even to the extent of turning a good story into a moralistic lesson.

There is an unevenness about the narrative. This may be due to the way in which the story seems to have gathered various bits of folklore in the telling. Some suggest that its history progresses from international fairy-tale to Jewish fairy-tale to Jewish Tobit legend, and via various kinds of editing en route. Although these can underline key concerns of the original writer and his successors, the unevenness tends to hold up the progress of the main storyline. One of these concerns Ahikar and Ahikar's deceitful kinsman Nadab (see the notes on 1.21–22; 14.10). Tobit (speaking in the first person – *Ahikar was a relative of mine*, 1.22) confesses that he owes much to Ahikar (2.10) and draws the moral from Ahikar's ultimate vindication: because of his good works Ahikar escaped the snare Nadab laid for him. That is a version of the Ahikar story known to us from a document perhaps as many as four centuries earlier than the book of Tobit, and one which shares with Tobit features of wisdom teaching and in particular the negative form of the Golden Rule: 'Son, that which seems evil to you, do not to your companion', or, as Tobit 4.15 offers it, *Do to no one what you yourself would hate* (see the role of the negative form of the Golden Rule in Hans Küng's work for the Global Ethic Foundation).

Another element from Tobit which is at home in folklore reminds us of some of the similarities between Tobit and the gospel narratives. In Tobit it concerns the story of how Sarah is rescued from the demon which every wedding night murders her newly-wed husband. Just as Raphael enables the prayers of Tobias and Sarah to be heard by God (see Matt. 18.10), so also Raphael provides the means by which the demon can be driven out (see Tob. 6.13–17). These are ideas which appear elsewhere is various forms (see 1 Enoch 10.4); they are found in books such as the *Testament of Solomon* (a book ascribed to King

Solomon but written about 100 CE, which tells about Solomon and Asmodaeus).

There are various versions of the book of Tobit. Fragments in two different Semitic languages have turned up among the Dead Sea Scrolls, and the REB (on the whole) translates the Greek text found in Codex Sinaiticus (which is marked by Semitisms) rather than the shorter text in Codex Vaticanus. The likelihood is that originally Tobit was written in Aramaic, copied inaccurately several times and translated into Hebrew; this too was copied, so that the context in which Greek translations were made was, to say the least, varied. The evidence of the Dead Sea Scrolls also shows that Tobit cannot be dated later than the end of the Qumran community (70 CE). Jerome claimed to have access to an Aramaic text of Tobit via a translator, but recent work on the Vulgate suggests that Jerome's hurried use of what was possibly an Aramaic text of Tobit has resulted in what is virtually an editing of the Old Latin text of Tobit, betraying perhaps more of Jerome's style and concerns than earlier and valuable readings.

It is worth reading through the prayers in Tobit; for example, Tobit's prayer of distress in 3.1–6 and Sarah's prayer of distress in 3.11–15. Tobias and Sarah's prayer in 8.5–8 has had considerable influence over the years on wedding liturgies, and the prayer of thanksgiving in 13.1–18 draws in the theme of Jerusalem as the place where God's praise is to be heard. This theme may be a later addition. Tobit and Tobias are described as belonging to the community of exiles from the Northern Kingdom of Israel, living in Nineveh, the capital of the Assyrian empire. Whether by the time the story was written Assyria had come to stand for the Greek or the Roman Empire depends on ascribing the book to a period such as the Maccabean or post-Maccabean. Certainly the theory that the written book of Tobit might have come from the Maccabean tradition could explain why the Jerusalem theme might have been added.

The Assyrian setting is one of several links with the book of Judith: the same designation for God (Lord of heaven), agreements of vocabulary (various people 'leap up'), similar rhetorical devices, the use of parallels to the book of Judges, the celebration of Jerusalem and, as we shall see, similar expressions of piety. They could well have emerged as literature in a similar or the same context, probably in the Maccabean period or post-Maccabean period.

The book is full of insights into Israelite piety. One of the most interesting of these highlights the importance of the family meal: the meal at Pentecost in Tobit 2 is thrown open to all the poor. The Israelite meal and its rich associations with hospitality, acceptance and recognition, suggest parallels with the eating practices in the life of Jesus and of the Early Church. Interestingly too, Tobit leaves the feast to attend to a corpse and secure for it, following Israelite law, a proper burial. Associated with the meal is a concern for a kind of purity associated with individual rather than priestly principles. Both in the book of Judith and in Tobit the practices of washing are a form of piety associated with eating. That may well have been a development due to the desire of individuals to discover forms of holiness, some of which were linked to a depth of understanding and faith. If in Pharisaic times this kind of concern for holiness became a matter of social standing rather than, as it was in its origins, a matter of personal piety, it would not be surprising if Jesus took exception to the kind of activities which in Tobit and Judith have a quite different justification.

Chapter 1

Tobit (his son's name is similar, and his father's too, meaning 'God is my good', and with an ancestry some of whose distinguished names reappear later: 1.4, 8, 22; 4.1; 5.13; 7.1; see also Deborah in v. 8) is described as a Galilean (see v. 5, or did Tobit come from the neighbourhood of Samaria?). He was *taken captive* to Nineveh in the time of *Shalmaneser of Assyria* (v. 2). As we have seen, Assyria may represent Maccabean or post-Maccabean empires. *While I was quite young . . . my ancestor broke away from the dynasty of David and from Jerusalem* (v. 4) refers to the breakaway of the Northern from the Southern Kingdom in 922 BCE. Shalmaneser, however, was king 727–722 BCE. Dates here are unimportant; what is important is that Tobit belonged to the Diaspora; he had before his exile (unlike his colleagues and his idolatrous tribe) fulfilled, to the letter, responsibilities to Jerusalem, including the first, second and third tithes enjoined by the Law (vv. 6–8; Deut. 18.1–5; 14.24–29) and the teachings of his grandmother Deborah (note the reference to proselytes in v. 8). He had made *truth and righteousness* his way of life (v. 3). Similarly, in his exile he did charitable acts for his fellow-exiles (v. 16; Tobit affirms ungrudging almsgiving to those in need and to those who practise righteousness, as a sacrifice to God to purge away sin and avoid death, but see the note on 4.16–18); and – again in this he differed from his *family and nation* – he *scrupulously avoided* eating gentile food (vv. 9–11; Deut. 14.3–20). His reward from God was *favour* and *presence* before Shalmaneser, which lasted until the latter's death (vv. 13, 15). So we have an emerging picture of an ideal, if in some ways lonely and isolated, Diaspora Jew (an ideal for the Maccabean period), following dietary restrictions (Dan. 1.8; Judith 10.5), marrying one's kin (v. 9; Judith 8.1–2; the language defines this in Tobit as marrying within one's own tribe); to that picture can be added burying one's kin (1.17–18; Judith 8.3; burial becomes a key motif in Tobit; see vv. 18–19; 14.12–13), prayer (Judith 9.2–14; Dan. 2.19–23) and being *mindful of God* (only found in Tobit at 1.12 and 2.2; a parallel expression is found in the Sinaiticus text of 14.7, where Vaticanus has 'sincere love of God'). Crucial for the book of Tobit are the family relationships: he marries Anna (unnamed in this Greek text of 1.9; see 2.1); they have an only son Tobias; he lodges ten talents of silver with his kinsman Gabael in far-off Media while Media was still accessible (1.14–15); he claims Ahikar as a *relative* (1.22). Because of the Israelite murders associated with Sennacherib's rebuff by Jerusalem, burial becomes an issue for Tobit and the cause of his first fall from grace and into penury (1.18–20). After Sennacherib's death Ahikar is *appointed* or confirmed by Esarhaddon as a key official; he *interceded on* Tobit's behalf (1.22). The name Ahikar is, as we have seen, a curiosity: it is a name used of a counsellor to Assyrian kings (the Old Latin tradition here calls him 'kindred of the king'), and a name of one whose wisdom writing is preserved in an Aramaic papyrus from Elephantine; and at this verse a Qumran Aramaic version (4QTob^a 2,9a) reads: 'he (Ahiqar) was son of my brother, of my father's house and of my family' (see 2.10 for Ahikar's help to the blind Tobit and his departure to the Persian Gulf).

Chapters 2–3

The next two chapters describe how on one and the same day Tobit in Nineveh and Sarah in Ecbatana, unaware of each other, pray simultaneously out of deep trouble and distress; God hears them and sends Raphael ('God has healed') to heal them both (see 3.17; 12.12). The story as it unfolds reveals aspects of divine providential care at work across the Diaspora. Tobit's family has now been restored to him, and he speaks in the first person of a feast prepared for him at which he takes his place; the patriarchal character of the meal is evident. *Pentecost*, the wheat harvest feast fifty days after the Passover, was, as we have noted, a time to invite in the alien, the fatherless and widow

(Deut. 16.11; 15.7–9), so Tobias, the son, is despatched to find from among the captive people *a poor man who is wholeheartedly mindful of God* (2.2; see the note on 1.12). Tobias finds one of their nation murdered in the market-place, and Tobit rushes out to retrieve the body and hide it till night makes burial possible. He bathes before eating (see the earlier note on purity and piety). At nightfall, to the jeers of his neighbours, he once again risks everything by burying the corpse. He falls asleep in the courtyard, where sparrow *droppings* cause *white patches* on his eyes, which the doctors' ointments turn into blindness (2.10–11; on issues concerning doctors, prayer and divine providence see ben Sirach 38.1–15; some suggest a hidden polemic here against magic medicine as taught to humanity by fallen angels, see 1 Enoch 8.3). Anna, his wife, becomes the bread-winner (2.11), so effectively that during the winter she is given as an additional gift over and above her earnings, a young goat. Did Tobit blush *with shame* or flush with anger? In either case he accuses Anna of stealing the goat, refuses to believe her, and his wife snaps back, '*So much for . . . all your good works! Everyone can now see what you are really like*' (2.14). Interestingly, Jerome's Vulgate omits this altercation; perhaps Jerome did not appreciate any suggestion that pomposity in Tobit's piety could be challenged here. Tobit appears to regard her as Job did his wife (Job 2.10), as lacking in understanding of the deeper things of God (although it is comforting that the *Testament of Job* takes a different view). The question remains: Did the story-teller approve of the attitude that Tobit expresses in his prayer (on the same grounds as are expressed in Job and in some Psalms) *in its entirety* (3.1–6)? '*I had rather die than live in such misery, listening to such taunts*' (presumably including those of Anna). Or did the story-teller recognize Tobit's aloof, self-opinionated piety, and even perhaps contrast the altercation here with the preferred mutuality of Tobias' and Sarah's relationship (8.7)?

In Media, at the very same moment, Sarah is in a similar suicidal mood; she also is troubled by insults, undeserved as she sees them (one of the Qumran fragments calls them 'false reproaches' 4QTob^c 61. 2–3). In her case it is *her father's servant girls* that complain; they accuse her of murdering seven husbands and they complain at the trouble she is causing them. At this point in the story the demon Asmodaeus is introduced. According to the text it is Asmodaeus (probably a Persian name) who has killed each of the husbands on their wedding night, following a folktale known as 'The Monster in the Bridal Chamber'. The world of Tobit resembles the world of the New Testament, in that individuals in conditions of desperate need, illness and helplessness turned to traditions of deliverance which depended on magic, exorcism, religious belief, physicians, charismatic healers etc. which, as we have seen, could be interpreted in different ways, and from our modern perspective can only partially or theoretically be distinguished one from the another. In both Tobit and the New Testament the question is why the stories are recounted, and there is little doubt that in both they are indications of God's gracious, creative, effective, restorative and renewing power. Precisely how Sarah's problem and her eventual deliverance were being described (there is an incredible mixture in Tobit of exorcism, pharmacy and angelology), or precisely how they might be described today, is less important than the extraordinarily creative ways in which divine providence is seen as working with human need. Sarah resists the temptation to suicide, out of concern not to bring her *aged father in sorrow to his grave* (3.10; an attitude with strikingly modern parallels). Her prayer intends to ask for deliverance from the taunts either in death or in life if she must continue to live; but, as in the Psalms of individual lament, her prayer typically includes praise (see the Prayer of Manasseh). Having protested her purity, and innocence, she admits that she can see no solution; her father *has no other to be his heir, nor has he any near kinsman or relative who might marry me* (3.15). What she does not know, and what we are told by the omniscient narrator, is that Tobias is waiting in the wings to be part of Raphael's overall solution to her problem and Tobit's (3.16–17).

Chapter 4

Providentially Tobit remembers *the money he had deposited with Gabael at Rages in Media* (v. 1) and sends for Tobias. Tobit begins as if this is a farewell: *When I die, give me a decent burial. Honour your mother, and do not abandon her as long as she lives* (v. 3). The commandment in Deut. 5.16 includes both parents as deserving of honour and the honouring of both carries its reward. Tobias adds a special comment about the hazards of motherhood, requiring that Anna be buried beside him (v. 4). Regarding reward for good living, Tobit is positive (v. 6a) but he concentrates on winning divine counsel (v. 6b). The REB here translates the Sinaiticus text of Tobit – *the Lord will give good counsel*. Since the Sinaiticus text lacks vv. 7–19cd (although a manuscript akin to Sinaiticus has a version of these verses) the REB turns to the other main Greek tradition. Here the feel of Tobit's speech changes from a farewell utterance to wisdom advice commending a life-style such as Tobit himself has embraced and concentrating not on areas related to the story-line but concerned with economic features of patronage, as in the Greco-Roman environment: on almsgiving (vv. 7–11), on fornication, and on choosing *a wife from the race of your ancestors* (for Noah's choice see *Jubilees* 4.33), a practice which is underlined by powerful arguments. The ancestors possess the promise of the land; refusal to marry within the race or tribe comes from pride (the Vulgate concentrates just on the danger of pride) and pride leads to ruin, disorder and starvation (vv. 8–13). The advice continues: pay promptly for work done (*If you serve God, you will be repaid*, v. 14); *Do to no one what you yourself hate* (v. 15), the negative form of the Golden Rule (see Matt. 7.12 for the positive form); avoid drunkenness; *Whatever you have beyond your own needs, distribute in alms* (v. 16; see 12.8–9; 14.10–11; ben Sirach 29.9–13); honour the righteous dead, not sinners (it might be said that the Vulgate over the centuries has done some damage to the reputation of the Apocrypha; here it Christianizes the text, imagining Jews as unwilling to eat with publicans and sinners!). 4.20–5.3 reverts to the question of the money residing in Media. Tobit and Gabael have each kept a half of a document as guarantee of the deposit.

Chapter 5

Raphael appears, offering himself as a guide and companion for Tobias on his journey to Media. The parallels between Tobit and the books of the Old Testament are too many to recount. But as in the case of the book of Judith, Judges provides important parallels. One such parallel concerns the angel who came to Ophrah while Gideon was threshing wheat in a winepress (Judg. 6.11–22). As in the case of Raphael, the angel is not initially recognized as such, is prepared to wait around and holds conversations with Gideon which alert Gideon to the strangeness of the visitor, but the full truth only dawns when the final miracle occurs and Gideon at last grasps that he has 'seen an angel of the Lord face to face' (see Tob. 12.6–22). Raphael not only knows Media (although his estimate of two days' travel is at an angelic, not human, pace!), he also says that he knows Gabael before Tobias reveals where in Media they are to go. Tobit is harder to convince and fails to grasp what Raphael is saying to him: *Take heart; in God's design your cure is at hand* (v. 9). Indeed Raphael, having chosen the name Azarias (meaning, God helps), is forced to concoct for himself a (for Tobit) believable and convincing parentage. Satisfied at last, Tobit tells Tobias to get ready, saying (in one of the many examples of double-talk in the book): *May his angel escort you both, my son* (v. 16). Anna is less easy to convince; she would be happy with their current lot, hard though it is. Only the idea of a *good angel* going with them consoles her (v. 21). Her strength of character, her indomitable hope which shines through her actions even during their anxious wait (10.1–7) and her deep affection for both Tobias and Tobit are only allowed to emerge at the end of the story, providing an important commentary on what seems initially to be a patriarchal household (11.5–9).

Chapter 6

The appearance of a dog following Tobias out of the city (see also 11.4) has caught the imagination of artists and writers (see the half-invisible, almost ghostly companion in Verrochio's Tobias painting in the National Gallery). It is an unusual feature and may belong to an earlier narrative, since the dog does not seem to have any particular function. The Tigris route is also a surprise, but this does provide the opportunity to struggle with a large fish which attacks Tobias (see the Caucasian folk-tale of the 'Red Fish'). The fish serves as food (for Tobias; the various traditions differ on whether or not Azarias ate), and two key moments of the story depend on the fish: the healing of Tobit and Sarah: *the gall, heart, and liver can be used as remedies* (v. 4). Lest the point should be missed, Tobias asks Azarias to spell it out: *You can use the heart and liver as a fumigation for any man or woman attacked by a demon or evil spirit* and the encounters will cease permanently. *The gall is for anointing a person's eyes when white patches have spread over them* and they will recover (6.7–8). Tobias and Raphael arrive in Media and approach Ecbatana. Raphael now acquaints Tobias with the fact that they are to stay overnight with a relative of Tobias, Raguel, and with the existence of Sarah, Raguel's only child, *sensible, brave, and very beautiful* (v. 12), whom it will be Tobias' duty on their return from Rages to marry and Raguel's duty on their return to release. Judged by our knowledge of the Jewish law, Raphael somewhat overstates his case: *Raguel . . . cannot betroth her to another without incurring the death penalty according to the decree in the book of Moses* (6.12) – perhaps a touch of divine exaggeration, or of humour for the hearer. But the point is clear: Tobias has the legal right to marry Sarah and Sarah is his providentially appointed bride (6.17; 7.12; one scholar finds 33 connections with Gen. 24!). What is not so clear is precisely what timetable Azarias proposes. He appears in v. 11 to propose an immediate promise of marriage, then their visit to regain the money, then the wedding celebrations. By v. 15 Azarias is sure Sarah *will* that very night *be given to* Tobias *as* his *wife*. By 9.1 Sarah is his wife and they are still at Raguel's, from where Tobias has to send Azarias to make the journey without him to carry the *note of hand*, collect the money from Gabael, and bring Gabael back with him to join the wedding feast. The timetable is fulfilled in its general outline, but not quite as Tobias anticipated. Perhaps the acceleration of events is intentional; as we might say, because of Tobias' cold feet (vv. 13–14) – somehow he has heard about the seven previous fatalities, is concerned that his father and mother will have no one to bury them, and has drawn the conclusion that the demon, while deeply attached to Sarah, is not so happy about her successive suitors. Raphael/Azarias becomes the traditional guardian-cum-pedagogue (v. 15). Rather spoiling the story, Azarias says exactly what the couple need to do in order for Tobias to deliver Sarah from the demon. Once again, in the Vulgate of v. 17, Jerome appears to have his own agenda in translating this section of Tobit: far from quoting an older source he seems to be shaping the story to attack those who argued for a married clergy. In v. 19 Tobias gives in and sets his heart on Sarah.

Chapter 7

In this chapter Tobias seizes the initiative. *Azarias*, my brother (the more literal sense of the texts), *take me straight to our kinsman Raguel* (v. 1; see also vv. 8c, 11). They greet Raguel first, and Raguel remarks to Edna his wife on Tobias' similarity to Tobit. In v. 6 the narrative is somewhat telescoped in the REB and its Greek text; there is no opportunity to spell out what 'He is alive and well' means, and Raguel's next words imply that the news about Tobit's blindness has somehow been communicated. In the other Greek tradition this sequence of events is given more space. The compressed version of the REB has the advantage of a sense of drama and emotion. Washing and bathing before eating are practised here in Media too (v. 9; the Diaspora is a place where piety is to be practised). Tobias again takes the initiative: *Azarias*, my brother, *ask Raguel to give me Sarah my kinswoman* (v. 8).

Raguel overhears, concedes that such a marriage is appropriate and in terms of kinship the only legal option (i.e. the only proper Israelite option), but warns what has happened to the seven previous husbands. In the REB Raguel also adds a comment (v. 11c is rather vague in the Greek) which is clarified in v. 12cd – a formula committing the couple to God's care. This is part of the formal handing over of Sarah to Tobias and of an ancient marriage contract not mentioned in scripture but known from various Aramaic texts (v. 14; in one text the contract is 'sealed'). The marriage bed is prepared. Raguel's actions (8.11) suggest he fears the worst; his words in 7.18, however, '*Take heart, dear daughter*', are reminiscent of the healing promise in 5.9 and may be the omniscient narrator's rather obvious hint that what is to happen to Sarah will in fact be a healing.

Chapter 8

Escorted to the bride's bedroom Tobias follows instructions (see REB 6.16). The incense is perfuming the room: Tobias removes *the fish's liver and heart from the bag in which he had them, and* puts them on *the burning incense* (v. 2). The stench of the fish repels the demon and Raphael pursues the demon to that ancient home of magic, Egypt. According to the Greek text Raphael did his work there thoroughly: he tied him hand and foot, and *bound him* on the spot (see Matt. 12.29). The prayer that follows became the pattern for the blessing of bed and board in medieval marriage liturgies: Tobias praises God the creator, especially for making Adam and his wife Eve. Importantly, Eve is made *to be his partner and support* (see Gen. 2.18–20), and they are *the parents of the human race*: that is, the purpose of marriage is both mutual companionship and procreation. Furthermore, Tobias acts not *out of lust but* in truth (v. 7). Jerome again adjusts the Vulgate to his viewpoint by changing 'in truth' to 'solely for love of posterity, through whom may your name be blessed for ever and ever'. Tobias prays that they *may find mercy and grow old together* (v. 7). Both add *Amen* and sleep through the night. The understanding of marriage presented here stresses mutuality and companionship, a stress to which Jerome's Vulgate does not do justice. The Greek serves to correct the impression given by earlier parts of Tobit of a strictly patriarchal understanding of marriage. Sarah is healed; and the hopes and prayers for divine mercy have been answered. Meanwhile, Raguel has risen and arranged for a grave to be dug so that the embarassment of yet another corpse can be avoided. He sends a servant girl to find if Tobias is dead (vv. 9–12). At the good news that the couple have survived the night the whole household (according to Sinaiticus, although see the singular in v. 16) breaks out in praise to God. The prayer has God's universal blessing as its focus, and specifically the gift of joy and his mercy shown to *these two, these only children* (vv. 15–17). The grave is hurriedly filled in – and all this *before dawn came*. Raguel's instructions for an extended celebration are detailed, generous and pastoral, as is the position which Raguel gives his new son-in-law (the Vulgate differs here).

Chapter 9

The extended celebration creates problems – delay in the visit to Rages and concern back at home (see 10.1). So Azarias is entrusted with the task of taking Tobit's part of the bond, ensuring the money is retrieved and bringing Gabael to the wedding feast. Gabael proves entirely trustworthy (v. 5). Again, distances are an irrelevance. Gabael is soon with Tobias and breaks out in a prayer of blessing (v. 6).

Chapter 10

Tobias' parents are indeed concerned. Anxiety grows there and with it yet another sharp exchange between Tobit and Anna (softened somewhat in the REB; in the Old Latin translation the exchange is quite acrimonious). Again the narrator has fun with the words: there'll have been quite a distraction, says Tobit helpfully (v. 6). And what a distraction! Anna keeps a continuous daytime and night-time watch (v. 7). Tobias finally prevails in his determination to leave for home, and the theme becomes *prosperity to the end of our days* (vv. 10–12). The commandment 'Honour your father and mother' (see 4.3–4) becomes now '*Honour your husband's father and mother*' (v. 12; see also 11.1); and the family ties are sealed with Edna's words to Tobias: *I entrust my daughter to your keeping; do nothing to cause her distress throughout your life* (vv. 11–12). The Vulgate instructions to Sarah lack the warmth, close relationships, kinship terms and affection of the Greek.

Chapter 11

Raphael's work is not yet finished. Near Nineveh he reminds Tobias of his father's condition and suggests they go on ahead of Sarah to *see that the house is ready*, Tobias bringing the *fish-gall* (v. 4). Anna sees them coming; the narrator chooses the language carefully: she tells *his father*: He's here – *your son and the man who went with him* (v. 6). So that we know what is to happen, Raphael instructs Tobias precisely how to apply the remedy to his father's eyes and what to expect. The contrast between Anna and Tobit is dramatic: Anna rushes out to fling her arms around her son (v. 9); Tobit stumbles and manages to reach *the courtyard gate*. Only when Tobias has fulfilled Raphael's instruction, gently and considerately, can Tobit throw *his arms round him . . . burst into tears* and cry, *I can see you, my son, the light of my eyes* (v. 14). Tobit's thanksgiving interestingly concentrates on *all the angels* (v. 13). The interpretation of his blindness as a scourge is paralleled in the language of Mark 3.10, 5.29, 34, except that in Tobit God is spoken of as the cause of the punishment, not 'unclean spirits', as implied in Mark. It is important to say that this ancient view of suffering as punishment is one area where biblical ideas are incompatible with a contemporary understanding both of God and of illness. Rejoicing now takes over. Tobias tells of his success and breaks the news of his marriage to Raguel's daughter, Sarah (12.14–15). Tobit's ability to walk *without anyone to guide his steps* causes amazement in Nineveh. When he welcomes Sarah: *Come into your home, and may health, blessings, and joy be yours; come in, my daughter* (v. 17), all the Jews in Nineveh share *a day of joy*. As in a finale, Ahikar (from v. 22, 2.10) arrives to join in too, with Nadab (see 14.10).

Chapter 12

The instruction in 4.14 to pay a workman immediately is fulfilled to the letter by Tobit and Tobias, generously, since the promise had been made to Azarias in 5.15–16 of a bonus on top of any wages. In one of the folk-tales linked with the book of Tobit, 'the Grateful Dead', the guide is given half of what the hero acquires; that is what is offered to Azarias (vv. 1–5). Raphael's response calls them to the praise of God, to the proclamation of what God had done, and to true piety: *Better prayer with sincerity, and almsgiving with righteousness, than wealth with wickedness* (v. 8; see 4.7–10, 16). In place of the cult (4.9–11), almsgiving preserves from death and wipes out every sin (v. 9a; see Prov. 15.27a LXX; in the Greek text almsgiving and righteousness appear together in Tobit 1.3; 2.14; 12.8–10). This is the basis for the increase of and the maintaining of life (v. 9b). Raphael now tells Tobit and Sarah what the hearers have known from the beginning of the story. His revelation of his identity is modelled on Judg. 13, and his exhortation in 12.17, '*Do not be afraid, peace be with you*', recurs only elsewhere in the Septuagint in Judg. 6.3 and Dan. 10.19 (Theodotion's version). His identity shows him to be a tester, healer and intercessor, one of the seven angels who can *enter* God's *glorious presence* (v. 15), sent by God and now *about to ascend to him who sent me* (v. 20: Raphael only takes the form of an *apparition*, one that does not take food or drink, so is able to disappear and resume his former glory). Tobit and Tobias praise God and give thanks for *the great deeds he had done when an angel of God appeared to them* (v. 22).

Chapter 13

The Tobit Psalm provides a suitable conclusion to a book which began with Tobit honouring Jerusalem. But it is difficult to be sure how the various traditions of the Psalm developed. The REB is a cocktail of traditions, shaken and stirred. It brings together the three themes of God's scourging, his mercifulness and his greatness in the Diaspora (vv. 1–6abc; see 9.10). REB adds from Vaticanus and Alexandrinus the declaration to the sinful from among the nation: *turn and do what is right in his eyes; who knows, he may yet welcome you and show mercy* (v. 6d). Parallel to the references to Jerusalem in 1.6–8, Vaticanus and Alexandrinus turn to the city of Jerusalem, applying to the Holy City the theme of punishment and restitution (v. 9). At v. 10b the REB returns to the Sinaiticus text: *Your sanctuary will be rebuilt*. The promise to Jerusalem is that *Your radiance will shine to the ends of the earth. Many nations will come to you from afar* bearing gifts for the King of Heaven (v. 11; see Isa. 60.1–11; 66.10–14). Those who pull down your walls will be punished (see Judith 16.17); the parallel phrase in the REB, *for ever blessed will be those who rebuild you*, is introduced here from the Old Latin and Vulgate texts. Reminiscences of Isa. 54.11b–12 complete the picture of the new Jerusalem, where God's *holy name will be praised for ever and ever* (13.18c). What is clear from this survey of the chapter is that when Tobit was completed as a literary unit Jerusalem has been destroyed and rebuilt, and that in relation to the coming of many nations to Jerusalem a New Temple is promised as God's house for ever.

Chapter 14

The righteous, those who practise almsgiving, worship and piety, are seen to prosper, and to live to a ripe old age and be buried with joy. That is true for Tobit, Raguel and Tobias and their families. The book proves to be about different people from the Diaspora, experiencing misfortune but in the end receiving God's promises. Tobias's last words concern the evil within Nineveh (see the reference to the book of Nahum and the note on Ahiqar and Naban); following the Deuteronomic tradition of retribution he prophesies its downfall (which the hearer knows has indeed happened) and Tobit warns Tobias to leave the city, which Tobias does eventually on Tobit and Anna's death (v. 12) in order to join and inherit Raguel's household (v. 13). The significance of Tobit's prophecy is unclear: is it a warning, as the Maccabeans gave, to retain a strict Jewish piety in an alien environment? What the Psalm in ch. 13 foretold now becomes the prophecy of a conversion of the whole world to *the true worship of God; they will renounce the idols which led them astray into error* (v. 6b). Tobias lives to see the prophecy concerning Nineveh fulfilled and (a difficult perspective for us) to praise God for it.

Judith

The revelation that a speech during the Cold War by the President of the United States, virtually branding as Satanic his counterpart in the USSR, almost caused a nuclear holocaust, invites much greater care today in our use of language about evil. To make an outright condemnation of evil is one thing; to brand someone as Satanic today is quite another. Today the two need to be distinguished very carefully, not least because of their different levels of effect. The book of Judith comes from a period in the ancient world when that distinction would not have been observed. The book could belong to the time of the collision between Hellenism and Judaism in the second century BCE which will be described in our introduction to 1 and 2 Maccabees. (The book might perhaps be a little later, or a later rewriting of an earlier Judith story – the earliest fixed point for its creation is the reference to Judith in an early Christian writing, Clement's First Letter to the Corinthians 55.4–5; the date of this letter is much discussed – it was probably written 95–96 CE.) If the book of Judith does belong to the Maccabean period, then, as we know from the book of Daniel (which like Judith concerns Nebuchadnezzar, see Daniel 4), the view would have been current that the ruler of the world could well be the embodiment of evil. Such a view was reflected in the angry response of the Assyrian commander-in chief Holophernes: *What god is there besides Nebuchnezzar? When he exerts his power he will wipe them off the face of the earth* (Judith 6.1, 2b–3a). The mixture of idolatrous claims and threats to the Temple (Judith 8.21) would have been sufficient warrant, for the ancient Jew, to brand the claimant as evil personified.

Of course the name Nebuchnezzar belongs to a much earlier stage of history than the second-century date of the Maccabees. Indeed, parts of Judith reflect different periods of history. The enemy are Assyrians, i.e. the eighth century. In ch. 4 the Judaeans are alarmed because they have returned from exile, and their temple in Jerusalem has only just been rededicated. In ch. 5 Achior, the commander of the Ammonites, gives an account which so enraged Holophernes that it nearly cost Achior his life. That account of Israel's history takes you to the reoccupation and restitution of Jerusalem, which is well into the Persian period, if not into the Maccabean period itself (Judith 5.17–19). The links with the book of Daniel point in the same direction, and there are hints (2.28) that the book must have been written before Alexander Jannai, about 100 BCE. So the Maccabean or post-Maccabean period could well be the time of the origin of Judith as a book (see also Judith 7.8 and 1 Macc. 5.3–6). The result of all this is a strange amalgam of history and strange associations of events. Who destroyed Ecbatana? Certainly not Nebuchnezzar (Judith 1.14). And how do you get from Africa to Asia Minor to Mesopotamia and so on back to Cilicia in three days except by El Al (Judith 2)? Sometimes author's errors in information reveal something about the writer's own geographical setting, but not so in this case. Here the geographical and chronological material points instead to a universalization, a distention, an inflation of places and events, which gives the book a cosmic breadth and significance.

War, destruction, tyranny, pillage and rape provide a good half of the book of Judith. As in many powerful novels, the opening chapters hold the reader's attention through the horrors of what is being described, which then become the setting within which the crucial incidents that follow can be evaluated. It is only with ch. 8 that Judith appears on the scene with her town of Bethulia (no one knows where exactly Bethulia was, except that it appears to have been on a key route into Judaea near Scythopolis, perhaps indicating Samaritan interests. Its name could be a symbol of Jerusalem – for the importance of Jerusalem in the book see 8.21, 24; 10.8; 13.4; 16.18–20). It is a town starved, parched and about to be pillaged. Judith envisages a brilliant personal coup (*by a woman's hand*, 9.10; 12.4; 13.15; 16.6), and to achieve this she sets off with her trusted maid-servant from Bethulia toward the Assyrian outpost.

Often novels betray the author's self-understanding, or the understanding of a people or race (a kind of internal history), and that may well be true of the book of Judith. Reading Judith 10.19 one senses not only the author's national pride embedded in the camp-followers' comments but also the author's quick-witted humour, sense of irony and amusement, not least perhaps at the situation which begins to develop within the female–male relationships.

The translation in the REB sounds a little coy (see 11.5) and it would be hard to pick up in translation all the double-talk, innuendos, salacious hints and ironies of the Greek text. Do these suggest that the form of the book we have was written in Greek? Jerome claimed to be using an Aramaic source for his Vulgate translation of Judith and there are hints of a Semitic background to the language, but how they got there and by what route we can only guess. Nevertheless the Greek we have in Judith is elegant and carefully nuanced. Probably to have picked up all those Greek nuances in an English translation would have made it less suited for public reading. For the book of Judith describes quite brilliantly how, within all the agonies of war, pillage and rape, the male is still capable of being trapped like a spider in a web by an astute, determined, beautiful and none too principled young woman. Judith emerges throughout (probably, although some doubt this) as a person of the highest sexual standards and (certainly without question) a truly pious nature (13.16), except that she is not averse to a few purposeful untruths, not to mention her determination to mislead, her utter ruthlessness in killing Holophernes and her brilliance in executing a dare-devil get-away, as neatly planned as anything in *Where Eagles Dare*. Some regard as a key to the book this contrast between sexuality and death and see the book as a series of dualities such as are listed in ben Sirach 33.14–15.

What the book reveals of Israelite faith is fascinating. It reflects cleverly and intriguingly on the great traditions of Israelite thought at a time when Judaism was seeking to re-establish its own sense of identity, perhaps, if the Maccabean theory is right, against the background of Greek culture. Does Israel continue to suffer because of her sin (present or past) (Judith 5.20–21; 8.18)? Should Israel try to test God by giving God a deadline for deliverance (Judith 7.30; 8.12)? Should Israel simply let go of the story of divine protection (Isa. 37.33–35), and concentrate on faith in the hearts of the people, accepting whatever fiery test of faith God requires (Judith 8.25–27)? Is determination in prayer the answer (Judith 4.9, 12)? Or is the place of the Jerusalem Temple what matters? Or are there past injustices which require the courage to avenge (Judith 9.2)? Should Gentiles like Achior be accepted into Judaism and on what terms? And – the major question of them all – what is the relation of God's omnipotence and omniscience to his exercise of justice and mercy (Judith 9.5–6)?

The book of Judith can best be described as a novel. Some novels are didactic and others have a capacity to raise a raft of important questions without labouring or even defining the answers. Recent studies of Judith which explore the plot and the characters, their interplay, parallelism, interchange, opposition and development, underline this factor in fictional writing. Novels can also make use of cross-references to other literature which deepen the level of the narrative.

Judith was written with references to the Judges (see Judges chs 4–5, and the same comment on Tobit), to Abraham and Jacob, perhaps in its final form with references even to Greek culture (see 12.15; 15.13) and even Greek historical writings. All these factors prevent the reduction of the text to a single function. It is a complex communicative act.

Nevertheless, part of the book's function is probably contained in Judith 16, an act of praise and thanksgiving (see 8.25) which rehearses events and affirms God as, above all, the defender of the defenceless (16.11; see 9.11: *You are the God of the humble, the help of the poor, the support of the weak, the protector of the despairing, the deliverer of those who have lost all hope*). Certainly some of the many attempts of artists, painters and sculptors to capture key features of the book of Judith, from the sixth century CE to the present day, have highlighted this particular aspect.

Chapter 1

The original Greek shows the setting for the book to be an imaginative conflict of two massive forces: between, on the one hand, Nebuchadnezzar (actually Jerusalem's Babylonian destroyer, but here called 'Assyrian', i.e. Israel's Northern Kingdom's destroyer) and, on the other, Arphaxad (an otherwise unknown King of the Medes) who prepares his capital Ecbatana for war. The Palestinian area (as was in fact usual) is caught in the middle, treats Nebuchadnezzar as *a mere man* (v. 11; contrast 3.8), refusing to join his forces. *This roused Nebuchadnezzar to fury against the whole region; he swore . . . to exact vengeance from all the territories of Cilicia, Damascus, and Syria . . . the Moabites, the Ammonites, the people throughout Judaea, and everyone in Egypt* (v. 12). Arphaxad and his monumental defences were destroyed (v. 14).

Chapters 2–3

How was Nebuchadnezzar's oath implemented? The REB translation of vv. 1–2 implies that a conference was held about implementing Nebuchadnezzar's threat; he called his officials to discuss *his secret plan for the region* and his declaration of an intention *to put an end to the disaffection*. The Greek, however, might imply a slightly different picture: that initially 'there was talk in the palace'; some of the officials thought that the king was not implementing his determined policy (ch. 1), and such mutterings caused the king to confer (2.2). That slight difference would underline the literary character of the setting. It is closely parallel to events during the campaign of a Persian King, Xerxes, against Greece. Judith 2.7 adds further probability to this parallel: *Bid them have earth and water ready* was also a feature of Persian policy; the Persians required earth and water as a *token of submission* to avoid slaughter. Although 'as a token of submission' is not actually in the Greek text of Judith, the REB adds it by way of explanation. Holophernes was sent by Nebuchnezzar to overrun the whole area (2.19). He was to prepare the way for punishment (2.10: *If they submit, hold them for me until the time comes to punish them*). So 'bid them have earth and water ready' is a tiny nugget of information about Persian war strategies to underline the ferocity of their intentions. Holophernes, as the text shows, far from limiting his role to occupying the territory, *devastated Put and Lud, and plundered all the people of Rassis, and the Ishmaelites* (2.23). These are remarkable, even miraculous, feats of travel; and the names too are suspiciously odd: we know of Put, Lud and the Ishmaelites, but not of Rassis or Cheleans. He *sacked the towns, laid waste the countryside, and put all the young men to the sword* (2.27). *Fear and dread* are appropriate (2.28), but so also, given the style of the narration, is a degree of sarcasm, mockery and fascinated horror: *Accompanying them went a motley host like a swarm of locusts, countless as the dust of the earth* (2.20). The campaign results in widespread capitulation, and an advance towards *the Judaean ridge* (3.9). In these opening chapters Nebuchadnezzar is set up as a god-like figure with god-like power (1.12), and Holophernes, his *commander-in-chief*, is commissioned to *destroy all the gods of the land, so that Nebuchadnezzar alone should be worshipped by every nation* (3.8). But there is one sarcastic hint of what is to come (a hint missed by the REB): he claims victory 'by my hand'. It is 'by my hand', the hand of a woman, Judith's, that he will be put to shame (see 2.12; 9.10).

Chapter 4

The Judaeans are understandably very, very frightened (v. 2). The surrounding areas are alerted and preparations made for the expected onslaught. Jerusalem itself is put on high alert, with the high priest Joakim and the Gerousia (a Greek name for *the senate* (v. 8); the name is a hint of Seleucid times) calling for a public response. For the first time in the book the name of *Bethulia* appears (v. 6). Bethulia is to be responsible for holding *the passes into the hill-country, because they gave access to Judaea* (v. 7). Just why Holophernes' troops should have been expected to choose such a treacherous route is yet another mystery. Three times the writer stresses *the great fervour* with which the inhabitants of Jerusalem are to throw themselves into a public lament – even the animals are to put on sackcloth (see Jonah 3.8)! The public laments in the Psalms echo the concerns expressed in Judith 4.12, and the writer comments that *the Lord heard their prayer and took pity on their distress* (v. 13). Nevertheless, for the moment the fasting has to continue; it will be some time yet before the people can know what the writer knows.

Chapter 5

When Holophernes asks why, *Of all the people of the west . . .* the Israelites *alone disdain to come to meet me*, Achior, the commander of the Ammonites, gives an account of the Israelites' history. The detail of Achior's account reveals it to be as cunning a piece of writing as is to be found anywhere in the Apocrypha. Achior promises 'the truth, the whole truth and nothing but the truth' (v. 5), and ends with the concern that Holophernes may be disgraced (v. 21) – which is indeed what is to happen. Achior is commander of the Ammonites (distinguish this name from that of the Amorites, see v. 15), and he describes Israel's conquest as taking *possession of the entire hill-country* (v. 15) driving out *the Canaanites, the Perizzites, the Jebusites, the Shechemites, and all the Girgashites* (v. 16). It is difficult to believe that this writer was not fully acquainted with the books of Joshua and especially of Judges. The book of Judges knows of several women who killed or incapacitated great heroes (Judges chs 4–6, which has many parallels with Judith 9.53; 16.19). Judges also describes how Israel took Amorite territory but none of the Ammonite (Judg. 11.15), only attacking the Ammonites under provocation. Included in the list above of the tribes driven out are also (unusually, see Josh. 9.1) the Shechemites (see Judg. 9, and Judith's implicit condemnation of the Shechemites in Judith 9.2–6 because of the rape of Dinah by Shechem in Genesis 34). Ironically too it is Achior who sets out the theological principles behind Judges and the rest of the Deuteronomic history (vv. 17–18): that when Israel is obedient God raises up a judge to rescue Israel (in

Judges as in Judith 5.23, by means of the few); when Israel is disobedient Israel falls under the yoke of foreigners. Achior also slips in numerous challenges to the worship of Nebuchadnezzar ('God', that is, the one true and only God – the REB reads *'their God' – dried up the Red Sea for them*; v. 13; there is also a word-play in v. 21 contrasting Holophernes as 'my lord' and Israel's lord, again not in the REB). Little wonder Achior is almost *hacked to pieces* (5.22).

Chapter 6

When *the uproar . . . had died down*, Holophernes attacks Achior as an associate of *Ephraimite mercenaries* (that is, of the Northerners whom the Assyrians had already conquered). He is claiming prophetic power, and suggesting that a god other than Nebuchadnezzar exists (v. 2). He fills out Nebuchadnezzar's oath against his detractors with his own violent picture of *mountains . . . drenched with their blood* (v. 4). This is a passage in which the reader understands what Holophernes says rather better than Holophernes himself – a form of irony typical of literary story-telling: *You shall not see my face again from this day . . . you will be allowed to live until you share their fate . . . you need not look downcast* (literally: do not let your face fall, see 13.8) . . . *I have spoken, and not a single word of mine will go unfulfilled* (vv. 5, 8, 9). The reader knows that what Holophernes has done is unwittingly to declare that he will lose his head and Achior find the eventual safety in which to identify it (14.6). This is made possible initially by Holophernes despatching Achior to the spring of Bethulia, where he is set free, welcomed and testifies to Holophernes' boast. The prayer which follows (v. 19) establishes the basis of Israel's hope: the arrogance of the enemy and Israel's humble condition (see Judith's prayer in 9.7–14).

Chapter 7

The deployment of Holophernes' *immense* army terrifies the Israelites. On the second day the springs of Bethulia are seized, and the siege begins. The idea of starving Bethulia into submission so as to avoid even a single casualty, rather than becoming involved in *a pitched battle*, is credited to *the rulers of Esau's descendants and the Moabite leaders* (vv. 8–15). These names recall two features of Israelite history which are centuries apart: the enmity of Moab going back to the time

of Elijah and Elisha (e.g. 2 Kgs 3.5) and the war which Judas Macca-
beus waged against 'Esau's descendants' when the latter opposed the
rededication of the Temple (e.g. 1 Macc. 5.3–6). The story is proceed-
ing at different levels: there is the literary level (so e.g. no male person
will be allowed out of Bethulia (v. 13); whereas we know that Judith
and her maid will be); and there are the different historical levels, with
themes which are common to the different generations: the lasting
dependence of Israel on God, the continual fear that Israel's sins may
incur divine judgement (v. 28), and the desperate recognition that
there is no human help that can save them, and that slavery has
sometimes been a better fate than death (vv. 23–27). Ozias (the
Hebrew name is Uzziah), one of the town magistrates, thinks to win
sufficient time: *Let us hold out for five more days; by that time the Lord our
God will again show us his mercy, for he will not abandon us for ever*
(v. 30). The chapter ends with Bethulia in a desperate condition.

Chapter 8

The setting is now complete within which the Judith story proper can
begin. She is presented, as her name suggests, as the perfect Jewish
woman: *No one had a word to say against her* (v. 8a). Her family includes
patriarchs, judges and prophets; she marries within her tribe; when
widowed, she remains in that state and practises a strict piety. She is
perfect for the part she must play: beautiful and influential, with a
favourite and competent woman slave in charge of her property
(v. 10), who can summon the elders to Judith's roof-shelter. Judith
acknowledges the people's evil pressure on the leadership, but criti-
cizes the latter for provoking and testing God; they are presuming to
know and dictate how, what and when God will act (vv. 9–17). She
maintains, in agreement with the tenor of Achior's report in 5.17–19,
that unlike past generations this generation has not succumbed to
idolatry and so it has cause to hope for deliverance (vv. 18–20). She
spells out the consequences for Jerusalem and Judaea of losing
Bethulia, in the desecration of the Temple, *contempt* from enemies and
divine *dishonour* (vv. 21–23); what is happening is that God is testing
his people's loyalty, as he tested Abraham (Gen. 22) and Jacob (Gen.
29), and he deserves thanksgiving (v. 25) and attention to his warning
(v. 27). Ozias is caught between Judith's evident wisdom and his oath
to the people, and so pleads with her to pray for *rain to fill* their
cisterns. The initiative is now in Judith's hands. She promises, without

disclosing what it is, a memorable action: *the Lord will deliver Israel by my hand* (v. 33; see 9.10). As distinct from the leaders who look for divine relief, Judith is recognized as acting to *take vengeance* on the enemy, with God going before her to guide her (a point evident in the original: see 5.13, Judg. 4.14). There are several theories about Judith's relation to Uzziah and the leadership; but perhaps the distinction between waiting for vengeance on the enemy and acting with that effect is the crucial one.

Chapter 9

The parallels between this section (chs 9–11) and Esther 14–15 cannot be resolved by assuming one to be the source of the other. They both rest on a tradition of prayer, used in two separate contexts. Judith prays *at the moment when the evening incense was being offered in the house of God at Jerusalem* (v. 1). Action, as in Simeon her forefather's *vengeance on those foreigners* who raped Dinah (v. 2; see 5.16), is a vengeance divinely planned. Everything, past, present and future, is in the mind of God and what God conceives is realized (see the discussion of providence in 1 Esdras). God's ways are *prepared beforehand* (v. 6c), to punish those who seek to rape the city (there is a play on the name Bethulia, which is similar to virgin and to the house of God*)*; God's *judgement rests on foreknowledge* (v. 6d). The theme of the divine overthrow of overweening arrogance (v. 9), and the empowering of the weak with that intent, links Israelite and early Christian thought (v. 11; Judg. 7.2; 1 Macc. 1–2; Luke 1.51–53). What distinguishes the two traditions is the recognition, on the one hand, that God *stamps out wars* (v. 7; see also 16.3a), and, on the other, that God, by the violence of a woman's hand and her deceptions, can bring down *wrath on the heads* (v. 9) of those who threaten the covenant and the Temple.

Chapter 10

The detail of Judith's preparation for her mission becomes of evident importance as the story unfolds. With coiffure, perfume, festival robe and other of the feminine attractions which Isaiah had formerly denounced (Isa. 3.16–26), she plans carefully what her favourite maid should carry (still available to her, apparently, despite the stringent conditions of the siege): *a skin of wine and a flask of oil . . . a bag with roasted grain, cakes of dried figs, and loaves of fine bread*, together with other *utensils* (for the significance of these see 10.19; 11.21–23; 12.2–4; 12.15, 19; 13.10). She and her maid meet the elders of the town as arranged, commit the mission to God, ask for the gate to be opened and leave the men of the city gaping after her. *Confronted by an Assyrian outpost* (v. 11) she describes herself as a *Hebrew* escaping in order to reveal to Holophernes how, without casualties, the *hill-country* could be taken. Dazzled by her beauty they give her a hundred-strong escort to *Holophernes' tent* (vv. 14–17). The general reaction in the camp is totally blind to the possibility that Judith might outwit them; quite the contrary, they comment that if Israelites have wives like this their menfolk could *outwit the whole world*; hence Israelite men must not be despised or ignored; they must be killed, every one of them (v. 19). The army's attitude to women is implied as a blindness by which God will eventually punish them.

Chapter 11

Judith's conversation with Holophernes is laced with double-talk, of which these are a few examples (Judith is assumed to be aware of them, Holophernes unaware of them even when he is speaking): in *this night* (vv. 3, 5) *the information . . . is the truth* (v. 5; 11.9–10, 12); *through you God will accomplish a great thing, and my lord* (Holophernes/God; see Judg. 4.18)) *will not fail to attain his ends* (v. 6) . . . So that my lord (Holophernes/God) may not *be thwarted or cheated* (v. 11; see also in Holophernes' response vv. 22–23!) . . . *the things that God has sent me to do with you will be the wonder of the whole world* (vv. 16, 23). There are misleading half-truths: *the living might of him who sent you to bring order to all creatures* (v. 7) . . . *I have been given foreknowledge of this . . . and I have been sent to announce it to you* (v. 19c); and there are deliberate, clever, fawning deceptions: *they are doomed to die, and sin has them in its power, for whenever they do wrong they arouse their God's anger* (v. 11bc); the pretended appeal to Jerusalem for permission to break a food prohibition which will seal their fate, and of which Judith will have direct information from God; *I shall set up your throne in the heart of the city* (v. 19). There are also preparations for Judith's fulfilment of the task and safe escape: all the things that God by his laws has strictly prohibited (Judith and her maid have food and drink to substantiate this and prevent her having to share in the coming feast; 12:2); *and each night I shall go out into the valley and pray to God* (v. 17b).

Chapter 12

The details of Judith's plan are now reinforced: her food will enable her not the break her law, and *I shall not finish what I have with me before God accomplishes by my hand what he has purposed* (v. 4); shortly before the dawn watch she asks: *may it please my lord to give orders for me to be allowed to go out and pray* (v. 6), and returning to the camp sets up a similar pattern over three days. In this chapter the innuendos leading up to Holophernes' attempt to seduce Judith (v. 16) are more evident in the original than in translation, both because of the use of euphemisms in the original and the deliberate avoidance of suggestiveness in translation. Judith dresses herself up to kill, explains to Bagoas the eunuch that they will be going out to pray later (13.3) and Judith's maid makes all the necessary preparations. Judith's continued banter is salacious: *Who am I to refuse my lord?* (v. 14); *Certainly I shall, my lord . . . for today is the greatest day of my life* (v. 18). The contrast with Esther is interesting. Holophernes drinks himself into a stupor (as the Greek text suggests his attendants also did, 13.1).

Chapter 13

The servants hurry away; Bagoas excludes everyone and departs himself; Judith sends her maid outside to wait for her, *as she did on other days*, and so is left alone with Holophernes. After prayer (*this is the moment to come to the aid of your heritage*: v. 5), like Jael before her (Judg. 5.26, although Jael covered Sisera before she killed him), Judith takes Holophernes' short sword, strikes twice at his neck and decapitates the Assyrian leader. She rolls the body off (and behind?) the couch (Bagoas will find it flat on its back on the ground; see 14.15; 14.18); she disentangles *the mosquito-net from its posts* (v. 9; again not quite a parallel to Jael's activities, since Judith takes the bed-canopy with her) and shortly afterwards she joins her maid outside, gives her the head for her to put in the food-bag, and the two set off for prayer, through the camp, round the valley but then up the hill to the gates of Bethulia. The guards are alerted to their presence by the cry *God, our God is with us* (v. 11) and the whole town turns out to welcome them back. Repeating the themes *this very night* and *by my hand*, Judith calls for praise to the God *who has not withdrawn his mercy from the house of Israel* (v. 14), and produces the head from the bag and the mosquito-net (which presumably is evidence of the circumstances of the beheading, albeit one in itself which might arouse suspicious thoughts). She repeats the refrain *The Lord has struck him down by a woman's hand* (v. 15; see Judg. 4.21) and swears by God who protected her on her road that *my face lured him to his destruction* [but] *he committed no sin with me* (v. 16). The people praise God and, to the people's acclamation, Ozias acknowledges that as long as people (the REB translation 'men' at this point is misleading) commemorate God's power, *the sure hope which inspired you will never fade from their minds* (v. 19). In the people's time of humiliation Judith had *firmly held to God's straight road* (v. 20). The contrast between Judith and the leadership is clear, but this is no grudging acknowledgement of her greatness nor any admission that the leadership has been humiliated or criticized.

Chapter 14

As often, the enemy's head is to be impaled on the battlements (see 2 Macc. 15.35), in this case at Judith's command. She has the plan of attack ready: after the sun has risen the city's forces are to feign an attack on the Assyrian outpost, which will alert the camp and the Assyrian generals; the failure to find Holophernes will produce panic and flight. As in the book of Judges (Judg. 4.22), the head of the enemy commander has to be identified and Achior the Ammonite is available to do this. The parallelism between Barak (Judg. 4.22) and Achior offers interesting comparisons and contrasts. In particular, unlike Barak, Achior is a foreigner and that adds a new factor to the Judith story. *Achior, realizing all that the God of Israel had done, believed wholeheartedly in him; he was circumcised, and admitted as a member of the community of Israel, as his descendants are to this day* (v. 10; qualifying the commandment of Deut. 23.3). In this respect Judith's story again resembles the Daniel episodes where the foreign ruler is converted (see Nebuchadnezzar in Dan. 4.34 and Darius in Dan. 6.26). Everything happens as Judith said it would. Bagoas knocks on the screen behind which he thinks the couple will be sleeping, pulls it aside and discovers his master's headless body. He rushes to Judith's quarters and finds her gone. *He burst out, shouting to the troops . . . One Hebrew woman has brought shame on King Nebuchnezzar's house* (vv. 17–18); and the camp goes wild.

Chapter 15

The Israelites now pour out in pursuit of the fleeing enemy. Ozias takes over, mobilizing support from all the neighbouring areas. Jerusalem and the hill country rally at the news, and forces from Gilead and Galilee outflank and pursue the fleeing Assyrians. Bethulia and the returning victors find *booty in plenty*. The Jerusalem high priest and senate gather to greet Judith: *You are the glory of Jerusalem, the great pride of Israel . . . God has shown his approval* (vv. 9–10a). What follows, the dance of the Israelite women led by Judith, is described using vocabulary also found in the celebration of the purification of the Temple in 2 Macc. 10.7. In the context of a beheaded ruler overcome in a drunken stupor, the language would have recalled the Greek story of Pentheus, torn apart by the Bacchantes (significantly included today in one of the scenes at the Cornish Eden Project!). *Thyrsoi* (the word used in v. 12) have been described as wands wreathed in ivy and vine-leaves with a pine-cone at the top carried by the devotees of Bacchus, alias Dionysus; and it is possible that the writer was adding to the celebration of the Israelites a mockery of 'arrogant, drunken, defeated foreigners'. Judith and her companions crown themselves with olive leaves as symbols of victorious endeavour, and *the men of Israel, in full armour, followed, all wearing garlands on their heads and singing hymns* (v. 13d).

Chapter 16

The hymn of Judith provides one of the closest parallels to Judg. 4–5, where Deborah and Barak also begin a song of celebration. In both the heroine sometimes speaks in the first person (*I will sing a new hymn to my God*, v. 13; see Judg. 5.3) and sometimes in the third person (*Judith, Merari's daughter, disarmed him by her beauty*, v. 7d). Both hymns begin with a direct address from an individual (*Strike up a song to my God*, v. 2); then follows a poetic reference to events just recounted (vv. 4–6), and a third person reference, *The Lord Almighty has thwarted them by a woman's hand* (v. 6), parallel to the description of Jael's attack on Sisera. Both use language about the disruption of nature: 'Mountains shook in fear'(Judg. 5.5), 'the stars in their courses fought' (Judg. 5.20), *Mountains will shake to their depths like water* (Judith 16.15). Finally, both songs end with Israel at peace: 'The land was at peace for forty years' (Judg. 5:31c), *No one dared to threaten the Israelites again in Judith's lifetime, or indeed for a long time after her death* (Judith 16.25). The parallels could well suggest that the Judith story provided the opportunity for a writer in the Maccabean or post-Maccabean period to celebrate the safekeeping of the Temple through a heroine such as Jael (see vv. 18–20). The place of Judith at the end of the book, where she reverts to her widowed estate, has been treated as her removal to a sphere where her otherness could no longer endanger her male-ruled world and she could be reintegrated into the traditional pattern of her society. That almost rings true, but not quite. *She had many suitors . . . her fame continued to increase,* [and] *no one dared to threaten the Israelites again in her lifetime.* It is true that Ozias has taken charge again of the army and the high priest remains central to the piety of the Temple. But it is Judith with her reputation and openness to God's word (v. 14) who remains a challenge to any threats to Israel's life.

The Rest of the Chapters of the Book of Esther

The Jewish Festival of Purim is not the best time to expect seriousness, clarity and coherence even from Jewish scholars (Esther 1.8). A British university once made the mistake of expecting a lecture on Purim from a scholar, only to find that the latter had entered fully into the spirit of the festival and was in no condition to communicate its significance. It has, however, been an important festival at many periods of Jewish history when Jewish communities were under pressure. It has been and remains today a time of joy, merriment and giving of gifts; and care for the poor is explicitly commended by the book of Esther.

But describing the book of Esther is no easy task. The REB Introduction to Esther explains some of the circumstances. The REB Old Testament text of Esther is ten chapters long, translated from the Hebrew and exhibiting oddities such as an absence of explicit references to God and some unusually un-Jewish morality – part of it is a kind of *King and I* romance in which the lowly heroine melts the heart of a proud king. In the REB Apocrypha the text is a translation of a Greek text, and in the course of that story there are relatively frequent references to God which appear alongside denials that Esther acted immorally. In this Greek text are some six special sections which have been the subject of long and detailed studies in an effort to find why they were added, where they came from and how they fit in to the whole text. The end product reads something like a novel, but not one with the consistency to win a Booker prize.

The Greek text itself is something of a mystery. It exists in two forms, the Septuagint (the LXX) and the so-called Alpha text (the AT). The relationship between these and the Hebrew text (the Massoretic text: MT) is a major area of debate. So, for example, the Septuagint ends with 11.1, which tells us that the translation had been made in Jerusalem and had been brought by a priest and Levite Dositheus to Egypt; the Alpha text ends at 10.13 with the joy and gladness of the fourteenth and fifteenth of Adar; and the Massoretic text ends with a verse about Mordecai (see Old Testament Esther 10.3). In all probability the Alpha text itself has a long and complex a history, including a Proto-Alpha form, so complex indeed that its relationship to the Massoretic Hebrew text cannot be exactly defined. The relation of the LXX to the AT and the six additions will be illustrated as the commentary proceeds.

So the story of Esther has a long history, stretching from before the Hebrew text was written to the Slavonic version of medieval times. One important moment in its history was the collecting together of the six traditions found in the Greek text but not in the Hebrew (or Syriac). The person responsible for this collecting process was Jerome in his preparation of the Vulgate. He gathered the six traditions into a single unit and placed them together at the end of the book. They were given a sequential numbering so that the six traditions followed Esther 1–10 and, in the Authorized Version of the Bible, were numbered Esther 11–16. Hence the odd appearance of the REB Apocryphal text of Esther. In the REB the six additional traditions have been returned to suitable points in the Esther story, but their numbering 11–16 is retained, high numbered chapters being interspersed with low numbers. As a result our Apocryphal Esther, a translation of a major Greek text of Esther, begins with chapter 11.2!

The total effect is, as we said, a kind of religious novel, although how different from the modern religious novel such as those which Susan Howatch writes! There is more than just a suggestion of unreality in the story. Could the Persian king have authorized a document with reference to 'the Living God'? There is more than just a suggestion of improbable comedy too. You cannot imagine all the husbands among the Medes and Persians going into a panic at the possibility of rebellion in their homes because of Queen Vashti's (or, as the Apocryphal Esther calls her, 'Queen Astin's') disobedience (1.18). That belongs to ancient comedy, such as the Greek writer Aristophanes' *Lysistrata*, or to some melodramatic film portrayal, or perhaps to a parody of the modern suffragette movement. It could hardly belong to an actual history of ancient Susa.

Most important of all is that the providential hand of God is expounded explicitly, and that the history of the text of Esther shows changing attitudes to those who belong to other nations. It could well be that the slow acceptance of Esther among Jewish scholars was due to the picture which, according to the Hebrew text, was painted of the Jews as unreliable citizens who could gather their resources and 'work their will on those who hated them' (Esther 9.5 in the Old Testament section). Such disloyalty and insubordination would have been a difficult message for Jews in the Diaspora to stomach, and presumably later would also have raised issues for Christians. Such changes of emphasis point to the different moments in Jewish history at which these various traditions emerged, and the commentary on the REB text will take some of them into account.

The violence towards the end of the novel is horrific, unbelievably so. It would be judged by international law today as totally unacceptable. Even so, it is worth noticing that whereas the Greek version has fifteen thousand slaughtered on the thirteenth of Adar (Esther Apocrypha 9.16), the Hebrew version has no less than 'seventy-five thousand of those who hated them' (Esther OT 9.16). So we are dealing not merely with six additional traditions; the REB is a translation of a Greek text which itself has a history, and a history which reflects changing opinions among Jewish communities and, as we shall see, also important responses even among Christian communities.

Three examples of this history must suffice for the moment. 3 Maccabees, written in Greek about 50 BCE, has parallel sections to the book of Esther which note how God gives providential direction to the pagan king (see Esther 16 and 3 Macc. 6.28), but the text of Esther used there seems independent of our Greek text. Josephus, the Jewish historian, presents the Esther story (*Antiquities* XI.184–296) with material from the six additional traditions but, sensibly for a historian who sought to commend the Jewish history to a non-Jewish audience, omits those sections which would have given offence. The Old Latin Itala translation similarly allows the enmity of the Jews with those of other nations to slip into the background, and in some of the additional material translates a Greek text of which we otherwise have no textual evidence. In every chapter we are to expect different levels of traditions and editing.

Chapter 11

The Hebrew text of Esther begins with the Vashti episode and leads to Esther becoming Persian queen. The Apocryphal text opens with a vision of Mordecai or Mardochaeus (as this text calls him) to which God gives a response. This is one of the additional traditions, given a date in the year before the Hebrew story begins. Unlike many dreams in the Jewish tradition, this one receives its interpretation only after its fulfilment. Initially Mardochaeus is unable to understand it and has no one to explain it. In 10.1–9 he recognizes its significance himself: that the battles of the dragons concern himself and Haman; that the gathering of the nations is an attempt to blot out the memory of Israel; that the river depicts Esther, whom the king married and made queen; that she is God's response to the people's prayer for a deliverer (Jer. 31.7). Other verses in the dream, 11.5, 7, 10, have no specific interpretation; they resemble Isa. 24.18–20 and may be colourful additions. An odd feature of the interpretation is that it links closely with another additional section: Mardochaeus' prayer in 13.8–17. There Mardochaeus defends himself before God against the criticism that he showed insolence and arrogance before Haman; he had refused to bow before any but God. One explanation of these oddities is that the additional traditions mentioned so far have links with the Daniel stories and could well represent Mardochaeus speaking for the Maccabean and Hasmonean leaders who, criticized for their arrogance, argued that they could bow only before God and not before the Seleucid rulers (the history of the Hasmonean struggle against the Seleucids is set out in the commentary on 1 Maccabees). The reference to Esther becoming queen could be a defence of Hasmonean policies extended later into the reign of the mother of Alexander Jannaeus, someone who was an actual Jewish queen, Queen Alexandra Jannaea Salome (76–67 BCE).

Chapter 12

Mardochaeus overhears discussion of a plot, reports it, is given an appointment at court and rewarded; in the concluding verse Haman is mentioned as one who *enjoyed the royal favour* and looks for a chance to harm Mardochaeus *and his people*. This is a doublet of 2.21–23 (it gives similar information); there Mardochaeus' service is recorded to his honour, which seems to fit better with the two letters (13.2–7 and 16.1–24). The two letters show signs of composition in a style of diplomatic correspondence which belongs to the Diaspora, probably to Alexandria. They concern particularly the issues raised by the presence of Jewish communities within the Diaspora: are they good citizens and can they be relied on?

Chapters 1–3

When Queen Astin refuses to obey the Persian king, a search for a new queen (and the search shows several differences between the LXX and the MT) results in the king falling in love with Esther and planning to marry her. Now Mardochaeus has a place at court by virtue of Esther; and on his advice she does not disclose that she is Jewess, although she makes *no change in her rule of life* (2.20). Haman's promotion *above all the king's friends* (3.1) means that Mardochaeus, in refusing to *do obeisance* to Haman, is defying royal orders and Haman responds by planning a pogrom on *the thirteenth day of the month of Adar* on the basis of 'lots' (the Hebrew for 'lots' is *purim*, hence the name of the festival). 10.11 interprets the lots as the divine judgement on the nations and the divine verdict for his people. The reference to the thirteenth in this text is a mistake; it fails to see the neat way in which the problem of the irreversability of a Persian king's decree is resolved (see 8.8): the Jews will be allowed to act on the thirteenth (8.12; 16.8; see 1 Macc. 7.48–49, 2 Macc. 15.36: 'it is the eve of Mordecai's Day') so that by the fourteenth there will be no enemies left to enact the royal decree.

Chapter 13.1–7

This first of the two letters supports the royal desire for a safe and quiet kingdom. Written on the king's behalf by Haman it is self-congratulatory, replays for the reader the criticisms made in the Greco-Roman world of the Jewish way of life, and sets out the arrangements for the violent end they are to meet so that *our government may henceforth be stable and untroubled* (v. 7).

Chapter 4

The relationship between Mardochaeus and Esther is interesting. There are the problems of her distance from him in the royal palace, his assumption of the right to advise her in this time of extreme danger, his recognition that she alone might be in a position to speak against Haman, but he warns that she should not presume on her safety. She responds regally and Mardochaeus does *everything Esther had bidden him* (v. 17).

Chapters 13.8–14.19

The prayers by Mardocaeus and Esther are two of the many prayers of supplication to be found in the Apocrypha which express the Jewish faith in God in times of persecution and oppression (see Judith 9, Tob. 3, Baruch, Prayer of Manasseh, 1 Macc.). Mardochaeus affirms that his refusal to do obeisance to Haman, which has caused the disastrous plight of the Jews, was his refusal to bow to any except the Lord, *God and King, God of Abraham* (13.15). Esther's prayer is offered in the context of every physical feature of penitence (14.1–3), all of which will contrast with her *robes of state* in 15.1. It reverts to the themes of the people's suffering because of their sin and the call upon God to show his sovereignty over *gods that have no real existence* (14.11). She expresses her loathing at sharing *the bed of the uncircumcised* and, like Judith, confirms (to the readers' relief) that she has avoided Gentile food and drink (14.15–18). In this moment of danger she prays for deliverance for herself and her people (14.19).

Chapter 15

This is a further addition to the Septuagint (15.1), albeit an interpretative commentary on Esther 5.1ff. (MT). No longer is this the self-possessed Esther of the Septuagint. She is externally stately and *radiant* (v. 5), but inwardly vulnerable and weak and in an extraordinarily emotional scene swoons helpless before the kind of majestic near-divinity of a king in the Ptolemaic mould (vv. 13–15), who is revealed in his omnipotent *towering anger* (v. 7). The text shows consistencies with the Alpha and perhaps the Proto-Alpha text, and with *The Letter of Aristeas*, all of which suggests an Egyptian version of her audience with the king. There are major changes from the Hebrew text, however, in v. 8: *But the king's mood was changed by God to one of gentleness*, and from the Alpha text in vv. 13–15, where his appearance like an angel of God (see Judg. 13.6) again overcomes Esther to the king's distress. The passage has quite a distinctive textual history.

Chapters 5–7

Between Esther's invitation to the king and Haman and the banquet itself two events move the story forward: Haman sees Mardochaeus in the court and in fury has gallows set up for him; but the king, rendered by God unable to sleep, finds the record of Mardochaeus (see 2.23, and contrast 12.5) and demands from Haman how such a one should be honoured (6.6–11). He names the man to be honoured as Mardochaeus, to Haman's grief. Haman's family warn him: *the living God is on his side* (6.13). At the banquet the queen draws the king's wrath on Haman, who is hanged on the gallows he had prepared for Mardochaeus.

Chapter 8

The importance of this chapter lies in Esther's request for the decree to be recalled and in the king's permission, since it is impossible for a Persian decree to be recalled, for another writ to be sent in his name. It is important too in that it demonstrates in vv. 1–9 the extent to which concerns found in the additions of chs 10, 11, 13, 14, especially Esther's position via-à-vis Mardochaeus, are already present in the Septuagint of Esther over against the Hebrew text: e.g. in v. 1 Mardochaeus is *summoned*, in the MT he comes of his own volition; in v. 7 the king addresses only Esther, in the MT he addresses both Esther and Mardochaeus (see also 9.3, where verse-long, expansive praise of Mardochaeus in the MT is reduced to a mention of fear in the LXX). The Septuagint was fertile land in which the additions concerning Esther could be planted.

Chapter 16

The replacement edict is prepared. It is parallel in style to ch. 13 and lays the blame at Haman's door; as a Macedonian he had sought to transfer Persian *sovereignty to the Macedonians* (v. 14). As a message to the Empire, using subtle switches of tense (see v. 8 which parallels *The Letter of Aristeas*, as vv. 17–18 do explicitly), it warns those who from evil intent threaten the State's benefactors of the avenging *justice of the all-seeing God* (v. 4); it authorizes the continued presence of Jewish communities as a contribution to political stability, and Jewish vengeance on the thirteenth of Adar (v. 20); as a feature of the Greek book of Esther it affirms that Jews can *live under their own laws* (v. 19) in the Diaspora and sanctions Purim as a festival of divine intervention for his chosen people.

Chapters 9–10

The events of the thirteenth include the bloodthirsty decision of Esther to hang up the bodies of Haman's ten sons (somewhat parallel to the sex/death motif in the book of Judith), and the fourteenth and fifteenth days include the characteristic events of Purim, now confirmed by Esther and Mardochaeus and established by Esther's decree.

The Wisdom of Solomon

Anyone who wants to understand the apostle Paul needs an acquaintance with the Apocrypha, and in particular with the Wisdom of Solomon. In his major commentary on Paul's Letter to the Romans Professor J. D. G. Dunn makes this comment on Rom. 1.23:

> By this time it would be clear to Paul's readers and listeners that he was leading them along the familiar path of Jewish polemic against idolatry. It is probable indeed that Paul was consciously modelling his exposition on the Wisdom of Solomon: the echoes of Wisdom's thought and language are quite marked in this section of the argument, particularly the Wisdom of Solomon chs 13–15, so much so that Romans 1.19–21 almost constitutes a summary of Wisdom 13.1–9, and Romans 1.24–25 of the powerful anti-idol polemic in Wisdom 13.10–15.19. It is sufficiently clear that Paul also had in mind the figure of Adam and the narrative of the fall (Genesis 3), as of course is true also of the Wisdom of Solomon (2.23–24).

Perhaps it is not altogether surprising that the Wisdom of Solomon should have been included in one list of the Christian Canon along with the New Testament books.

It is not at all clear how Paul and his readers might have become acquainted with the Wisdom of Solomon or with that book's traditional lines of argument. Usually the Wisdom of Solomon is associated with the ancient city of Alexandria in Egypt, and dates for its composition have ranged from 110 BCE to 37 CE. We shall work with the theory of a date at the beginning of Augustus' Empire (perhaps 23 BCE).

It has been said recently that most of the world's great religions are concerned with the critique of idolatry; that is certainly true of Judaism. It has also been said that each of the great religions provides a discipline by which idolatry can be recognized and corrected, and that all humanity, including the righteous of each faith, stands in need of that discipline every day. If, as is implied, that applies to Christians as well, the Wisdom of Solomon remains a text with a message.

Identifying those idols in the life and history of contemporary Christianity is a question to be addressed, not perhaps to the writer of the book of Wisdom, but certainly to ourselves; his answers would inevitably be different but ours must be as honest and authentic.

The key issue in interpreting the Wisdom of Solomon is to whom it is addressed. The answer that we shall work with in this commentary is the only one which offers a way of understanding the book as a whole (most answers divide the book into two or three separate parts): the book is written in a context of Alexandrian hellenistic education by a Jewish scholar concerned to express the traditional faith for his own context, when some Jews brought up in that educational tradition had embraced a theology and anthropology inconsistent with what the writer takes to be the traditional faith.

There is no clear consensus regarding its interpretation. One cause of this is the difficulty of translating the Greek text. Its syntax, vocabulary and punctuation often raise questions. Even the REB is open to criticism at some crucial points, notably at the beginning and the end of the book; it can be questioned precisely at those points which often give an indication of why the book is being written. As far as vocabulary is concerned, some assume that the Wisdom of Solomon maintains an accurate and consistent philosophical position; other scholars recognize that the theology and anthropology remain consistent but the language is drawn from different contexts, without the writer fully appreciating its implications. This commentary represents the second option.

Chapter 1

Many interpretations have been suggested for the opening section. What it does *not* stress is how God's people came into existence (contrast with this chapter the opening ten points of Virgil's *Aeneid* which clearly explore Roman origins); nor does the conclusion of the book stress Jewish origins. A possible way to read the book is to recall how education can shape people's attitudes, from those who lead nations to those who lead households. If on the basis of that education some Jews develop false ideas, argues the author, that spells disaster (v. 5; see chs 14–15). Only a true understanding of the providential leading of God can establish human wellbeing, flourishing community and justice (19.18–22). In this way the opening section sets out the main concerns of the entire book. *Rulers* are to seek the Lord in righteousness, in goodness and *singleness of heart*, since God is manifested only to the trustful (v. 2). Wisdom will not enter a soul committed to evil practice. The holy spirit will avoid falsehood, especially falsehood based on education (probably, as some older commentaries suggest, the word *discipline/education* goes with *falsehood*, not with holy spirit); the holy spirit (see 7.22) will *withdraw at the approach of injustice*. Wisdom is well disposed towards *mortals* but will not grant immunity to a *blasphemer* (v. 6). God is witness, visitant and hearer. God's spirit . . . *fills the whole earth, and that which hold all things together knows well everything that is said*. So a godless person will be brought to account. Avoid *futile grumbling* and false speaking which destroy life (v. 11; see Exod. 16.2–9, and Wisd 11.4). *God did not make death* (v. 13); the world was made for existence, and the created world is the means by which God brings deliverance (v. 14; 5.20; 16.17; 19.18). *Death has no sovereignty* since righteousness is *immortal* (see 8.13, 17). The *godless* counted *death* in their *company* and waste away (see Odes 1.15) because *they are members of his* (death's) *party* (see 2.24).

Chapter 2

The thoughts of the godless are set out in direct, argumentative style. They cannot be placed in any one tradition, Epicurean or Stoic. *Our life is short* is expounded in terms which suggest medical judgements, although passages such as Job 7.9 could be in mind. *By mere chance* (v. 2) may be what the godless said of their birth, in harmony with Lucretius' *De Rerum Natura*. *Our body* will prove to be dust; again the presentation could fit various philosophies (v. 3), but it marks a departure from a Jewish anthropology: the body has been separated off from the divine gift of life. Life is shadow, say the godless (v. 5). 2.5 contains extraordinary vocabulary, including the astronomical notion that time cannot turn back. Life, say the godless, should be enjoyed to the full (vv. 6–9; as classical literature said, *carpe diem* ('use the day well')). In the next section (*Down with the poor and honest man!*) power becomes the godless one's 'law of righteousness'. Might is right! Two features of the passage are worth underlining: first, in this section the godless person clearly belongs to the Jewish tradition; second, the writer allows his own self-description to enter the text: he is an inconvenience; he accuses the godless of sins against the law; and calls the godless traitors to their education (v. 12); he professes to know God and be a child of God (vv. 13, 16b), and avoids godless ways as he would something ceremonially impure. Since he claims to be a son of God, the ungodly will set out to test him, to see if the claim is genuine. If it is genuine, God *will save him from the clutches of his* assailants (v. 18; Ps. 17.7). The godless plan is to unmask the honest man (an ironical comment, since that is the word used of God's unmasking of kings in 6.3). The godless will use *insult and torture . . . to measure his forbearance* (see God's forbearance in 12.18), by condemning *him to shameful death* (v. 20).

The writer comments: *how wrong they were!* Their testing of the righteous is a sign of *malevolence* and of blindness to the rewards of holiness. They have forgotten that God created the human being *imperishable, and made him in the image of his own eternal self* (note that Adam is created in God's image and so can share his immortality). The godless are unaware of this. The devil's spite brought death into the world; but v. 24b has probably no reference to the devil: they are of *death's* company, those who put the righteous one to the test (see 1.6; 2.21). The chapter has addressed the deluded thoughts of the ungodly from the standpoint of traditional truth about God and about humanity. Their thoughts have been depicted from many sources which may be found in the education of the time. But the truth which has been set out is Israel's traditional faith.

Chapters 3–5

The Greek translation (LXX) of the Psalms includes the promise to the just that they will have life in the world to come as recompense for the trials they experienced in this life, and that their assailants will die (see Pss 73 (72 LXX) and 88–90 (87–89 LXX)). These chapters agree with the Psalms, but make a host of positive statements about the *just* (Isa. 57.1–2). Some statements use the present tense: they are *in God's hand* (3.1); they are *at peace* (3.3); they have *a sure hope of immortality* (3.4); God proved them. Other statements are future: *after a little chastisement* (3.5; see 16.4) they will have great kindness shown to them; *they will shine in glory* (3.7); they will judge the nations (3.8); they *will attend upon him in love* (3.9). The *godless*, on the other hand, who despise wisdom in its association with education (3.11) will meet with *punishment* in the future (3.10); but in the present also their *hopes are void*, their labours unprofitable, their actions futile; their lives are lived under humanity's curse (3.13; Gen. 3.15–19). This double effect of being *unjust* is experienced whether life is short or long, and applies to those who sprang *from a union forbidden by the law* (3.16–19). The writer makes two exceptions to this: *the childless woman if she is innocent* of sexual transgression; and eunuchs (Isa. 56.4–5) who *in return for their faith* will enjoy the most delightful of roles *in the Lord's temple* (3.13b–15). Traditional views of immortality are included (see ben Sirach 39.8–11): even without a successor a reputation for virtue wins recognition *from God, and also from mankind* (4.1); it has influence now and is mourned thereafter, and wins an untarnished *victory* (4.2). The godless, on the other hand, however prolific, can be *snapped off* like sucker offshoots and brittle branches (see Plato, *Laws* 741a on education); they find at the time of their judgement that their children are witnesses to their wickedness (4.3–6). The *just person* is judged by *understanding* and not by his age, as Elijah was; Elijah was snatched away so that deceit could not beguile him (4.11) and the malign influence of evil dims *the radiance of the good* (4.12); perfected briefly, he fulfilled what many years can bring. God in his mercy *comes to the help of his holy people* (4.15; 19.22). The just in death (4.16a) will condemn the godless living, and youth, perfected swiftly, will condemn the long years of the unjust (4.16). When a just person dies, the unjust cannot grasp God's plan and purpose. But it is the unjust that God will *laugh to scorn* (4.18); he uproots them; all *memory of them will perish* (4.19) and *on the day of reckoning* they will cringe before their conviction of lawlessness (4.20). That is the moment when the *just* person will *confront those who oppressed him* (5.1); in terror *they will be astounded* at the remarkable way salvation is found among the people of God (19.2). Repentant, the godless will recognize their departure from *the way of truth* (5.6–7). Their overweening arrogance proves to be of no assistance to them. A series of pictures suggest how their boasts have disappeared without anything to show (like the passage of the messenger, the ship, the bird, the arrow). They have nothing, no virtue, to show for their lives, which they have *frittered away*; their *hope* is like a *transient memory*. And judgement will come. The present and the consequent future rewards of the just are reaffirmed (5.15–16). God will afford protection to them when, like the mighty warrior, he comes in righteousness, justice, holiness and wrath (Isa. 59.16–17), and all creation (lightning, hail, sea, floods, *tempest* and *whirlwind*) will fight with him against *his frenzied foes* (5.20; see 19.6, 15) – those whose lawlessness will be responsible for the land becoming waste (4.20; 5.23; 10.7; 16.19) and royal thrones undermined (5.23; Hag. 2.21–22). The judgement of the mighty warrior God takes a particular form here and frequently throughout the book (see 19.18–22): the created elements of the world fight with him. The parallels with Isaiah are significant from many points of view; not least because the parallels concern God as deliverer of his people, even of those who repent of their rebellion.

At many points in these early chapters the criterion of judgement has been the Law, explicitly or implicitly (1.9; 2.12; 3.14,16; 4.6, 20; 5.7), so that the godless have been under the Law. God's justice and righteousness are the concern of all, especially rulers and princes (Isa. 66.16; Prov. 16.10–15; Ps. 72), since their education includes wisdom as their study (see *The Letter of Aristeas* §209, where the Egyptian ruler enquires of a guest, 'What is the most needful characteristic of kingship?' The reply was, 'That (he) should keep himself uncorruptible, practise moderation throughout all his life, respect justice beyond all else, and cultivate such men as friends, because God himself loves justice.' See also §267).

Chapter 6

From such a declaration of future judgement (v. 5) it follows that kings, lords and judges should give full attention to what is written here (see 1.1–4), both because their power is from the Most High, who will therefore *scrutinize* their acts and intentions, and because they *have not been upright judges . . . have not maintained the law* nor walked according to *the will of God* (v. 4). The lowly are well acquainted with mercy; the powerful will be unmasked by the *Master of all* (v. 7), for he shows no special favours to the great. *Under his providence* the small and the great are equal; but his *sternest inquisition* is for those in authority (vv. 3–8). This is King Solomon himself who is speaking, and Solomon's words (see 7.7) contain wisdom, holiness, learning; these provide a future defence in time of judgement, and promote an eagerness to be educated by him (vv. 9–11; see 10.15 and 2 Sam. 22.26–28; Ps. 18.20–34; Prov. 1–4). The contrast between some forms of education and that which leads to wisdom is made, first implicitly, then explicitly. The dynamics of knowing wisdom are explored in ben Sirach (see also Prov. 2.6), and Wisd. 6.12–16 is compatible with ben Sirach's emphases: the dynamics include a loving, eager, receptive attention, an unwearying, costly search, meditation and vigilance, and the promise that *on their daily path* wisdom will meet them *halfway in all their purposes*. The disciplines which form the beginning of knowing wisdom are a genuinely true desire for education: including love, wisdom's law as the *warrant for immortality*, and growing near to God and his kingdom (vv. 17–21; 7.14; 8.9–16). Solomon it is, therefore, who is able to reveal the *mysteries* of wisdom (see 1 Kgs 3.9), to trace wisdom's way from his own birth to her true revelation (7.1–6 fulfils this task of tracing wisdom from his birth; the NRSV translation of 6.22 is possible: Solomon will trace wisdom's way 'from the beginning of creation'; but the REB translation that he will trace her 'from *her* first beginnings' is the least likely). Unlike the godless, Solomon refuses to allow his sharing of wisdom to be tainted with jealousy or ill-will. *Wise men in plenty are the world's salvation, and a prudent king* gives communal stability (v. 24, an emphasis central to 14.22–31). All this explains why Solomon calls for education according to his teaching (v. 25) as leading to the common good.

Chapter 7

Solomon begins his personal story concerning wisdom from his birth and the fact of his mortality. In terms reminiscent of 2.1–9 but establishing his understanding of humanity, he recalls that, like Adam, he was born of earth, laid on the earth, beginning the single path by which all come and all depart (vv. 1–6). Behind this declaration of his mortality are two qualifications: the spirit of wisdom, granted as the response to prayer, leads to unexpected possibilities for human happiness (vv. 7–12); and God's providential care for Adam supported him even after he sinned (10.1); hence Wisdom's theme that God is the unfailing helper of his people. The dynamics of coming to know wisdom and discovering her riches (see 6.12–21) are being redescribed in terms of Solomon's own life-story (vv. 7–13). Verse 13 makes the contrast explicit between Solomon's way and that of others: his learning involved no deceit and he taught ungrudgingly (see 6.23; and ben Sirach 39.1–15). This leads to the same conclusion as 6.25: those who possess wisdom have taken up friendship with God and are established by the gifts her education provides. What follows is a request that his teaching and thoughts may be worthy of what he has received; after all, God is a director and corrector of the wise; in his hand are our lives, our teaching, *prudence* and understanding of *craftmanship*, and he has given an unerring knowledge of *things as they are* (vv. 16–17a;1.10). It is important here to note that true wisdom is, according to the writer, compatible with forms of hellenistic philosophy and science (vv. 17b–22). The writer is not representing a wisdom confined to natural knowledge such as Solomon displayed in 1 Kgs. 4.33, nor necessarily forms of knowledge as they are defined by hellenistic philosophy. Solomon knows how the elements of the physical world actually operate (19.18–22). The writer of the book of Wisdom stands between the Jewish and the hellenistic traditions, unwilling to part with either and unwilling that either should discredit the other. This is essentially his understanding of how all, from rulers to craftsmen, should be brought up, and the clarifying of this process and its importance will be part of his task in the forthcoming chapters; they should know what the Jewish tradition says about God and his providence, and what contemporary knowledge knows of astronomy, its practical calculations of the calendar, zoology, human nature, meteorology, botany and pharmacology. Moreover, they should know this because wisdom is the deviser of everything, and it is wisdom that has given Solomon instruction (vv. 21–22).

Wisdom appears in the book of Proverbs to shift between personification (Prov. 8) and an abstract quality, a quality of the world in its manifold interrelationships, so that Prov. 31.10–31 is a portrayal not just of a capable woman overseeing her household but rather of a woman embodying what it is to be wise. Wisdom may be found (24.14) – found particularly in the sayings of the wise (22.17–21) in more than just one tradition or religion (Egyptian or Mesopotamian), where assiduous cultic use of wisdom could, parallel to sacrifice, mysteriously assist both political stability and individual well-being. In ben Sirach this is related specifically to the Jewish Law, but related in such a way that the Law is comprehended and experienced in the totality of Jewish piety and faith as a way of life, a totality which includes the divine influences by which revelation, obedience and personal transformation take place. A similar development can be traced in Baruch. In the Wisdom of Solomon we have already seen the relation of wisdom to political stability and well-being, and in 7.23–8.1 wisdom takes on not only the function of subtle interrelationships in the world (7.22; 1.6–11) but also of divine sustaining activities which express the providential, creative care of God (v. 23; 8.1). There are parallels here with the Stoic world-soul which animates and renews the universe, but this is achieved in the book of Wisdom in tune with divine creativity. Wisdom's nature can be spoken of as *a clear effluence from the glory of the Almighty* (v. 25), as a *radiance that streams from everlasting light, the flawless mirror of the active power of God, and the image of his goodness* (v. 26). As in ben Sirach this wisdom can enter *holy souls, and makes them friends of God and prophets* (v. 27).

Victorious over evil, wisdom *gently orders all things* (8.1) and expresses the divine freedom and creativity of activity (see 8.4) on which the writer of the book of Wisdom insists. It is not surprising that in the hymn in Col. 1.13–20 the work of Christ parallels the work of Wisdom (see also Heb. 1.3).

Chapter 8

Solomon now returns to the illustrations from his life. As in ben Sirach it is important that the search for wisdom begins in youth. The language here is erotic. Central to the argument is wisdom's sharing of the divine life (vv. 4–18; see 1.6–11 and 9.9): the Master of all loves her and she is an initiate of his understanding and *chooses* his works. This sharing of the divine life means that if riches are a desired possession, what could be richer than wisdom? If good sense is at work, what operator could be preferred to wisdom? If anyone loves righteousness, what in human life could be more valuable than the cardinal virtues (see 4 Macc. 1.4)? If one longs for experience, here is the source of inference, understanding, prophecy and foresight (vv. 5–8). *So*, says Solomon, *I determined to take her home* to share life with her, *knowing that she would be my counsellor in prosperity and my comfort in anxiety and grief* (v. 19). Honour among elders, the capacity to speak in public, leaving behind a lasting reputation – these are wisdom's gifts, here and in ben Sirach (37.16–26). But wisdom offers immortality, along with good government, a fearsome reputation, brave leadership and joyful companionship. She offers *immortality in kinship* with her (vv. 11–17). Aware of all this, says Solomon, *I went about in search of some way to win her* (v. 18). In Solomon's favour were high birth and a noble soul (understood in the tradition of the Jewish philosopher Philo, a near contemporary of the book of Wisdom); he was not from any forbidden union (3.16–17). But only with God's permission, as God's gift (how important is that recognition!), could he *gain possession of her* (v. 21). Solomon then begins his extended prayer to God.

Chapter 9

Unlike 1 Kgs 3.1–15 and 2 Chron. 1 this prayer is a direct appeal to God. He addresses God as *God of our forefathers*, as Creator by his *word*, fashioning humanity for *sovereignty over . . . creation* as a holy and righteous *steward* and with the responsibility of administering *justice*. Solomon declares himself a *slave*, weak, mortal, unable to fulfil humanity's vocation without wisdom. Without the wisdom who sits by the divine throne (see 8.9), he is unable to rule and judge God's people, and cannot build a temple and an altar in Jerusalem as a replica *of the sacred tabernacle prepared by you from the beginning* (v. 8c; see Odes 1.17). He pleads for wisdom, the one *familiar* with God's works (v. 9), *present* at creation, aware of God's desire and commands, so that she may work with him, guide him and *guard* him *with her glory* (returning him to Adam's true state), so he may judge *justly* and *be worthy of* his *father's throne* (vv. 9–12). To know God's will and purpose is beyond humanity, uncertain and fallible as we are; the mortal body is a weight on the spirit, and the earthly frame on the mind. Verse 16 interprets this not so much as a denigrating of the body and the physical frame (it is not a kind of material dualism), so much as stressing our incompetence to understand even earthly matters; how much greater our inability to track out the heavens! The association of wisdom with the mission of the holy spirit in v. 17 leads to the conclusion in v. 18: with help from on high, mortals *were kept safe by wisdom*. All this suggests that the book of Wisdom's use of language is flexible rather than precise. The conclusion of this section, typically for the book of Wisdom, leads into the next.

Chapter 10

In the Greek text the shape of the chapter is made clear by the repeated pronoun *she* (referring to wisdom and alternating with *wisdom*: 10.1, 4, 5, 6, 9, 10, 13, 15, 21). The chapter offers illustrations of how wisdom has kept mortals safe. Wisdom guarded God's unique creation, the *father of the human race*, Adam, even after his unique sin, so that he could fulfil his role of ruling *over all things* (vv. 1–2). The earth was threatened by a flood (see the parallel in Virgil's *Aeneid* 6.106) following Cain's angry betrayal of wisdom. Wisdom piloted the righteous Noah's barque across the waters (see 14.6 and the parallel with Homer's *Odyssey* 5.33), his *plain wooden hulk*. Wisdom recognized the righteous Abraham, following the complicity that built Babel, and kept him blameless despite his *pity* for Isaac (v. 5; Gen. 22). Wisdom delivered the righteous Lot as he escaped the destruction of the Five Cities, to whose wickedness in ignoring wisdom the wasteland (5.7), stunted plants and *pillar of salt* remain a lasting, unforgettable testimony (Gen. 19). Wisdom protected and guided Jacob as a fugitive, gave him a vision of God's kingdom and knowledge of holy things, prosperity at the expense of Laban, safety in the face of treachery (2.12), and victory at Peniel (Gen. 32), showing godliness to be the *mightiest power of all* (vv. 10–12). She delivered the righteous Joseph, being with him in the dungeon, giving him eventually royal authority and proving his accusers false (Gen. 39), and *bestowed on him undying fame* (vv. 13–14; see 8.10–15). The longest reference in the chapter is to wisdom's deliverance of God's oppressed people. She inspired Moses so that he (or wisdom?) *defied formidable kings* (again see 8.10–15), guiding Israel on its *miraculous journey*, bringing them through the Red Sea so that the righteous *despoiled the ungodly* (Exod. 11.1–3; 12.35–36) and praised God's holy name: *wisdom enabled the dumb to speak, and made the tongues of infants eloquent* (v. 21; see Ps. 8.2).

Chapter 11

In 11.1–14 terms reappear which we met in chapters 1–5. In those chapters they served to clarify the opposition between the righteous and the ungodly. They reoccur in 11.1–14 in a form which stresses a new and significant factor. The righteous too are seen to require disciplining and those very disciplines are seen in relation to the discomfort of the ungodly, and indeed they deepen that discomfort. If, as we have argued so far, the issue is how the traditional Jewish faith, presented from the background of a common education, can be defended against adherents of a different theology and anthropology, the form of comparison we meet in ch. 11 would seem to raise the stakes for both parties. The more traditional must recognize what is involved in such discipline; the more radical must face the increased pain and damage their programme involves.

To present this in a programmatic form: the Exodus story is being used, first, to set out the relation between the godly and the godless under three themes:

1. The means by which their oppressors have been punished were used to help the victims in their hour of need (v. 5).
2. The instruments of someone's sin are the instruments of his punishment (v. 16).
3. When the righteous were put to the test, though their discipline was tempered with mercy, they understood the tortures of the godless who were sentenced to anger (v. 9).

These will be referred to as programmatic statements nos 1–3.

Second, the comparison or opposition between the godly and godless is presented in seven Exodus situations: thirst (11.4–14), hunger (16.1–4), animal pestilence (16.5–15), fire (16.16–17.1), darkness (17.2–18.4), death by conspiracy (18.5–25), death by drowning (19.1–5).

As a background for the first of these comparisons, the writer takes Deut. 8, especially 8.15, 'he led you through that great and fearful desert . . . where he drew out for you from the hard rock a spring of water.' (This, including the hard rock, is from the Septuagint version.) This presents the desert wandering as a time of the humbling discipline and testing appropriate to God's children, to unmask their complacency, self-approval and pride, so that they may recognize their dependence on God and be warned to keep God's commandments, on pain of suffering what the nations suffered. That time reminded them that strength and prosperity come only from the Lord. They must be purified, so that the people serve only the Lord God and no other gods.

So *wisdom, working through a holy prophet, gave them success in all they did* (11.1); as they made their way through untrodden wastes she fought off assaults. The cry for help is a feature of the book of Wisdom (7.3–14; see Ps. 63.1), and God's response is water from the hard rock. The writer uses programmatic statement no. 1, supported first from the negative side: the great river Nile in its continual flow usually provided all the Egyptians needed, but (Exod. 7.20) as a punishment for the killing of the innocents, when Moses barely escaped with his life, the Nile turned *putrid*; on the positive side, the Jews *when they had lost hope* received *abundant water* (vv. 6–7). The thirst the Jews endured introduces programmatic statement no. 3, illustrated from the positive side by Deuteronomy's comment about a *father* disciplining his children, and on the negative side by *torture like a stern king passing sentence* (v. 10), a suffering expanded by a form of programmatic statement no. 1 (v. 13), leading to an anticipation in v. 14 of programmatic statement no. 2: Moses, whom they have abandoned, exposed and mocked (see 4.17–18), the means of their sin, became the one through whom they were punished. *They* (the godless) *saw your hand in it, Lord* – this recognition is an all-important stage in the process of divine judgement (12.27). The final comment stresses the intensity of the opposition between the righteous and the godless: *their thirst was such as the godly never knew* (v. 14c). Presumably this was, according to the writer, because the Egyptians, in threatening Moses, took an initial step towards denying the reality of God (see the continuation in

vv. 15–16, and the commentary on 12.27). No wonder Moses was accorded a prophetic role in v. 1!

The writer now introduces four principles by which to understand the divine activity:

A. You set all things in order by measure and number and weight (v. 20).
B. You are merciful to all (v. 23).
C. You correct offenders little by little (12.2a).
D. You act for judgement and mercy by means of your creation (vv. 15–26).

These four will be referred to as Principles A, B, C and D.

Pointers to Principle A are examined in vv. 15–20. Verses 15–16 point in that direction (v. 16 is programmatic statement no. 2: instruments of sin become instruments of punishment). Since the Egyptians worshipped mindless reptiles and worthless beasts, these were the means despatched against them to punish them (v. 15; see Principle D). But God's total potential, as the creator of the world from *formless matter*, could not be limited. Possible punishments would have been bears, lions, dragons, volcanos, meteors, that which fatally wounds or frightens to death (vv. 17–19). Or just a single breath would be an appropriate punishment. Hence Principles A and D (v. 20).

Pointers to Principle B (God is merciful to all) also emerge from God's *great strength* (v. 21a), for which the pictures could have been drawn from classical Greek tragedy and Isa. 40 alike, but especially from the latter because of its association with the critique there of idolatry. Principle B (a very rhythmic line) – you are merciful to all – follows *because you can do all things* (v. 23b); all things include: overlooking sin to *bring* people *to repentance,* care for what you have made and the reason in making it, the holding of everything in existence and its maintenance, consideration for everything since *your imperishable breath is in every one of them* – O Lord and lover of the soul! (see a similar comment in a different context 1.6; and Charles Wesley's hymn 'Jesu, lover of my soul').

Chapter 12

Pointers to Principle C (God corrects *offenders little by little,* v. 2) include the arguments from 11.15–12.1, especially the purpose of bringing people to repentance and to trust in God (v. 2c). The historical argument runs as follows: the Canaanites were responsible for *their loathsome practices*, including sorcery, cannibalism and child sacrifice, yet God decided that room should be made for his people in the promised land by *the hands of our forefathers* (v. 6). Yet even so the principle of 'little by little' applied (Exod. 23.30), since hornets were sent as an advance guard (Josh. 24.12), so that the Canaanites were *exterminat*ed little by little (v. 8; see Deut. 7.22), the purpose being (v. 10) to give them room for repentance, for all their *evil stock* and *innate wickedness*, and their permanent inability to understand the nature of God truly. Nor can a different motive for the amnesty be imputed, for no one *can challenge your verdict. You are just and you order all things justly, counting it alien to your power to condemn anyone to undeserved punishment* (vv. 12, 15). In 2.11 the ungodly claim strength as their own decree about right and wrong (Might is Right); here God's strength is the very *source of justice*, and his mastery over all actually makes leniency a possibility for all. It makes possible the distinction between those who doubt his absolute power and those who, though aware of it, are insolent and are consequently punished. As Master of strength you *judge in mercy and rule us in great forbearance* – Solomon's prayer is still continuing – and the power is yours to choose (vv. 15–18). So the children of God learn from *acts like these* that the just one is also kind-hearted (v. 19; 11.26); they are filled *with hope* of repentance. If that is how God has dealt with his children's enemies, *with what* accurate *discrimination* has God judged his own people, whose forefathers received covenants full of good promises (vv. 19–21). Therefore God educates his people, while scourging their enemies in countless ways. He teaches his people to meditate on his goodness when they are sitting in judgement, and to hope for mercy when judged.

Precisely how the argument proceeds from here on is affected by the translation of the complicated syntax of vv. 26–27. The writer infers from the previous argument a gradually modifying form of his programmatic statement no. 2: the means of sin is the instrument of punishment; first, *heedless folly* (see 10.8) and *abominations* characterize the sin; and *torment* replaces punishment. Verses 24–27 probably explain the modification: *they had strayed far down the paths of error*. They had considered as gods the most repugnant things, the most repugnant of animals (frogs?) and shameful things (a stage worse than 11.15; see also ch. 13). Deceived, like foolish children, they were fittingly made to look ridiculous by God's judgement (they worship what is ridiculous and so are made to look ridiculous: programmatic statement no. 2). However, those not warned and censured by such ridicule tempt God to give a further judgement, a judgement worthy of God (see 11.15–16). Punished by those very animals which they took to be gods (punished because of what is about to happen), they saw the One of whom previously they had denied knowledge, and they *recognized* him to be the true God. The means of sin (treating things as god and denying they know God) become the instrument of punishment (once they saw and recognized God for who he truly is, they knew their denial to be the ultimate sin and itself the most fundamental punishment: dismissal from the presence of God: v. 27; 11.13). The following chapter provides a commentary on this.

Chapters 13–15

Ignorance of God (13.1) can mean many things: ignorance of God's existence or ignorance of what or who God is (see Acts 17.23, where a reality is recognized and worshipped without it being named). Here it is the second. *Born fools* could be general or specific; here it belongs within a context such as Isa. 44.9: the ignorance of worshippers of idols shows up their foolishness. Fools could not even know the 'One who is' from the good things which are seen, or know the architect by attending to his works; instead they selected from a host of elements or heavenly bodies what they considered to be gods (13.2). On the one hand, *delight in the beauty* of such things (v. 3) might cause them to reckon them as gods; but in that case they must recognize *how much better is the Master of them*, since the one who created them is the one who originally brought beauty into being (the Greek word *genesiarchos* belongs to no hellenistic philosophical system; it was deliberately coined to carry Jewish scriptural connotations). On the other hand, the *power and influence* of such things (v. 4) might have impressed them and caused them to worship; but in that case they should consider how much more powerful is the one who fashioned them. As against some contemporary philosophers, the writer is arguing that the effects seen in the universe must be distinguished from the one who is their original cause; there is a qualitative difference between created and Creator; it is only by analogy that the creator can be seen in the beauty and greatness of what was made (13.5; the REB is rather imprecise here). Nevertheless such people are *not greatly to be blamed* (13.6); perhaps they erred in seeking and wanting to find God, and in their search *were persuaded by appearances*. But, again, they cannot *be excused* (13.8); they had enough knowledge to try to track down the goddess Aion (REB speaks here about 'speculation' concerning the 'universe'; but the verb can to mean to 'track down' (a suitable verb for tracking down a deity), and Aion was the name given to a Greek goddess who has been associated with the Emperor Augustus and the everlasting character of the Empire: see Virgil, *Aeneid* 1.278). If they could try to track down Aion, could they not somewhat sooner have discovered the Lord and Master (13.9)?

Those classed *degraded* (or miserable) set their *hopes* on the dead rather than on that for which humanity and creation were made (2.23): they give *the title of gods* to precious metals artefacts, man-made representations of creatures or useless stones – dead things. An example of this class is the carpenter, and the passage is a reconstruction of Isa. 44.9–20, a typical prophetic polemic against idols. The carpenter's initial work is evidence of wisdom's inspiration; it is skilled, deft and elegant. But having produced a *household vessel suitable for everyday* he uses the last *bits* of wood that are *left over* for cooking and has a good meal (13.11–12). What is left over from that is a *crooked* (1.3), knotted, totally useless piece, which he works (see 7.2), with the experimental attention of leisure hours, to resemble the *image of a human being* or *some worthless creature* (the language again recalls 2.23–24). It is smeared and raddled, *so that every flaw in it is daubed over*, and for it he makes a *suitable shrine* or paltry niche (the contrast with a temple increases the irony) and secures it firmly to the wall with a nail. So he takes every precaution against it falling down, well aware that, being just an image, it cannot *fend for itself* (13.15–16). The next verse is unfair to the ancient theories of worship via statues (*he feels no shame in addressing this inanimate object*), but 13.17 does provide an obvious counterpoint to Solomon's prayer: Solomon prays for wisdom; the carpenter prays about *possessions* and his family. The inappropriateness of the wooden image – *weak, dead, incapable, cannot put one foot before the other, ineffectual* – is mocked, as is also the carpenter himself. He is himself *degraded* (13.10), and has failed to embody humanity's true nature.

Or again, the seafarer *invokes a piece of wood more fragile* than the ship itself (14.1). A useful background to this section is provided by a poet of the early Empire and a contemporary of Virgil, Horace, writing in his *Odes* 1.3. He is wishing godspeed to Virgil for his sea journey, but does so with a typical twist. There is the appropriate reference to protection from above (from the divinities, Castor and Pollux; see Acts 28.11), but Horace also mentions the divine purpose of the sea which humanity dares to cross with their accustomed foolish pride. A translation of lines 21–24 reads:

> Alas, how vainly Heaven planned
> With pathless gulfs to sunder land from land,
>   If naughty ships can break their bounds
> And overleap the unpermitted sounds!

Horace is carping at progress, to a degree the book of Wisdom would probably not have approved of. As 10.4 has indicated, wisdom can instruct the ship's pilot and come to the rescue (see 14.6–7); 14.2 probably makes wisdom the ship-builder (rather than, as in REB, giving the credit to the shipwright's *skill*) and the book of Wisdom prefers to speak of the God-given pathway through the sea, a safe course among the waves rather than 'pathless gulfs', and divine providence to pilot the ship even if the seafarer is inexpert; and 14.5 suggests that the things made by wisdom should not lie unused. There is another side to 14.1–14: the hints of greed (14.2a, *desire for gain*), *superstition* (14.14), pride (14.6; see Gen. 6.4–5 and the Greek parallels), straying from God's way, judgement (14.8, 11), and above all the failure to see the divine purpose at work among the righteous in fulfilling humanity's vocation and potential (14.6). The creator's work is imperishable; the carpenter and his work are not: *While a blessing is on the wood through which right prevails* (Noah again!), *the wooden idol made by human hands is accursed – and so is its maker – he because he made it, and the perishable thing because it was called a god* (14.7–8). The connection with chs. 1–5 is made in 14.9: hateful to God are both the *godless* and *ungodliness*. So the section concludes with the warning of the divine visitation on idols (5.17–23) and *the devising of idols* (it is a human conception and invention). Idolatry is *the beginning of immorality* (as a corrupting of life, entering like death into the world via human vainglory). It had no part in creation and will have no part in the future.

The form of the prayer in 14.3 uses the singular address, *Father*. It is sometimes assumed that this form of address is a Christian prerogative. We shall find in ben Sirach that God is invoked as Father in time of need, in reliance on the relationship of son to the Father (see 23.1, 4; 51.1, 10). Such an address is also found in Qumran 4Q372 : 'My Father and my God, do not abandon me to the hands of the nations' (see also 'my Father and my God' in 4Q460). It is an address of intimacy, yet recognizes God's universal claim. The address 'our Father' appears in Tobit 13.4, and simply 'Father' here in Wisdom 14; as a prayer of the believer intimate with the Father of heaven it is found in the *Apocryphon of Ezekiel*. Nevertheless the address 'Father' on the lips of Jesus does have a new audacity, claiming the unique personal relationship of Jesus, the embodiment of the Son of God.

A rationale for idolatry begins with a father overwhelmed with grief at the untimely death of a child (14.15). The natural response to that situation is sympathy for the father, but it is not clear that Wisdom responded in that way. The turning of the child into an *image . . . honoured . . . as a god* becomes a cultic imposition on his household and a legal obligation. The similarities between that and tyrannical orders to worship *graven images* (14.16b) cannot be obscured simply by the wider honouring given to a prince by his people (14.17a). For then it is the people who *produced a visible image of the king*, because they live at a distance and wish to *gratify* him *by their zeal* (14.17bc). Furthermore, it is *ambitious craftsmen* who have a vested interest. They widen the cult's appeal to include those ignorant of the original image. They skilfully turn the wood, perhaps *to please the monarch*, changing the likeness of the image into an idealized object of beauty (14.18–19). Only a short time before, the image was simply of someone honoured; now the populace, *beguiled by the beauty of the workmanship*, take it to be an *object of worship* (14.20). So beauty, which in other contexts could be a feature of wisdom's moral transformation, became a snare and an enslavement *by mischance or misgovernment*, the damage to life and society arising because people conferred on stone and wood the divine name *that none may share* (14.21; see the first two commandments in Deut. 5.7–8 which link chs 13–15).

As if it were not sufficient to have erred in the matter of knowing God, people experience the damage done to the fabric of society and the relationships distorted by idolatry *in the constant warfare of ignorance* – involving a massive range of evils – all of which they designate *peace* (14.22). The gap between reality and such distorted experience and between human potential and its massive failures is indicated by a list of sins not dissimilar to the Caananite sins of 12.3–6, and associated with ritual ceremonies and cults. The ties which enable people to maintain a purity of life and to live and work together are broken (14.24), and *chaos* ensues (see 5.23), endangering life, property, values, trust, order and truth. *Honest folk* are *driven to distraction*, and personal and sexual relations are polluted. Heathen idol worship, unnamable in its depravity, is *the beginning, the cause, and the end of every evil* (14.27) – self-indulgence to the point of madness, deceitful lies offered as prophecy, dishonest living, quickly broken vows – all because trust is placed in lifeless idols, before which vows are debased and no ad-verse judgement is anticipated (14.29). On both counts justice will *overtake them*: by *devotion to idols they have thought wrongly about God*; by despising holiness they have debased vows through deceit. Not that making vows before idols implies a power at work in idols; rather, they are made before the *nemesis of sin*, constantly visiting *the trans-gressions of the wicked* (14.31).

As in 11.15–26, the acknowledgement of God's power (15.3) com-prises both judgement and mercy, and at the Exodus Israel experi-enced both. In 15.1–3, parallel to some of the Psalms, God is addressed as the *merciful ruler of all that is*, to whom his people belong even if they sin, although, because they are reckoned as his people, they will not sin. This is summarized in the central statement, registering Israel's vocation: *to know* God is *the whole of righteousness* and *to acknowledge* his *power* is *the root of immortality* (15.3). So his people are not *led astray* by malicious human inventions or through the use of skill or artistry; they do not respond to the sight of images *without life or breath* (15.4–5). That is for fools who, whether making them, desiring them, or wor-shipping them, are *in love with evil* (contrast 8.2) and deserve what they get.

Parallel to the carpenter of 13.11–18 is the potter of 15.7–13. In Isa. 45.9–13 the potter is the divine creator; in Wisdom 15, by a deliberate contrast, the potter is a human being, choosing what he makes of the clay and choosing to make false gods, while *the living soul that was lent to him must be returned on demand* (15.8). Unconcerned about his short *span of life* (and sceptical about immortality) he vies with other crafts-men, considering it to his *credit to contrive fakes*. Because he did not recognize the one who moulded him and breathed the breath of life into him (thus offering him life, vocation and purpose, and the wis-dom to share in the divine life), his own life is actually worth less than the clay he works (since just as the clay is for him to work and judge, so is he to the divine potter). For the potter our life is a fairground, and anything goes, providing he makes a living. Yet even that shows he has a clearer grasp than most that what he is making is wrong (15.9–13).

Solomon has dealt with the fools (13.1) and the miserably ignorant (13.10). But most foolish and *infantile* of all are those who oppress God's people, supposing *their* own *heathen idols* to be gods, when in truth it is God who made us living beings so that we might be in the likeness of his immortality. A mortal who by *impious hands* shapes a god in his own likeness can only create for worship what is dead and so something less than himself (15.14–19). It is the worship of animals, the lowest form of idolatry, for which the final place is reserved in the writer's critique. Such idolatry involves creatures left out of God's original blessing of creation (see Gen. 1.20–22): the reptiles. Once again the author ends a section where he intends to begin the next.

Chapter 16

The author returns now to the comparisons within the Exodus setting.

The comparison: hunger (16.1–4)

Parallel to one of the Psalms (Ps. 78.12–55) this comparison sets Egypt's disasters over against Israel's protection; it uses all three programmatic statements and the principle of God's mercy and judgement via creation (Principle D). The Egyptians were *chastised by creatures* such as they worshipped (programmatic statement no. 2), creatures so revolting that they were turned off *even from essential food*. In Ps. 78 the reason suggested for the Egyptians' hunger is locusts and hailstones (see Ps. 105.33–35), but those causes belong to the next comparison rather than here. Here in 16.1 hunger is caused by revolting reptile idols (16.3; not *vermin* as in REB), probably by the plague of frogs. These are an imagined consequence of the pollution of the Nile, showing how the punishment could open their eyes to the nature of their offence (through the plague they too were revolted by the worship of such creatures). This was to fulfil the divine principle of encouraging repentance 'little by little' (Principle C). The Egyptians were punished by hunger; the Israelites were sent the *novel food* of quails to quicken their appetite and satisfy their hunger (programmatic statement no. 1). The *short spell* of *scarcity which* Israel suffered (in Ps. 78 it is an extended period because of Israel's disobedience, grumbling and punishment) taught Israel the nature of *their enemies'* torture (programmatic statement no. 3).

The comparison: animal pestilence (16.5–15)

The emphasis here is on the third statement, that the righteous were put to the test and, though their discipline was tempered with mercy, they understood the tortures of the godless who were sentenced to wrath (see NRSV). The discipline and punishment here were *fierce and venomous* (literally, crooked) *snakes*; but even this was *a short-lived* lesson. Central to this experience was Israel's act of repentance followed by the lifting up of the bronze snake (Num. 21.6–9), not as something to look at (this is a safeguard against any suspicion of idolatry), but as a symbol of God's saving *word* (v. 12; Ps. 107.20); it was a reminder of *the requirements of the law* (v. 6). The contrast is explicitly made between the Israelites who were healed and the Egyptians who were not. The latter were *convinced* that God delivers his own, because when Egyptians *died from the bites* (v. 9a) *no remedy . . . was found* for them, their punishment corresponding to the seriousness of their sin (16.9b). The swiftness of the healing of the Israelites after they were bitten was in case they should *fall into deep forgetfulness* and become distracted from God's *kindness* (v. 11). As in Tobit 13.2 God can bring a person down to the *gates of death* and return them back; that no mortal can do (vv. 13–14; see Ps. 107.18).

The comparison: fire (16.15–17.1)

There is no escape from divine judgement (v. 15); the godless discovered this, and also discovered, pursued by hail and destroyed by fire, that this was God's judgement upon them. Principles D and C explain why the Egyptians learnt that this was indeed God's judgement: (Principle D) God uses his creation in both judgement and mercy; fire in the case of the Egyptians burned more brightly in the water (i.e. through the hail and the rain), showing that *creation . . . fights to defend the righteous* (v. 17). Yet it is also moderated, so that (Principle C) judgement proceeds little by little, giving room for repentance (v. 18). Furthermore, fire destroyed the *produce* of the *sinful land* (v. 19), offering a contrast with Israel via the story of the manna (*angel's food*, bread from above, suited to *every taste*: v. 20). The blazing fire which destroyed the enemies' crops is contrasted with the sweetness of manna (notice that the time sequence of the Exodus story is irrelevant here). For this to be possible the fire had to forget its own power otherwise it would have destroyed the manna as well! (A form of programmatic statement no. 1; see also Principle D and 19.13–22 where, again, the elements strain to punish the unrighteous but relax to be benevolent to the faithful.) The effect for the Israelites was that the manna became associated with the sustaining, unfailing, instructive divine word (see Exod. 16.15–16, particularly the LXX). Here too fire worked miraculously: although the fire did not destroy the manna, the first rays of the fiery sun did melt it (v. 27; see 19.21b) – a miracle understood as counselling daily piety (prayer *as daylight dawns*) and a warning against being ungrateful to God.

Chapter 17

The comparison: darkness (17.2–18.4)

Programmatic statement no. 2 – that the instruments of someone's sin are the instruments of his punishment – suggests that the darkness in which the Egyptians were punished is one with their false worship and their oppression of Israel (they lie enclosed by darkness as they enclosed Israel). Separated from each other, the Egyptians were *fugitives from eternal providence* (v. 2). The darkness of their *secret sins* creates an inner disorder, fear (see v. 11) and nightmares, which no known hiding place can resolve (v. 4). The language hints at fears from the underworld, stygian darkness, the waters of Lethe (where the dead forget all they knew), the *grim faces* of those in the keeping of Hades and Persephone. Sometimes it is difficult to tell which element of a text is lived experience and which is a literary cross reference. Here and in 18.19 the language describes with an uncanny accuracy the 'entry into the underworld' in the Bulgarian mountains of Rodope in all its dark fearfulness; the darkness is impenetrable. The pillar of fire (Exod. 13.21) in the darkness serves for the Egyptians only as a blaze to play tricks on their imagination (v. 6) and the stars cannot pierce the darkness around them (contrast 10.17). Their dark *sorcerer's art* and boasted wisdom serves only to ridicule their sickness and dread (v. 7; see 5.4–7). Evil, when inwardly condemned, becomes craven, and leads to *forebodings of disaster* (v. 11). Fear sets in with the abandonment of reason's aid (v. 12), and hope cannot understand the cause of the torment (contrast the Egyptians in 16.18). This darkness in v. 14 is impenetrable, whereas Israel recognized in the stories of the patriarchs (10.1–11.1) how wisdom's aid can deliver from any circumstance. Night brings a glimpse of the depths of hell which, though *powerless*, haunts their sleep and paralyses them in their inner treachery. The prison without bars and the workers anticipating their doom depict a world where failure to recognize wisdom (as with the carpenters and potters) leaves no possibility of escape. The terrifying experience of the entry into the underworld contrasts with the reality which the Israelites know of *the bright light of day* (v. 20). For the Egyptians alone suffered the *heavy night*, but what was worse than the darkness was the *burden each was to himself* (v. 21; see 17.2, 11, 13, 15, 16).

Chapter 18

The bright light of day continued for God's *holy ones* (v. 1), who could be heard by the Egyptians but not seen by them. The positive reaction of the Egyptians to Israel in Exod. 11.2–3 and 12.33–36 becomes in vv. 1c–2 a blessing on Israel (Israel had not suffered what the Egyptians had; see 17.20), and a thanksgiving to Israel for not doing the Egyptians mischief *under provocation*. So the Egyptians *begged* them for the *favour* of their departure. A reflection on the *pillar of fire* as Israel's guide and light leads to a contrast between Israel's light and the Egyptians' imprisonment by darkness – an appropriate punishment (programmatic statement no. 2) for those who imprisoned Israel (*kept Israel in durance*). They had imprisoned a people whose vocation was to mediate *the imperishable light of the law* (v. 4).

The comparison: death by conspiracy (18.5–25).

In v. 5 the means by which their oppressors were punished becomes assistance to the victims in their hour of need (v. 8; programmatic statement no. 1): the conspiracy *to kill the new-born infants* results in Passover night (v. 5; see 11.14 on Moses and 19.7 on the drowning in the sea). Prior warning of Passover night gave Israel hope, and by means of the assailants' punishment Israel was made glorious (see v. 4; 19.22). Verse 9 brings together features of Israel's common life: the sacrifices, covenants (v. 22), law, the forefathers and the sacred songs of praise (whether specifically Passover features or reflecting the Chronicler's traditions is unclear: 2 Chron. 30.22; 1 Esdras 1.1–22). This will prove important in the second stage of this section (vv. 20–25). The clamour of Egyptian *lamentation* contrasts with Israel's songs (v. 10) as the scale of the 'single stroke' is described (vv. 11–20), and unbelievers, previously misled by *magic arts* (v. 13; the Greek of 1.14; 12.4 uses the same root), confessed that the Israelites have God as their Father. All was *in peace and silence* (the source of the Christmas 'Silent

Night'?) when, like the warrior victor of 5.17–23 the *all-powerful word* (wisdom, from the heavenly throne) descends, spreading death everywhere, a death anticipated in dreams and recognized in reality *so that they should not perish still ignorant of why they suffered* (v. 19). The second part of the section finds the agent of death at work among the godly, with a trial *of death* there too, although there *the divine wrath did not long continue* (v. 20; Principle C) because of Aaron's action in interposing the weapon of the word (see Num. 16.1–50, where again 'the single moment' of destruction is mentioned), and *bearing the weapons of his priestly ministry, prayer and the incense that propitiates* (v. 21), with an appeal to the covenants with the forefathers (v. 22). The high priest's robes halt the destroyer with their universal claim, their link with the *glories of the fathers* and, above all, the divine *majesty* symbolized by the diadem (see Exod. 28 for a full description of the robes and their significance). The divine purpose at work in Israel's history and life intervenes (see 19.22) even in the face of sin and destruction within God's people.

Chapter 19

19.1–5 summarizes the situation and adds that, by contrast with Israel, *the godless were assailed by pitiless anger to the very end*, since they *pursued as runaways those they had entreated to leave* (another classic illustration of programmatic statement no. 1, since the completion of the Egyptian punishment was the means by which Israel achieved a miraculous *journey*; 19.5).

The comparison: death by drowning (19.6–17)

The whole creation . . . was refashioned in subservience to your commands (see Principle D): first, to preserve Israel as, overshadowed by the cloud, it passed safely via an open road out of the Red Sea, *after witnessing amazing portents* (vv. 7–8). Perhaps v. 9 is suggested by Isa. 63.13–14 and Ps. 114 (see the parallels there with the Red Sea and the Promised Land); some suggest a sequence similar to Gen. 1; some suggest a touch of Greek mythology as in Apollonius Rhodius' *Argonautica*. All three suggestions could be right at what is a climactic point of Solomon's praise: *they praised you, O Lord, by whom they were* delivered (v. 9; see the recapitulation in vv. 10–11 of miracles by which the refashioning of creation (Principle D) brought chaotic disaster for Egyptians – earth produced flies or gnats, and the water produced frogs – and, as relief for Israel, the sea produced quails; see also 16.5–14; 19.22). Hence, second, creation was refashioned to punish sinners, with a warning from the *thunderbolts* (v. 13). The sin here was that of turning *guests* into *slaves* (a hint perhaps of the traditional complaint that Jews, who had common rights and were benefactors in the Diaspora, were nevertheless treated as slaves and outcasts). The punishment was appropriate: they were struck with blindness (like the Sodomites who mistreated strangers; see 10.6 and Gen. 19.11). In *yawning darkness* they could not find their own home.

The final section (19.18–22) is an act of praise as a commitment to the Creator. Israel has been given a vocation by God and safeguarded by divine providence. Some, by denying the true nature of God and substituting an inadequate understanding of humanity, have threatened that vocation and the stability of the world, in ways such as idolatry and the comparisons offered by the book of Wisdom. The true nature of God, however, is that he is One who can help in any circumstances; he can adjust the created order to meet every contingency; the universal elements, far from being the determinative principles which human vanity made of them in one of the most significant misjudgements regarding the nature of God and the world (14.14), can appear in fresh arrangements and effects. Fire proves to be a subtle instrument for judgement and blessing. The simple pattern of earth, air, fire and water which the writer has earlier worked into the pattern of the Exodus is here insufficient. All that God made of pre-existent matter has an unbelievably creative constitution (11.17). The whole universe is seen as God's creation, all the mysterious elements which have appeared in the story of the Exodus, far from being separate objects of veneration, co-operate in an infinite variety of possibilities. The stages of the Exodus illustrate the astonishing versatility of creation (v. 19). Verse 21 refers to the contrast between the fire's destructive power and its capacity to be protective and gentle. The final summary is a theological statement in which the writer seeks to challenge all the parts of the Jewish community (in as much as they wrestle in various ways with the splendour, beauty and attraction of the hellenistic world) to return to the true God. In vv. 18–22, not least in the musical analogy, the writer presents a superior faith and a vastly superior object of faith, of which Moses' priestly robe is symbol (18.24). It promises the secrets of the universe (7.17). This is not a transposition of elements in the pattern of an alchemy but a pattern of divine creativity built into the very fabric of existence. Verse 18 has a syntactical structure which no printed translation adequately represents. The clue to the syntax is that the real subject of the whole sentence is 'the elements', for it is the elements which are creatively transmutable in the hands of the Creator God. A possible translation would be: For, 'modulated' between one another (just as on a harp the strings can between them vary the type of musical structure) are the elements, remaining always 'resonant', as you can accurately surmise from observing what has happened.

It is this Creator God who has glorified his people with such a great vocation, and has the unfailing resources to secure their continued pilgrimage (vv. 9, 22).

Ben Sirach: Ecclesiasticus or The Wisdom of Jesus Son of Sirach

'Forgive us our sins as we forgive those who sin against us' – that sentence from the Lord's Prayer has a close parallel in the book ben Sirach: 28.2 reads 'Forgive your neighbour any wrong he has done you; then, when you pray, your sins will be forgiven'. The book ben Sirach was finalized, as its Prologue tells us, somewhere between 132 and 110 BCE and, as that illustration from the Lord's Prayer shows, provides an important background to biblical studies. It gives us close parallels to the gospel material; it fills in important details for the historical and theological study of the intertestamental period and of the New Testament. It offers, in particular, a portrait and illustration of what it was like to be 'a scribe', studying and reflecting on the Jewish tradition of law, wisdom and prophets (ben Sirach 39.1–11).

The title of the book is given in the Revised English Bible as 'Ecclesiasticus, or the Wisdom of Jesus Son of Sirach'. Ecclesiasticus is its title in the later Latin Bible (the Vulgate), presumably because, although not a part of the Old Testament canon, the book was nevertheless ecclesiastical; it was a church book. The alternative title, 'The Wisdom of Jesus, Son of Sirach', owes its form to a Greek text. It indicates that the Greek text has its place within Jewish Wisdom literature, and that it is a translation, made in Egypt, of an earlier Hebrew work (for this information read through the Preface to Ecclesiasticus in the REB Apocrypha, p. 90). There is also a third title. A recent modern volume has published the extraordinary mixture now available of Hebrew manuscripts and fragments of ben Sirach (3.16–51.30). These, with the Syriac traditions, associate other names with the book, in addition to Sirach and Jesus, for example, the names of Eleazar and Simeon. The third title, then, is the Hebrew title of the book, 'ben Sirach'; and 'ben Sirach' may mean rather more than simply 'son of Sirach'; it could mean 'grandson of Sirach'. It could be that several (as many as five?) members of the Sirach family were associated with the book. Presumably it would be the final member who wrote its famous

Preface; and he took on an enormous enterprise. Rather like some modern authors, he began by thinking that it was a small project, and eventually found that its fifty chapters took 'some energy and labour' (ben Sirach 24.30–34 is a vivid description of how the material had grown!). One problem with the family relationships which we have just described is that the names can be confusing. It is clear enough to refer to the 'grandfather' as Sirach. The book ben Sirach is a translation or version of the work of Sirach or the Sirach family. But the name ben Sirach can refer either to the book or to the person; it can refer to the Greek translation and its Prologue or to the person who wrote the Prologue and gathered the Sirach tradition together, translating it into Greek. Where the distinction between the book and the person is important we shall try to make clear how we are using the name.

The three titles go a little way to explaining why English translations of this book vary, and have different verse numberings (the verses referred to here are from the REB). We have various Hebrew versions and two major Greek versions. So the REB used critical editions of the Greek text but 'constant reference was made to the various forms of the Hebrew text'. No doubt the translators, given the printed collation of Hebrew texts now available, might have made even more adjustments! On the other hand there is something to be said for translating ben Sirach's work as it stands in the Greek, although of course using the Hebrew evidence as guidance in the translation process.

The structure of the book is in four parts: a prologue; 1.1–43.33; 44.1–50.29; and an epilogue. 1.1–43.33 has the following shape (hymns or poems concerning Wisdom are in bold type): **1.1–10**; 1.11–4.10; **4.11–19**; 4.20–6.17; **6.18–37**; 7.1–14.19; **14.20–15.10**; 15.11–23.27; **24.1–34**; 25.1–42.14; **42.15–43.33**). Between the hymns or poetic sections are extended sections of teaching. The clue to these and to their subsections (in some cases 12 or 13 in number) is in their summary sections and summary sayings.

Built into ben Sirach's picture of God's world (32.14–33.19) are two apparently contradictory features. First, there is a division between the wise and the foolish, the righteous and the wicked; and this division reflects a divine Wisdom according to which everything has its opposite. Such a division might be thought to reflect an in-built determinism, a fixed universe expressing a divine omniscience of everyone and everything, past, present and future. But second, there is an emphasis on human responsibility without which all the carefully summarized practical wisdom of the book would be pointless.

Each person is responsible for his or her own ultimate fate. That spells out a problem which is still with us, the problem of divine providence and human responsibility.

Sirach, the 'grandfather', together with the Sirach tradition, gives us a picture of the basic social structure in and around Jerusalem in 200–170 BCE, together with incisive and thoughtful comments upon it. Sirach himself was a conservative supporter of the high-priesthood and his life-style suggests a quiet, reserved approach to the changes around him. From other contemporary material we gain a somewhat different picture from Sirach's of the age in which he lived. They indicate intense conflicts, particularly surrounding the attempts to stabilize a regime in Jerusalem following the reform missions of Nehemiah and Ezra. Perhaps Sirach was somewhat oblivious to these impending social conflicts, or insofar as he reveals an awareness of them, perhaps he comments unfavourably on them, as his warnings about visions and dreams might suggest. Perhaps visionary scribes were part of the religious and economic opposition to the high-priestly party. He belongs to a period facing changes with the growth of new market forces. The society in which he lived was basically agrarian but in towns and cities new skills were developing. In some cases the book ben Sirach responds creatively to these new skills. Whereas older Jewish traditions had sometimes seen medical doctors as interfering with the process of divine judgement, the book ben Sirach will not deny the value of accumulated medical wisdom. How could that be denied when Wisdom is immanent in the world and the professions express that divine inspiration! In other cases the book is caught up in the patterns of the day. One of the fundamental shifts in society concerned the place of women, a subject on which the Sirach tradition has been subjected to a great deal of criticism. The changes which were taking place and the male reaction to them will be considered in the commentary.

A Hymn, extolling the fearful wonder of the only wise God
1.1–10

The clue to the opening hymn is in its parallel 42.15–43.33, itself a major section marker in the book. In 1.1–10 and 42.15ff. there appear the same special vocabulary (see the Greek term translated in 1.6 as 'subtlety' and in 42.18 as 'intricacies'), the same unanswerable questions (1.2–6; 43.31), the same emphases (see 1.8; 42.21; 43.29), and the same contrast between human knowledge and divine wisdom: what by divine generosity the astonished minds of humankind, especially those who love him (1.10; 43.32–33), are given to perceive of his divine works (*All wisdom is from the Lord*, v. 1a) is not to be compared with the God of all, the one who is beyond all his works and all our words (43.27–28) – *One alone is wise, the Lord most terrible, seated upon his throne* (v. 8; see v. 1b).

Between 1.1 and 43.33 are a series of interlocking, cumulative traditions, some of which are foundational or programmatic and others illustrative, for which the opening hymn provides a focus. Also there are psalms in praise of Wisdom which also develop and move beyond what we find in the opening hymn.

1.11–2.18 The foundation. Since God is to be feared (1.8), *the beginning of wisdom is the fear of the Lord* (1.14). Fear of the Lord is a recurrent theme: it sounds inhibiting, but in fact the writer's trust in God (as in some other Wisdom books) transmutes fear into reverent wonder (1.12), reverent wonder such as vocation, endowment or coronation evoke (all ways of looking at humanity's creation; see 1.14b): fear of the Lord brings a person honour, joy and long life (1.11–20); and *on the day of his death blessings will be his* (1.13; 2.3; 6.26–28). The context of ben Sirach's work is limited to earthly existence, and hence issues of blessings, salvation, punishment, reward, righteousness, vindication and death are dealt with by ben Sirach in that context (18.24). Nevertheless wisdom in abundance (1.16), enabling *peace* and *health* to flourish (1.18), shows the fear of the Lord to be fundamental for all humanity, from its beginnings to its end (1.15–20). That is as true of reverent wonder before God today as it ever was.

1.21, which appears as a marginal note in the REB, provides an appropriate link between 1.11–20 and 1.22–30: 'the fear of the Lord . . . averts anger'. However, the movement from 1.20, where the fear of the Lord is the root of wisdom from which long life sprouts, to 1.22, *unjust rage can never be excused*, does not really need a link verse. (Note that it is *unjust* anger tipping the scales of justice, not just any anger which is criticized; Matthew's gospel makes the same point: 18.23–35). The connecting links within 1.11–30 are already implied in what ben Sirach means by 'the fear of the Lord': 'the fear of the Lord' involves a practical pattern of living (see the Letter of James): to *guard* one's *lips* in patience, maintain the traditions of wisdom, *keep the commandments*, practise trust, humility and sincerity. These, which will be expounded in detail, belong to the 'fear of the Lord' as their opposites cannot: injustice, cynicism, arrogance and hypocrisy. For these are inconsistent with living in God's world in God's way – which is the heart of the Wisdom tradition.

2.1–18 *Testing, adversity, hardship* and *humiliation* are God's means by which uprightness, steadiness of mind and purpose are proved. Through four sets of triplets the relationship with God, as that of the fear of God (vv. 15–17), points also to his mercy: '*Let us fall into the Lord's hands, not into the hands of men', for his majesty is equalled by his mercy* (v. 18: a classic summary statement concluding 1.11–2.18).

3.1–4.10 Comments on family relationships involve key terms such as honour, humility, and stubbornness. The Hebrew text moves toward God's graciousness and deliverance from harm in this section. The Greek text concludes with the theme with which the section begins – honouring father and mother: *the Most High will call you his son, and greater than a mother's love will be his love for you* (4.10). The three intermediate sections concern: first, *honouring father* and *mother* (the Fifth Commandment); second, humility; and third, charity. The setting of the first is twofold: a concern with the social significance of honour, and problems within new (hellenistic) patterns of society where length of life was devalued and youth more highly prized (3.16). The danger attending the 'honour' society of hellenistic times is that honour can only be gained at someone else's expense and, as we shall see in relation to the role of women in ben Sirach, such a view of honour is disruptive of harmonious relationships. The setting of the second section is the concentration on proud theories (again hellenistic) rather than humble attention to what has been divinely commanded (3.29). The third recognizes that humility needs to be exercised within the area of charitable works (4.8), not least because the bitter prayers of the poor have access to God (see Tobit 3).

A central issue in these sections is what is meant by *Respect for a father atones for sins* (3.3) and *so almsgiving atones for sin* (3.30). Some scholars have regarded these verses as evidence for a belief that good works made possible an amassing of credit in the heavenly record book. Was this an example of salvation by works? There are good reasons for rejecting this view. First, ben Sirach worked with a this-worldly, not an other-worldly, pattern of belief, so notions of salvation implied in the phrase 'salvation by works' are foreign to his thinking. 'Salvation' in ben Sirach's language approximates to health and happiness, so that good works play an important part in the family's ability to cope with disasters and tribulations. Second, ben

Sirach views behaviour as a whole, not just as adherence to a code; he works with a holistic view of human works, not one which could be reduced to atomistic elements carrying merits, so that the amassing of credit is foreign to the relational picture described in ben Sirach 2.18. Third, the translation 'atones' has to be understood in ben Sirach's own context. The uses of this particular Greek verb in ben Sirach in relation to sin, wickedness and penitence are variously translated: 'pardon' in 5.6, 'secure pardon for' in 20.28, 'find pardon' (after self-examination:18.20), 'pardon' for those who pardon others, whereas those who cannot pardon their fellows find no one to pardon them (28.5), '(cannot) win forgiveness' (34.19), 'forgiveness' (17.29b), all of which fit within the general pattern of divine mercy in 2.11: *For the Lord is compassionate and merciful; he forgives sin and saves in time of trouble.* Alongside 'atone' are a series of other metaphors: e.g. 3.30a, *as water quenches a blazing fire;* 3.15, *when you are in trouble, it will be remembered in your favour, and your sins will melt away like frost in the sunshine.* Fourth, pardon is never to be taken for granted or lightly: the noun related to 'atone' is used in 5.5 to make this point; so, *do not say, 'His compassion is so great he will pardon my sins, however many.' To him belong both mercy and anger* (5.6; see 7.9); rabbinic discussions of the Day of Atonement make a similar point. Fifth, ben Sirach's thought is akin to the view that you enter the covenant by grace and remain in it by obedience (often called 'covenantal nomism'), where staying within the covenant, provided by God's grace, is made possible both by various means of dealing with sin, and by obedience to the divine will (21.1). Good works are both a response to the covenant and demonstrate that the dishonouring of the covenant has been dealt with. The holistic pattern is governed by grace from start to finish. Sixth, translations which appear to support the theory of amassed merit here are in fact dubious or faulty; e.g. 3.14, *will stand to your credit against your sins* should probably be translated 'it will be a provision toward your rehabilitation'. In 20.28 the context of 'atone for wickedness' is the shame/honour context, i.e. to gather respect from the great enables mistakes to be overlooked. One can be quite clear that the arguments against the Apocrypha which have been built on this and similar verses are today no longer acceptable.

As we noted earlier, the book intersperses the teaching material with short sections specifically about Wisdom, and in praise of Wisdom, as if Wisdom were a person. These are important structurally and are cumulative: they build up a total impression of what Wisdom is.

Wisdom and life
4.11–19

The blessings which Wisdom's sons/students enjoy are those which earlier in the text God provides: support, life, joy, happiness, honour (see also: *The Lord* blesses *the house she enters*: v. 13). The Isaianic description of God points to the holy nature of the (priestly?) service to Wisdom (v. 14). In v. 15 the REB reverts to the Hebrew text: those obedient to her *give true judgement*; whereas the Greek, translating a similar Hebrew word, reads, 'they will judge the nations' (see Wisd. 3.8; 1 Cor. 6.2). Wisdom's benefits can be passed on (v. 16). But the distinctive element of the poem is its emphasis on Wisdom's rigorous, fearful, puzzling, even dangerous disciplines (see 2.5 and the comments on 24.23); her education tests the trust and commitment of her sons on the touchstone of her decrees; to fail is to be abandoned (4.17–19).

4.20–6.17 Ben Sirach's world and our own need different warnings, and the practice of translation in the REB points to that. Ben Sirach's world needed a careful discussion of 'shame' (*There is a shame that relates to wrongdoing, as well as a shame that means honour and favour*, 4.21; Tobit's disgrace for burying his colleagues would illustrate the latter; see also 5.13). Today's world, however, looks for careful thought on personal integrity, and the REB translation reflects that: *Do not be over-modest in your own cause* (4.20), *Do not be untrue to yourself in deference to another or diffident to your own undoing* (4.22). The REB is therefore relevant to today, but it is not a translation of either the Hebrew or Greek original, and its policy here should surely be questioned. There are some useful parallels between ben Sirach's world and ours. Both ben Sirach's world and our own recognize the importance of timing: *never remain silent when a word might put things right* (4.23; see 4.29 and 4.20: 'Take an opportunity'; ben Sirach will return to the subject in 5.11). And both worlds value careful reflection on how we handle relationships (how to relate to those in some way dependent on you: 4.30; how to relate to those on whom you may be dependent: 4.27). Early Christian writers found 4.31 relevant (albeit in a different sense: *Didache* 4.5; *Barnabas* 19.9). But an accurate translation of scripture cannot always be relevant and to render it so may make its value temporary. It can be argued that the case for an accurate translation should take precedence over considerations of relevance.

5.1–8 This looks like a warning about reliance on money, which in a sense it is (vv. 1, 8). But its form, with the repeated *Do not say* (vv. 3–6, an ancient formula going back to Egyptian parallels) suggests something more important is at stake. Prosperity could be taken to imply divine blessing (Deut. 28.1–14), but that assumption has its dangers (vv. 1–3). What is at stake is whether or not God is just, and ben Sirach assembles his arguments on behalf of God's justice.

5.9–6.1 This section begins and ends with *This is the mark of duplicity.* The verses cover a range of pictures and examples (*faults, both great and small*, v. 15), including inconsistency, indiscipline, carelessness and thoughtlessness in thought and action.

6.2–17 A summary focus for some of what has been said and what will follow is: *Whoever fears the Lord directs his friendship aright, for he treats a neighbour as himself* (v. 17). The nature of ben Sirach's religion binds the relationship with God to our relationships with one another. The contrast between the destructive effect of *violent passions* (v. 2) and the possibilities which begin with a courteous greeting (v. 5) marks out (like the discussion of duplicity) an important but sometimes treacherous area of human relationships.

Seeking and finding Wisdom
6.18–37

As in the previous Wisdom poem (4.11–19), Wisdom is found only by means of testing circumstances: start early and don't be put off. The agricultural pictures would commend themselves to a variety of audiences: *If you cultivate her, you will labour for a little while, but soon you will be enjoying the harvest* (v. 19b). The fool is like the farmer who, while ploughing, has found a heavy stone, struggles to remove it and in the end, finding it too heavy, simply lets it fall (v. 21). The clue to v. 22 is a Hebrew pun, although which pun is not clear. The most approachable is a play on a Hebrew synonym for wisdom, letters of which appear in v. 33 for 'become wise' and which also form the word 'withdrawn': *Wisdom well deserves her name; she is* withdrawn from the reach of *many* (v. 22). The search for Wisdom indicates part of her character, and the reason why some do not find her; wisdom is partly a disposition involved in seeking, by means of determined submission to Wisdom's discipline (v. 24; see Matt. 11.29: 'Take my yoke upon you' – however,

v. 24 refers not to a yoke, but to a prisoner's collar; the same word, if read in v. 29, indicates a collar of honour; v. 30a, like the splendid collar of 30b here and in Prov. 1.9, could also be a golden ornament to the robe rather than a *yoke*). It is, however, partly also a disposition of finding, especially in joy at *finding the refreshment she offers* (v. 28). This transformation is depicted as the transformation of the bonds into *a splendid robe, a golden ornament* and a *violet cord* (according to Num. 15.37–38 this is woven into the tassel on the corners of the clothes as a reminder of the commands of the law; see 27.8). The process involves listening (rather than reading), attention, perception (of who is wise among the elders) and remembering (above all, maxims: v. 35). If a wise teacher is discovered, *wear out his doorstep* (v. 36). Pondering decrees, studying commandments, instruction of the mind (see 14.20) enable the *desire for wisdom* to be met (v. 37). The picture of Wisdom is becoming more complex: the processes of enquiry and discovery are as important as the maxims and the commands.

7.1–14.19

This long section is not easily divided into sub-sections, and commentaries differ in the divisions they suggest. One possibility is that the 'death and judgement' theme predominates, so that caution is advised at many points because *All human works decay and vanish, and the worker follows them into oblivion* (14.19), and God is the one who brings down or raises up.

Ben Sirach seems to operate with the policy of remembering every maxim and piece of advice, whatever its source. The nine *Do not*s in 7.1–10 concern the avoidance of evil and suggest the writer's mind-set is to play safe: *keep clear of wrong, and it will avoid you* (7.2). This appears to encourage the avoidance of the responsibility of high office, although 2 Macc. 4.1–20 paints a picture of Seleucid politics where corruption would be hard to avoid. Priests are respected in ben Sirach, especially with regard to the biblical commandments concerning the offerings (7.31), perhaps reflecting a current rise in their prestige (see 50.1–21). Care for the poor, the bereaved, the sick is extended also to the dead (on 7.33b see Tobit 1.18; 2.4–5).

8.1–19 Ben Sirach's aversion to risk-taking is illustrated in several fields: taking on *the great* and *the rich* (in v. 2b REB sees dangers in the power of wealth; the Greek text could equally warn against insisting on your own weights and measures), or taking a rise out of the *garrulous*, the *ill-mannered*, the penitent, the old or the dead. Such good sense rests on the *discourse of the elders* (v. 9). The conclusion is: *Do not tell what is in your mind to all comers or accept favours from them* (v. 19).

9.1–10.11 Women pose serious risks for ben Sirach (9.1–9; see 25.24). The mixture of caution and paranoia in these instructions belongs within the history of Wisdom literature (see also the story of Susanna); but here they may also have deep roots in changes within the writer's contemporary society. Men were beginning to lose some of the control they had enjoyed and this led to obsessiveness in areas they could control (see 9.7). Several references to banquets and drinking parties (see 9.9; 31.12–32.13) point to the unsettling impact of hellenistic socializing on Jewish life-styles and values. Again the advice is to avoid danger: *At table choose the company of good men whose pride is in the fear of the Lord* (9.16; see 9.15). A further element of caution involves taking the measure of your friends and neighbours (9.10, 14). Judgement before or at death awaits the ungodly, whatever their present success and pleasure (9.11–12).

The place of the ruler in the divine providence is dealt with here in terms of a series of generalities: *government . . . is in the hand of the Lord* (10.4), *it is he who confers honour on the legislator* (the Greek has 'scribe'; 10.5b). *Arrogance*, however, *is hateful in the sight of God and man* (10.7a); *because of injustice, insolence, and greed, empire passes from nation to nation* (10.8).

10.12–11.1 The association of *pride* and *anger* with sin and disaster, consequent on forsaking the Creator God, links the verses in 10.12–18 (see ch. 17). This applies at all levels, notably to princes and nations, when *the Lord overturns the thrones of princes and installs the meek in their place* (10.14–15; see Luke 1.51–52).

10.19 is a typical form of teaching which here contrasts *honour* and *contempt*. Those to be honoured are those who have pride in the fear of the Lord (10.20). 10.25–11.1 is a difficult passage, since it is not clear whether the Greek text is concentrating on poverty or on humility. Probably it argues that honour is seen to belong either to the poor or to the rich, since wisdom will raise up the head of the humble and will set anyone among the great, whichever he is, rich or poor (11.1).

11.2–9 This section belongs to the theme of God's reducing of the powerful and lifting up of the small and weak (vv. 5–6), and the consequent advice that pride is to be avoided. To support the theme of God's strange ways, ben Sirach draws on the tradition also found in ancient Egyptian Wisdom literature, that, as in the case of *the bee*, the appearance of the *small* can be deceptive (v. 3).

11.10–28 Here ben Sirach gathers a number of similar reflections which lead to a conclusion, found as a topic of ancient Greek thought: *someone's end reveals how he has lived. Call no one happy before he dies, for not until death is a person known for what he is* (v. 28).

11.29–34 Trust and distrust figure largely in these sections. Three sets of words establish the direction of 11.29–34: *home* in vv. 29 and 34, 'lure' or 'ambush' in vv. 31, 32 (see the Greek text; and Prov. 1.11) and *stranger/estrange* (v. 34). No opportunity should be given to those whose traps might disrupt your home, misrepresent you, threaten your life or your reputation.

12.1–7 Such an attitude of caution reaches an extreme position in these verses. *A good turn* (vv. 1, 2) done to the godfearer will have its reward, but *keep* it *for the humble* (vv. 5, 7); the persistent sinner is not to be helped, fed, or done any favour.

12.8–18 The translation here follows the Hebrew: since enemies are *friendly when all goes well with* you (v. 9a), prosperity does not show who your friends really are (v. 8a); nor, necessarily, does adversity (v. 9b). The enemy is totally unreliable, and if disaster overtakes you *he will wag his head and rub his hands* (v. 18a).

13.1–24 Relationships between unequals are also treacherous (see Eccles. 9.16; Prov. 14.20). The arrogance of another rubs off on you, and association with the rich and great can overstretch you, for as a relationship it is not evenly balanced (vv. 1–3). The rich person has status, can exploit you, drop you, deceive, drain you dry, and in the end laugh at you (vv. 4–7). The rich can humiliate, rebuff, be effusive, but be *weighing you up* at the same time (v. 11d). Trusting people with confidences is another treacherous area.

13.25–14.2 These last few sections have set out a dismal prospectus on the subject of relationships. The warnings have been severe and the cautions wide-ranging. These four verses seem like a thoughtful interlude. The micro-history of the heart is reflected in the face, from cheerfulness to the painful practice of thought and its expression. Consolation comes first in the form of the two wisdom beatitudes

(*Happy is the one . . .*): few people avoid errors and *remorse*, and few avoid self-reproach and disappointment. 14.20ff. will bring a little more cheer.

14.3–19 Miserliness (vv. 3b, 10) takes us back to the subject of wealth and towards the conclusion of the section, that *All human works decay and vanish, and the worker follows them into oblivion.* The absurdity of miserliness is placarded: it simply gives another *a life of luxury* (v. 4); it *brings no enjoyment* (v. 5); it *is its own retribution* (v. 6). God has declared to Adam and Eve: *you shall die* (v. 17; Gen. 2.17; 3.19). But death is not without its advantages; it enables one generation to fol-low upon another, like leaves, falling, decaying, so that new growth can appear. There is more to say about human fulfilment, as the following poem shows.

Wisdom and humanity's ideal state
14.20–15.10

So far the Wisdom poems have stressed particularly the terrible awe-someness of God, and the testing disciplines in following Wisdom. This poem concentrates on the blessings which Wisdom brings. The poem begins with a beatitude: *Happy is he who gives his mind to wisdom and meditates on understanding* (see 6.36). That requires determination and persistence – the pictures are of stalking, peeping, listening and camping. The reward is to be *sheltered by her from the heat* and to *dwell in her glory* (14.27). What has been said before about Wisdom is not forgotten: The fear of the Lord leads to mastering the law; only then can wisdom be truly possessed. But the warmth of the pictures that follow – coming to meet him *like a mother*, receiving him *like a young bride*, feeding him with the *bread of understanding* and the *water of wisdom*, supporting him – encourages the reader. Public honour and standing follow. It is as if the human being becomes or reverts to roy-alty (Job 31.36), *crowned with joy and exultation* (15.6), reverting, as it were, to Adam's true calling. So the praise of God is the true outward expression of humanity, a genuine expression of wisdom, prompted by God himself. The fool and the arrogant have no part in this. The *glory* (14.22) then, where those who seek wisdom live, is the fulfilment of humanity's ideal state, the true joy of living (see Ps. 8). The dark prospectus of caution has prepared the way for an enthralling reward.

15.11–23.27 This long section, using the theme of Adam, expounds the quality of life which the fear of the Lord makes possible (see 23.27: *Nothing is better than the fear of the Lord, nothing sweeter than obeying his commandments*).

15.11–16.23 Although God may test and discipline his people (2.1; see the notes there) and harden people's hearts (see the additional text in the margin: 16.15; also Isa. 6.9–13), and although his is a world where sin is possible (see the additional text: 16.16), nevertheless God opposed sin from the beginning. So the responsibility for making decisions (15.11–12), choosing to keep the commandments (15.15), choosing life or death (15.17), rests firmly on humanity; and God in his wisdom sees all (15.18). 15.18–20 and 16.11b–16, 16.18–19 are expressions of praise (i.e. they are doxological). On 16.19–23 see Ps. 139.10; Wisd. 1.6–7; Job 38.1.

16.24–18.14 True understanding begins with God's disposal of his works *in an eternal order* (16.27), where *one does not jostle against another, nor will they ever disobey his word* (16.29), and with God's filling of the earth with living creatures, *and to the earth they must all return* (16.30b). So who is Adam? The text deploys several key ideas: turning back, God's image, praising God's holy name and life, the life-giving law, God sees every sin, retribution in the end, God's patience, compassion and discipline. *The Lord created human beings from the earth and to it he turns them back again* (17.1; see 17.27–28, 32). He *made them in his own image* (17.3), with a power like his own, with lordship over all beasts and birds. He gave them faculties and minds to think, showed them good and evil, watching their hearts so that he could show them *the majesty of his works* (17.8) and *praise his holy name* (17.10). Grouped together are the divine gifts to human beings of knowledge, law, covenant, decrees; they saw his majesty and heard his teaching (*Refrain* from evil and fulfil one's *duty* to one's *neighbour*: 17.14). 17.30 should be taken with 17.31–32 and, like the Hebrew text, it includes 'dwelling on evil' (i.e. a failure to forgive one another) among the shortcomings of humanity (see 18.13). 18.1–14 reflects on what has been written, in the manner of a Psalm such as Ps. 90 (e.g. see the theme of 'Turn back' in Ps. 90.3, 13). As against the power and unfathomable mercies of the Creator God, *What is a human being?* (18.8; see Ps. 8.3–4). As in Ps. 90 humanity's limited life-span (extended here to a *hundred years*) is a major reason for the Lord's compassion: *That is why the Lord is patient with people* (18.11; see Ps. 90.13). *He sees and knows the harsh fate in store for them, and therefore gives full play to his forgiveness* (18.12). The Lord's compassion is for all; ours is a poor shadow of that.

His discipline, correction, teaching and decrees are brought together in the warmer metaphor of *a shepherd* and *his flock* (18.13).

18.15–29 This section moves from the book's basic understanding of humanity to a practical outcome. Since God is merciful and humanity often fails to be compassionate, *do not spoil all your generosity with hurtful words* (v. 15; see James 1.5). This all requires discipline and training: *They who are trained in learning prove wise themselves and pour forth apt proverbs* (v. 29).

18.30–19.30 A series of key terms gives shape to 18.30–19.17: passions, lust, wine and women (see 1 Esdras 3–4), gossip, tales, rumour, friends and neighbours, and the law of the Most High (19.17). Wisdom is defined by reference to *the fear of the Lord* and involves *the fulfilling of the law* (19.20). That makes it possible to distinguish wisdom from knowledge, cleverness, intelligence, duplicity, craftiness, subtle dishonesty and fraud (19.22–29; see 21.12); *clothes, the way he laughs, his gait – these* may *reveal his character* too (19.30; see 21.20). It is worth examining 19.18–19, which are printed in the REB margin. They contain a clear reference to 'immortality', a fairly clear sign that they are later additions.

20.1–31 This offers contrasts between the wise person and the fool, especially in relation to honour and shame, reverting again and again to speech (see the conclusion at 22.27: *O for a sentry to guard my mouth and a seal of discretion to close my lips, to prevent them from being my downfall, to keep my tongue from causing ruin!*). The wise know when to speak a word of *reproof* and when to be silent (Eccles. 3.7); the fool *is always speaking out of turn* (v. 7). This is a concern of both Jewish and non-Jewish wisdom literature, but it is a treacherously difficult area. Being silent could mean to *nurse one's anger* (v. 2), deny someone the chance to save *face*, or be *at a loss for an answer*; giving reproof could be useless if there is no chance of a moral or motivated response (see the picture in v. 4a), or be an abuse of *position* that *arouses hatred* (vv. 2–8). By contrast, speaking wisely *pleases the great* and *secures pardon for his offence*. But this kind of honour has its dangers too; *like a gag in the mouth* its expression in hospitality and gifts *silences criticism* (v. 29). That provides a neat picture about 'buried treasure being useless' and a saying: *Better one who hides his folly than one who hides his wisdom!* (v. 31; i.e. wisdom means, among other things, to express clearly a critique of aspects of both shame and honour).

21.1–22.2 This contrasts breaking the law (21.3) with keeping the law (21.11). The former leads to the *grave* (21.10), with *wrong* pictured as a venomous snake or two-edged sword (21.2–3); the latter *controls his thoughts* and leads to wisdom as a fountain of life (21.13; see 15.1–3; there are similiarities of style and content with *Pirke Aboth*, the Tractate 'Fathers' from the Jewish Mishnah which uses this and similar pictures; see *Pirke Aboth* 6.1: the wise man 'is made like a spring that increases and like a river that does not cease').

22.3–27 Each of the four sections has a particular focus: the first, on daughters (where the concern is that a daughter might shame her father and her husband, and that *the lash of wisdom's discipline is always in season*: vv. 4b–6); the second on fools (where mourning for a fool lasts, unlike mourning the dead, a whole lifetime, and nothing is more of a burden than someone who is stupid: vv. 7–15); the third on the mind (which when *backed by intelligent thought* is like a wall ready for painting, but weakened by *foolish fancies* is no proof against fear: vv. 16–18, see 21.14); and the fourth on friendship (that true friendship can be repaired but can also be destroyed by betrayal or, proving unreliable, will warn off the trust of others: vv. 19–26). Verse 27, reverting again to the subject of speech, concludes the section 20.1–22.27, and prepares the way for the prayer that follows.

23.1–6 Ben Sirach prays: *Lord, Father,* (see 51.10 and the note on Wisd. 14.3; also Luke 11.2; Mark 14.36) *and Ruler of my life* (vv. 1, 4) . . . *for wisdom's rod to curb my thoughts and to discipline my mind*, against the *onslaught of desire . . . gluttony* and *lust*. The personal character of the address and the acceptance that divine assistance is essential for true speech and thought – both are features which point forward to the scribe's deeper insights (see e.g. ch. 38).

23.7–37 Alongside such dependence on divine assistance stand the patterns of belief and practice which have characterized the opening section of ben Sirach: *the fear of the Lord* and *obeying his commandments* (v. 27bc). In practice these involve *discipline* of *the mouth*: avoiding scurrility and pride (vv. 7–8), avoiding use of the divine name in oaths (*anyone who has oaths and the sacred name forever on his lips* will never be cleansed from sin: v. 10), avoiding putting the welfare of his house at risk in the treacherous patterns of oath-keeping (v. 11), and avoiding *habits of coarse and filthy talk* which do not belong *among Jacob's descendants*. These habits can make a fool of you in high company and, once established, can never be cured (vv. 14–15). The fear of the Lord and obeying his commandments also involve, in practice, avoidance of many sins (v. 16), but one in particular, sexual promiscuity (see 1 Cor. 6.18; and compare the language in the Greek of vv. 16–17 with Col. 2.11: 'the body of his flesh').

Wisdom's declaration of her nature and task
24.1–34

24.1–22 So far the Wisdom poems have stressed particularly the terrible awesomeness of God, the testing disciplines in following Wisdom, and the blessings which Wisdom brings. Here Wisdom herself sets out her nature and task, speaking *with pride among her people, before the assembly of the Most High and in the presence of the heavenly host* (vv. 1b–2; see Ps. 82.1 and the commentary on the Wisdom of Solomon). Wisdom claims to be the word of God (see Wisd. 9.1–2; John 1.1), dwelling *in high heaven* (v. 4). The probable reference to Gen. 1.2b links Wisdom with creation (see vv. 5–6 for Wisdom encompassing alone the whole created order, the heavens, the earth and the abyss of Sheol); and *a pillar of cloud* (see Exod. 13.21 of God's accompanying presence) becomes Wisdom's throne. Wisdom then speaks of seeking a resting place on earth and finding it in Israel. (Other traditions suggest Wisdom found no resting place: see 1 Enoch 42; John 1.11.) The Creator's specific command (*he who created me decreed where I should dwell*: v. 8b; see Prov. 8.22) was to make her *home in Jacob* (v. 8c), thus associating Israel with God's creative presence and self-revelation in the world. Moreover, as the one created *before time* and enduring *until the end of time*, Wisdom *ministered in* God's *presence* in the wilderness tabernacle (Exod. 25.8–9) and so, again by divine authorization, in Jerusalem (v. 10). The language here stresses the closeness of the divine ties with Jerusalem: *in the city he loved* (v. 11a); *I took root among the people whom the Lord had honoured* (v. 12a). This 'taking root' is described in terms of Wisdom's presence in the trees and bushes of Israel and in their produce for the ritual of worship (vv. 13–16). 'Taking root', Wisdom also produces *a harvest of honour and wealth* (v. 17); the life of Israel exemplifies her presence. But Wisdom's praise becomes at this point more personal (see Prov. 9.1–6; Matt. 11.28–30; John 6.35): Wisdom offers (as if in response to ben Sirach's prayer, 23.1–6) protection from shame and help in following the right way (v. 22; see 51.2).

The relation of 24.23–29 to Wisdom's praise is one of the most crucial questions in the whole book. 24.23bc is, in the Greek, an exact quotation from the Greek of Deut. 33.4, Moses' final blessing on the people of Israel. It is possible to argue that *All this is the book of the covenant of God Most High* identifies Wisdom with the written book of the Law; all that is necessary is the following of the law (see Baruch 4.1). But it is equally possible, following the text and its grammar, that the written book of the Law is being identified with the amazing breadth of Wisdom's work as the divine creative word (38.7–8, 39.4; 43.6–10, 28; 44–50; 51.13–30). Hence the law is like the four rivers of the Garden of Eden, spreading wisdom and understanding, a wisdom the first man Adam did not grasp fully nor will the last one; Wisdom's *thoughts* are more abundant than the sea and *her purpose* than the great abyss. Ben Sirach's view of the law is, if the second view is taken, one which is understood within the full panoply of divine work, in creation (39.16–35), in ordering, deliverance, in praise of God, prayer and study, self-examination and self-understanding (38.34–39.11), through experience, travel, holiness of life, the teaching task, conversation with the learned, and in and with the mystery which is beyond thought and understanding. Wisdom is both one with the text of the Torah, and wider, in that it expresses the total living context in which the Torah operates, especially the personal aspects of living with the Torah, experiencing failure and danger and seeking and finding a personal or quasi-personal response (see 23.1–6; 24.19–22) and, with that, a fulfilment of life (17.8–10). Once established in ben Sirach's book, that understanding of the Law within the full panoply of divine work becomes the basis for all the remainder of the book, not least the teaching function it represents (24.30–34) which, *like a watercourse*, channels Wisdom's riches, watering his own *garden, soaking its flower beds* (vv. 30–31) and becomes available *for all who seek wisdom* (v. 34).

25.1–12 Two numerical proverbs provide a focus. The first summarizes three delights, and the second nine blessings capped by a tenth: *The fear of the Lord excels all other gifts* (v. 11).

25.13–26.27 In no sense can this section be regarded as balanced in its presentation. The language concerning women is unusually severe and the treatment of good and bad women unequal. While there are parallels in Jewish and Greek literature (particularly on the dangers of female beauty in enticing and trapping men), this section (see especially the extended discussions of money and sex) suggests, as we have seen in 9.1–9, that profound social changes (see 25.26) have taken place, altering what has been called 'the role of money and women as overdetermined symbols of male honour' (see 25.21b). Theologically, if 25.24 (*Sin began with a woman, and because of her we all die*) is to be taken as a careful statement, ben Sirach cannot be said to be consistent here, since in 41.4 we find 'This (i.e. death) is the Lord's decree for all mortals; why try to argue with the will of the Most High?' and ben Sirach nowhere qualifies 41.4 (see 14.17b, 17.1–32 and the comments there; contrast the alternatives offered in Wisd. 2.24, 'the devil's spite', and, in the light of the comments on 16.7, the sin of the giants in 1 Enoch 6–11). Theological statements concerning the death of all because of the sin of Adam would appear to belong to a period later than ben Sirach (see Rom. 5.12–21 and 4 Ezra 7.116–121). It would seem likely that 25.24 should be taken as deriving its heat from the difficulties of the social context, and linking ben Sirach's stress upon the universality of death with the *venom deadlier than a snake's* (25.15).

26.28–27.29 Characteristic of this section is the certainty of punishment for those who oppose the good: *for such a one the Lord will get ready a sword* (26.28e); *before they die they will be consumed with pain* (27.29).

27.30–32.13 The following sections present various positive qualities of life: forgiveness, compassion, firmness, health and good manners. The penitent's ability to forgive is contrasted with a sinner's vengefulness; the former enables the penitent to find forgiveness (see Matt. 6.12); but where can the sinner who *refuses mercy to his fellow* find forgiveness and *look for pardon* himself (28.4–5; see Matt. 6.15; 18.32–35)? Forgiveness is neither as easy nor as simple as it sounds. Relationships broken by foolish or wicked actions may be repaired; but how can the damage our actions caused be repaired? We may decide to set resentment behind us in an act of forgiveness, but find resentment reemerging like a stubborn weed. The relationship with God can be repaired, but that implies a continuing commitment to live mercifully. Ben Sirach is clear about one central feature of forgiveness: the close interrelationship between forgiving and being forgiven. An act of forgiveness requires attitudes of heart, mind and activity; the same attitudes are required in being forgiven.

Life as health, enjoyment and blameless prosperity – the *cup* filled *with* all God's *benefits*, 32.13 – features throughout 30.14–32.13, but how the author shaped this section is uncertain since the Hebrew,

Latin and Syriac texts order the material here very differently from the Greek.

At this point ben Sirach reflects further on his earlier emphases: the fear of the Lord as wondering awe and as life giving; the testing disciplines of wisdom involving the study and practice of the law; the wisdom of the Lord bringing the blessings of human fulfilment, excellent beyond all human language and honoured in the assembly of heaven. The climax will be in the psalm of praise in 42.15–43.33 (see the comments on 1.1–10). 32.14–33.18, as we saw earlier, holds together two apparently contradictory features. There is a determinism expressive of divine omniscience; there is also an emphasis on human responsibility without which all the carefully summarised practical wisdom of the book would be pointless. 34.1–36.17 stresses dependence on divine direction and the effectiveness of the prayer of the humble. Common to both those sections is the security (often apparently naively conceived) of those who fear the Lord.

32.14–33.18 As in 6.18–37, the study of the law can be fulfilling for those who fear the Lord but *a stumbling block* to those who do not (32.15). Those who fear the Lord and accept the discipline of his law are choosing a reliable, tried way; providing that once you have started you *do not change your mind* (32.19), your every step is secure (32.23). A Greek text (not translated in the REB here) has a warning to beware of being misled (among other influences) by children. (Is this the hook on which the Greek text hangs the warning in 33.19–23? The same cannot be said for 33.24–31 – and that is a warning not to expect clear literary organization of ben Sirach.) The major stress here is the security of those who fear the Lord.

Discussion in 33.7–15 ranges across festival and holy days and the nature of humanity. The writer concludes: this discussion illustrates a principle within *all the works of the Most High*, the principle of opposites: *Good is the opposite of evil, and life of death* (vv. 14–15). It would be difficult at the time when ben Sirach was written to find many places in the Mediterranean world where there was no philosopher of the Stoic persuasion. Certainly one of the most influential of Stoics, Chrysippus, argued that one could not posit the existence of good without the existence of evil. Stoics of that period were concerned too with a wisdom depending on a complete commitment, and on what is external to a human being. But ben Sirach's use of the principle of opposition is based on observation (v. 15), on an exploration of the wisdom of God in the creation of all things (43.33), on the gradual gathering of tradition rather than on the argument and logic of a philosophical tradition (see the autobiographical section in 33.16–18), and on the need to shape community leadership in the patterns of humble dependence on God. Individual responsibility, and modest households where slaves are ruled not with a rod of iron but with a care for justice, provide an appropriate model (33.19–31).

34.1–36.17 This passage, still within a general concern for security of life, stresses dependence on divine direction and the effectiveness of the prayer of the humble. Divine wisdom for *those faithful to the law* (34.8) needs no complement such as *divination, omens, and dreams* (34.5). Dreams are no more than an inadequate reflection of truth (34.1–4), unless *they are sent by intervention from the Most High* (34.6). Ben Sirach enters here an ancient area of dispute which still continues today. Jeremiah warned his contemporaries to 'pay no attention to the women whom you set to dream dreams' (Jer. 29.8), whereas dreams and their correct interpretation play an important role in other traditions such as the narratives of Genesis and Matthew's gospel; and in the modern post-Freudian era the debate continues.

35.1b–2 names different kinds of cultic offerings, for each of which there is in the sight of God an equivalent form of behaviour: *to heed the commandments, a kindness repaid, to give alms.* So 35.1a can be translated *To keep the law is worth* (is the equivalent of) *many offerings.* We noted earlier that priests are respected in ben Sirach, especially with regard to the commandments of the law concerning the offerings (7.31), as long as the poor, the bereaved and the sick are not neglected. Here the sense is similar. Those offerings, and especially the firstfruits and tithes, could, along with their equivalents in practical social care (as in Tobit 1.6–8), be presented to God with a generous and cheerful heart (35.6–9; see 1 Chron. 29.17), reflecting the generosity of the Lord (35.11) who responds with far greater generosity still. This leads ben Sirach to the subject of God's attention to the *prayer of the wronged* (35.13). As in Luke 18.7 God does not ignore the appeal for justice (35.13–15). The emphasis here is on the prayer of the just and the ultimate response of God who *shatters the power of the unjust* (35.18). Actions and intentions are both involved within the measure of divine judgement until mercy comes upon the afflicted as *rain-clouds in a time of drought* (35.20). It is a confident assertion which has often needed to be seen over a longer period of history than generations of the Jewish people have anticipated. The prayer itself (36.1–17) lays claim to *Aaron's blessing on your people* (see 45.15; 50.21) and prays that *all who live on earth* will *acknowledge that you are the Lord, the eternal God* (36.17; 50.22; the parallels with 50:21–22 suggest that this prayer also belongs within ben Sirach's own tradition). Those emphases are appropriate to the context, and several features of the prayer are reminiscent of the later chapters of Isaiah (Isa. 44.6–11, 24–26; 45.20; 46.10–13; 51.4–5; 63.3–4; 66.18b–24). Although some argue that 36.10 (in some texts it appears as 36.9) would be inappropriate in advance of Antiochus IV and the Danielic tradition, it is just as likely that the prayer is based on earlier prayer material. The prayer lacks the features characteristic of Psalms of Lament, such as the direct ascription of praise to God, and indicates an unfortunate shift which took place in prayer as a result of reactions to foreign oppression.

36.18–38.23 The focus returns abruptly to practical matters. In each case the issue is about preferences and choices (see *trust your own judgement*, 37.13). The initial example provides the key: *The stomach will accept any food, but one food is better than another* (36.18). So, *a man may prefer one girl to another* (36.21b). The parallel between choice of food and choice of a wife hardly appeals to our contemporary mind, particularly because 36.21b, curiously out of keeping with the issue being addressed, does not accord the woman the same room for discernment. Everything is seen from the male point of view. Nevertheless, discernment recognizes the qualities (beauty, kindness, gentleness, appropriateness, support: 36.22–24) which can direct one's preferences (see Gen. 2.18–20). The Greek text is marginally less offensive than the Hebrew, and the REB translation marginally less so than the Greek, since *He who acquires a wife has the beginnings of a fortune* (36.24) can be taken metaphorically, whereas the Greek has a direct reference to the wife as a possession, which, as we saw in the case of 7.26, is fundamental to ben Sirach's attitude to women.

38.24–39.35 Ben Sirach has been reflecting further on the fear of the Lord, on the testing disciplines of wisdom and on the wisdom of the Lord which brings the blessings of human fulfilment, and is preparing the way for the climax of the psalm of praise in 42.15–43.33. 38.24–39.35 offers an important contribution to this reflection. It depicts the life of the scribe in his study of the law and exploration of wisdom (39.1) as integral to the praise of the Lord's name (39.35). 38.24 (*A scholar's wisdom comes of ample leisure; to be wise* (or, to prove himself wise) *he must be relieved of other tasks*) is a natural inference from what ben Sirach has already said in 14.26–27: the *glory*, where those who seek wisdom live, is the fulfilment of humanity's ideal state. But ben Sirach also recognizes that God wins praise through the marvels of imparted knowledge (38.6). So although his preference for the scribe's life sounds similar to the Egyptian *The Instruction for Duauf* (dated 1991–1786 BCE), ben Sirach (by contrast to *The Instruction*) gives room to the positive aspects of concentration in the work of the farmer (38.26a, note the repetition of *he concentrates*), the craftsman (38.27d), the smith (38.28f) and the potter (38.30). These may not achieve high office or make legal judgements (38.33), but *they maintain the fabric of the world*, (see 38.32) *and the practice of their craft is their prayer* (or, 'their petition': 38.34). Nevertheless, the fervent, exemplary piety of the scribe's search for understanding sets him apart (39.1–5) and, *if it is the will of the mighty Lord, he will be filled with a spirit of intelligence* so that he has honour among the people and a secure reputation (39.6–11). Two important questions arise: first, given that in 39.1–5 the emphasis is not only on the past and the famous but also on *subtleties, hidden meaning* and *enigmatic parables* (39.2–4), how do these relate to *the law of the Most High* (39.1b)? The earlier discussion of 24.1 may point to an answer, namely that the law in ben Sirach is understood in the total context of the scribe's piety (see 39.5). Second, what is the significance of 39.6? It seems to suggest that *a spirit of intelligence* may be given to the scribe of 39.1–5 which affords the scribe particular insight into the secrets of God and so particular authority. It would then correspond with the autobiographical note in 24.30–34 and anticipate the similar note in 39.12: *I have still more thoughts to express; I am as full as the moon at mid-month.* Hence, as in similar passages from Qumran (see 1QH 11), the inspired teacher commends a theme for thanksgiving to his disciples: *All that the Lord has done is excellent; all that he commands will in due time take place* (39.16; see Eccles. 3.1–11). This is a theme which arises from the scribe's long research (39.32–33), and is written down to encourage his followers to *sing with full heart and voice, and to the name of the Lord give praise!* (39.35). His research is reflected in the form of comments introduced by *Let no one ask, 'What is this?' or 'Why is that?'* (39.17, 21 with a resumé in 39.34). The first comment illustrates from the story of Creation (Gen. 1.9–10) the might of the creative word of God which no one can limit, from whom nothing is hidden and for whom *nothing is too . . . difficult* (39.20b). The second caps the ancient discussions which suggest that one day the purpose of contradictory forces in nature may be understood, with illustrations of creation's obedience to the divine word (39.31), whether for blessing (39.22, 26) or judgement (39.23b, 24b, 25b, 28–30).

That obedience is *when the time comes* (39.31c), as *every need . . . arises* (39.33). So humanity can depend thankfully on God's goodness and recognize that it will be known in all things, not just when humanity's partial sight may understand something, but *at their proper time* as God decides (39.34). If that is the correct way to read this passage, then the 'proper time' is not so much a time which God has predestined as the time when God chooses to call creation into service (see 43.26 and the notes on Wisd. 19.18–22).

40.1–42.14 What follows in chs 40–43 picks up some of the key scribal reflections, culminating in the great psalm of praise which balances 1.1–10. 40.1–30 finds *a paradise* in the blessings and protection offered by *the fear of the Lord* (40.17, 26c–27a). The lot of Adam's race (see Gen. 3) is to suffer *troubled thoughts* and *anxious expectation of the day of their death* (40.2) – of death, the universal leveller, which returns us to the earth from which we all come (see 40.11). Some fears, terrifying as they can be, are, like nightmares, *groundless* (40.7); others, such as *disaster, famine, havoc, and plague* (40.9) are, like the flood (see 44.17), *created for the wicked* (40.10; see 39.29–30). Hence the *seven times over* in the experience of *sinners* (40.8b). The problem of the success of sinners (see Ps. 73.3–16) is not set out here; only the certainty of their ultimate and sudden failure (40.12; see Ps. 73.18–19) and the permanence of *good faith*, *kindness* and *almsgiving* (40.12–17). Again, it is a practical matter of well-chosen preferences or priorities which can enrich life despite all its anxiety and labour – *a pleasant voice* over against flute and lyre; *good advice* over against gold and silver; above all *the fear of the Lord* rather than *wealth and strength* (40.18–26a); and, as in 29.21–28, the choice of independence over against the *shame* and *resentment* that come from living *on the food of another* (40.28–30; see Prov. 14.16–17). 41.1–13 underlines the ultimate importance of such well-chosen priorities with another discourse on death: *Take thought for your name: it will outlive you longer than thousands of great hoards of gold* (41.11–13). For although death appears differently to the satisfied, rich, *vigorous* person as against the anxious, *destitute* cripple, it is pointless to argue with *the Lord's decree* since it is a decree *for all mortals*. There is no arguing about it *in the grave* (41.1–4)! Disgrace awaits the *children of sinners*; *a curse* greets *the impious* at birth and awaits them at death; so *the godless go from curse to destruction* (41.5–10), whereas *a good name lasts for all time* (41.13). Two contrasting sections follow, as instruction to be heeded publicly: the first designating areas where shame and disgrace are appropriate, the second where they are not (41.16). First,

41.14–24 associates a proper sense of shame with gaining or regaining the good opinion of everyone (41.24). Such a proper sense recognizes the dangers attaching to various levels of responsibility through personal behaviour or the behaviour of others (41.17–19), and also those day-to-day dangers of discourtesy, dishonesty, sexual attraction (especially with regard to female slaves), gossiping and *betraying a confidence* (41.19b–23). Second, 42.1–8 begins, *at other times you must not be ashamed* just because of what others might think, and concludes that this too can *win universal approval* (42.8d). Not being ashamed of the *law and covenant of the Most High* (42.2) marks out the main dividing line between the improper and proper shame, between hellenistic and Jewish values; and this carries the implications of justice for all (just and unjust), justice in matters of finance, business and trade, discipline for children and slaves, and anticipation of what the less scrupulous might do. Among these latter are counted women who might *bring shame and disgrace* (42.9–14). Daughters, for example, might do so at any and every stage; in order that no one, including older women, can corrupt them, they should be locked away in *a bedroom without windows*. At that level ben Sirach's fear of shame today sounds paranoid.

The great hymn of praise
42.15–43.33

This falls into three parts. First (42.15–25; note the link between 42.15 and 42.25), using the language of psalmody and wisdom (both Jewish and Egyptian), ben Sirach sets out what he has perceived and written of (42.15) in his previous psalms of praise (32.14–33.15; 39.16–35), both the glories of the physical universe and his wonder at its everlasting ordering (*all responsive to their several functions. All things go in pairs* 42.23b–24a). He also sets alongside these glories the limits ordained by God even to angelic understanding (see also 42.21d and Isa. 40.13–14), *so the universe may stand firm in his glory* (since it is safe with God and serves his glory alone: 42.17). His own knowledge encompasses everything from the fearsome mysteries of *the abyss* to those of *the human heart* (42.18abc). As each appropriate time, past, present and future (see 39.31), stands *under his eye* (perhaps a better interpretation of 42.18d–19 than REB's *signs of the times*, see 43.6), he makes known (note the present tense) *the traces of secret things* (42.19 has a rich content; the author has in mind both the issues found in 39.16–35,

Isa. 41.21–24 and some of the existential problems Job sets out in 9.1–10.22).

The second part of the hymn (43.1–26) praises the effective activity of God through his creative word, giving consistency of purpose to the amazing variety of the world and thus holding all things together (43.5, 10, 12, 13, 16, 22, 23, 26). Although the language of 43.26b might resemble elements of Stoic philosophy, like Rom. 11.33–36 it transfers such language into the very different context of God's unceasing creative, judging, healing and purposeful activity. The *sun* is presented according to its various effects as the *word speeds it on its course* (43.5; see the mythology and theology associated with 46.4); the *moon . . . serves in its turn, marking the divisions of time* and the means of reckoning a feast day (43.6–8; new moon in Amos 8.5 is the feast itself), and acting like a starting signal to the *armies of heaven*. The *stars* hold to their watch *at the Holy One's command* (43.10). On the basis of these verses various attempts have been made to define ben Sirach's chronological system, but his interest is more in the response of each to the creative word. The rainbow is *a bow bent by* divine *hands* (43.12, 9; without a reference to Gen. 9.13). Similarly, snow storms, lightning and hail fulfil his commands. Thunder shakes (or rebukes) the earth at *his appearing*. Different effects stem from the different weather patterns, and the sea (as in the Psalms and Job) adds astonishment and wonder.

The third part of the hymn (43.27–33) speaks of God in terms of everything (see 1.9), maintaining also that *he is greater than all his works* and fearsome, beyond any human praise. God's gift of wisdom has been set out over many chapters in its astonishing range, and that gift illuminates the affirmation: *The Lord has created all things* (43.33).

44.1–50.29

44.1–23 The following chapters 44.1–50.29 adapt the Israelite pattern of rehearsing God's acts on his people's behalf (see Ps. 78) to illustrate, by means of specific individuals, particular features of the earlier chapters and and to focus on certain of their emphases (see the parallel method in Heb. 11). Using an extensive list of passages from the Hebrew scriptures the author summarizes his argument (found particularly in the psalms of praise to Wisdom) that divine wisdom enables some individuals to enjoy the love, blessing and glory of the Lord (1.11–20; 4.11–19; 11.22; 14.20–27), to serve and praise him (17.6–19; 43.33) and to exercise influence and gain a reputation and praise that extends far beyond their nation and lifetime (see 15.6; 37.26; 38.24–39.11): *Nations will tell of their wisdom and the assembled people will sing their praise* (v.15; restating 39.10). Powerful rulers, wise *counsellors* and prophets, leaders through *deliberations*, through learning in the people's tradition and instruction, psalmists and writers, the wealthy living at ease – all were honoured in their time, and while some are forgotten, these who were *true to their faith* have passed on *their inheritance*. Some of the particular features of these individuals are found in the portrait of the scribe (38.24–39.11), and according to the later chapters some of them fulfilled the priestly office in blessing, teaching and directing the people's lives, a role which in 50.1–21 provides a climax to the section.

Some are noted because they stood out from their faithless generation (vv.10, 17b; 45.23b) and therefore received divine reward. Hence Enoch's appearance in v.16 (see 35.3, 49.14; Wisd. 4.10; Enoch's repentance refers to repentance for his pride in heavenly travels), and Noah's role (see Gen. 6.9) as a means of exchange *in the time of God's wrath*, and the survival of a remnant. 44.18 notes that a lasting covenant was made with Noah (The Greek text has the plural, 'covenants', presumably a later reflection on the various elements in the promise never again to flood humanity). The *fame* (lit. 'the glory') of Abraham also stood alone, and rested on his obedience to the law (perhaps ben Sirach saw the whole law as operative before Moses). Hence the *covenant* was made with him (set in his flesh by circumcision and tested by the divine command to sacrifice Isaac), and the *blessing* assured to him *on oath* which was to extend to the nations and *to the ends of the earth* (v.21). This was a *covenant* confirmed for Isaac also (v.22, because of Abraham), and duly laid on Jacob's head (v.23), together with the promise of the land divided among the twelve tribes (v.23; Gen. 48.4; 49.28).

45.1–22 Moses, *a man of faith who won favour in the eyes of all*, was made *equal in glory to the angels* and *the terror of his enemies* (vv.1–2). Along with the signs which impressed Pharoah, God gave him a commission *and revealed to him some part of his glory* (v.3; a consecration, a choice and a gift of the law as *the source of life and knowledge* so as to teach *his covenant* and *decrees*, v.5). Yet the commandments, the teaching of the decrees, the enlightening of Israel concerning the law and the authority to pronounce legal decisions were passed to Aaron by Moses. Moses ordained and anointed Aaron *to mark* that God had made with Aaron an *everlasting covenant* so that he might *bless his people* (v.15; see

50.21, Num. 6.24–26). What indicates the importance for ben Sirach of the priestly office is the contrast between the mere five verses on Moses and the extended description (parallel to the extended section in 50.1–21) of Aaron's priestly office, his vestments (see Wisd. 18.21–25, and 45.9 which may point to the priestly intercession for the people) and his responsibility *twice each day* to present his sacrifice, and *to make expiation for the people* (v.16). Even more significant is the *wrath* of the Lord which falls on the conspirators against Aaron, and the consequent provision of food for the priesthood (but not of land since *the Lord is his portion*: vv.18–22).

45.23–26 The motif of *standing firm ... when the people defected*, constituting an *expiation for Israel* (v.23), is applied also to Phinehas (see Num. 25.11; 1 Macc. 2.26), to whom the covenant, the sanctuary and the continuing priestly line were given. Verses 25–26 introduce one of the most complex sets of textual variations in ben Sirach and one of the most important. The most likely solution (see the discussion below on 47.1–25) is this: there is a parallel between the royal and the priestly succession (*as ... so*), but 45.25 recognizes the *royal succession* as passing *always* from father to son only, whereas the *priestly succession* passes from Aaron to all of his descendants. So the wisdom which is prayed for is for the priesthood – for the priesthood *to judge* the *people with justice*, ensuring prosperity for *future generations* (v.26). Behind the complexities of the textual tradition lies the issue of whether ben Sirach saw any hope of a messianic figure. Our reading of v.25 suggests that if there was a future hope it rested not with a messianic Davidic line but with the priestly, and, even so, it would need divine wisdom if that hope of justice and prosperity was to be maintained.

46.1–20 The common denominator in the stories of Joshua, Caleb, the judges and Samuel is their fidelity (vv.7, 11, 15) and the divine response of strength and help. By following the Lord (vv.6, 10) they crushed assailants (v.6; see 36.6–10) and produced signs. The associations of uplifted sword, hail, and the sun standing still (the legend of the long, extended day; see Josh. 10.7–14) are, according to Near Eastern literature and iconography, with divine warfare. Joshua and Caleb stood alone: *these two alone survived to bring the people into their heritage* (v.8). The judges illustrate in a vivid picture how the bones of the honoured faithful (see Ezek. 37) can give rise to the new life of the next generations (v.12). Prophecy also features in this section (vv.1b, 15), in Samuel's case proven as authentic both by his *faithfulness* and by subsequent events (vv.15–20; note the absence in this section of any explicit reference to Saul, although the king in v.20 is Saul; see 1 Sam. 28.8–20).

47.1–11 Nathan's prophetic work provides the link with David. David was chosen *as the choice fat is set aside from the sacrifice* (an important priestly reference: v.2). As a chosen one he too received divine *strength* and help (vv.3–7; the references in 1 Sam. 16–17 are understood similarly in the Syriac Psalms 151–153), so that he was hailed as a bringer of divine *blessings* (v.6c) and as permanent conqueror of the Philistines: *whose power remains broken to this day* (v.7c). David's piety matches the standards set by ben Sirach (vv.8–10), both personally (v.8; the title *the most High* is characteristic of 44–51: see 48.5; 49.4) and as securing the people's response in the worship of the Temple (see the Chronicler's tradition). 47.11 is carefully phrased, concentrating on David himself (God *gave him the kingship and a glorious throne in Israel*, 47.11cd), although acknowledging some permanent features of his reign (as in v.7c). A brief glance at what is coming explains the careful phrasing (49.4–5: so the royal line of Judah came to an end). David appears in the list of great ancestors as a religious figure, and not here as a initiator of a messianic hope.

47.12–48.16 Solomon (see *shalom* = peace, 47.13, 16; a peace due to David's reign) is honoured as the builder of God's house, a *sanctuary founded to last for ever* (47.13d) and, in his youth, for his wisdom and understanding (47.14–15). His *fame reached distant islands* (see 1 Kgs. 4.31–34) and he *amassed gold and silver* (1 Kgs. 10.14–22). Typically for ben Sirach (see 9.2–8), the author concentrates on the women who usurped Solomon's authority, causing the division of the kingdom (1 Kgs. 11.1–13). The continuation of the royal line in Rehoboam, *the fool of the nation* (47.23) (followed by Jeroboam as responsible for the shrines at Bethel and Dan: 1 Kgs. 12.29) is both a sign of divine mercy to his chosen ones (47.22) and the cause of the eventual exile and divine *punishment* (47.25). Even the great prophets Elijah and Elisha could not prevent that eventual scattering of the unrepentant people and the diminution of the nation *under a ruler from the house of David* (48.15). Elijah is celebrated for his miracles: *by the word of the Lord he shut up the sky* (48.3); he *raised a corpse* and *sent kings and famous men* to destruction, heard threats on the mountain of God (the identity of Horeb and Sinai is assumed here; Mal. 4.4), and was *taken up to heaven* (48.9). According to 48.10 Elijah is recorded in writing (see the prophecy found in Mal. 4.5) as the one who would return to *allay the divine wrath*, to bring reconciliation and the restoration of the tribes of Jacob (Mal. 4.6; see Mark 9.11–12) before the divine destruction of the wicked. 48.11 recalls Isa. 49.6; the Hebrew text refers to the individual who sees Elijah before death; the REB represents the plural of the Greek text, and the plural could represent either those who are blessed in alternative conditions (those who are alive/those who are asleep), or those blessed because, having seen Elijah, they have fallen asleep in love. As we shall see, the former is probably preferable. Much depends on 48.11c; there the section in brackets in the REB, *For we also shall certainly live*, is thought by some to be out of character for ben Sirach, since it could be held to assume life after death and ben Sirach does not elsewhere affirm life after death; it could therefore be a later addition to the text. More likely is the view that it refers to the confidence that those who are righteous 'live' (44.12–15), and that is a certainty which remains, at whatever point the people of God are brought together and the wicked destroyed. Happy are those who see you, happy are those who have fallen asleep in love, are then likely to be two alternative states, albeit both bound in the life-giving blessing of God to his people. The REB brackets are probably unnecessary. Ben Sirach is using Isa. 49.6 to interpret the prophetic language of Malachi concerning Elijah's return within his own world-view: the future vindication of the righteous against evil doers is certain, and the righteous are secure in the loving protection of God. Elisha too demonstrated his *prophetic power* through miracles as well as in his steadfastness before rulers; and the *marvellous deeds* he worked both *in life* and *in death* (48.12–14; see 2 Kgs. 13.20–21). Nevertheless *the people did not repent* and only a remnant under a Davidic ruler remained, some of whom *did what was pleasing to the Lord* whereas others *committed sin upon sin* (48.16).

48.17–25 The section on Hezekiah and Isaiah reveals a number of important features of ben Sirach's work. There is first the existence of two forms of the text. The two forms, the Hebrew and the Greek, follow the same outline and share important themes (e.g. that Hezekiah remained *firmly in the ways of David*, that Isaiah's hand was the means of Judah's salvation, v.20d, and that Isaiah revealed *the secrets of things* before they occurred); but the Greek is distinctively worded (especially in the first part, vv.17–21, where parallel ideas with 2 Kgs. 18–20/Isa. 36 are introduced), stylized (see vv.18, 23) and directed (by emphasizing Jerusalem's appeal to the *merciful Lord*, adding *his ancestor* to the name of David as in 2 Chron. 34.2, and stressing Isaiah's role as teacher and his addition *of many years to the king's life* via the miracle of the sun: contrast 2 Chron. 32.20–26). The REB, although translating the Greek text, fails to represent some of this distinctiveness (e.g. by using *in his reign* in v.18a, thereby destroying the parallel with v.23). Both Hebrew and Greek texts see the prophet, as in the Deuteronomic tradition, as a wonder worker (see v.14), but the Greek takes that emphasis further in relation to the miracle of the sun, and as a revealer of secret things to come. There is no evidence in this section on Hezekiah and Isaiah of a messianic hope. What might in the Hebrew text be classed as messianic terminology is used by the Sirach tradition of the person of Isaiah, not of the one who is to come; and in the Greek text the translation allows that terminology to disappear altogether (v.22). The only messianic hint that might remain is *the ways of David his ancestor*; but that serves here primarily to distinguish the southern kingship from the northern, to interweave Hezekiah's and Isaiah's functions and to prepare the way for 49.1–5.

49.1–16 The reputation of Josiah during the first part of the second century BCE is considered in our discussion of an early version of 1 Esdras (see pp. 1–4). Josiah too was *wholeheartedly loyal to the Lord and in a lawless age made godliness prevail* (v.3), but *the royal line of Judah came to an end* because of the abandonment of *the law of the Most High* by all *except David, Hezekiah and Josiah* (v.4). The Greek translation of Deuteronomy has a similar but slightly less restrictive list. By the hand of Jeremiah (for his call, see Jer. 1:5–10; and for his rejection by the people, see Jer. 41), or as *Jeremiah foretold*, Jerusalem, *the* holy *city*, was made desolate (vv.6–7). Ezekiel's vision is followed by reference to a storm and protection for the just (v.9, where the Hebrew mentions Job; see Ezek. 14.14, 20). 49.10 is evidence that the Book of the Twelve Minor Prophets was seen as a single entity and understood as encouragement (as in 46.12, dead bones produce new hope). The rebuilding of the *temple* is associated with both royal and priestly leaders (see Haggai and Zechariah), and with Nehemiah (perhaps as a precedent for Simon II) but not Ezra (vv.11–13). 49.14–16 prepares the way for the climax of the section, the *greatest among his brothers and the glory of his people . . . the high priest Simon* (50.1). His place belongs with those most highly honoured within creation: Enoch and his translation, Joseph and the watch *over his bones*, the honouring of the sons of Noah, and, finally, *Adam* himself *hold*ing *pre-eminence over all creation*.

50.1–26 The praise of Simon II (219–196 BCE) appears to have two purposes. Verse after verse picks up the values, concerns and the detail of ben Sirach's writing: Jerusalem (on the strengthening of the city see 50.3–4; and on Hezekiah, 48.17); the Temple (see 50.1–2; on its rebuilding see Zerubbabel, Joshua and Nehemiah); the glory of the priesthood, especially on great feast days (the text of 50.5–19 is too general to allow a definition of a particular festival; see 45.6–14); the privileges and sacrifices of the priesthood (50.12–15; see 45.14); and (one of the great themes of the Second Temple period and a constant theme throughout ben Sirach) *the blessing of the Most High*, here delivered in and through the high priesthood (50.20–21). There is, however, a second purpose. Simon's position had been strengthened by his own clarity of vision, political astuteness and personality. The hint in v.4 about fortification of the city, and the doxology in vv.22–24 in praise of *the God of the universe, who everywhere works great wonders* can be seen as a reminder that *Israel* was in need of *lasting peace*. The background to Sirach's work was a political, economic, religious struggle, a struggle between the Tobiads with their pro-hellenistic economic programme and the Oniads who under Onias II had brought his people to the brink of disaster, only for Simon II to re-establish the high priest's position in relation to the Seleucid king and the right of Jews to live according to their ancestral laws (with Sirach's support). Simon II was dead by the time ben Sirach wrote v.1 (*in whose lifetime the house was repaired*). The sequel to Simon II is to be found in the commentary on 1 and 2 Maccabees (which throws some light also on the hostilities against the Samaritans; see *the senseless folk that live in Shechem* in 50.25–26).

50.27–29 Ben Sirach's personal epilogue uses the imagery found in another autobiographical section, 24.30–34, and picks up various features of the Preface. The beatitude *Happy the man who occupies himself with these things, who lays them to heart and becomes wise* relates closely to the Wisdom section in 32.14–33.18. Some text forms conclude with the fear of the Lord, but the imagery of the *light* on the road is appropriate: see 32.21.

51.1–30

Three sections make up the final chapter. The first, the psalm of thanksgiving (vv.1–12), begins with thanksgiving and praise (vv.1–2;

see Ps. 116.1a), with the reason *because you have been my protector* (v.2; Ps. 116.1b) in the face of assailants (vv.2–7); the description of the past peril (vv.6b–7; Ps. 116.3, 10); the cry to God (vv.8–10; Ps. 116.4–5, 11) recalling God's act of deliverance from the peril (v.12a; Ps. 116.8,16); and ending with the promise of continual thanks and praise to God (vv.11, 12b; Ps. 116.9, and in Ps. 116.18–19 'in the midst of you, O Jerusalem'). This classic form of the Thanksgiving Psalm reflects the commitment to praise born of the experience of merciful deliverance in the face of opposition. On the cry to God, *Lord, you are my Father* (v.10), see 23.1–6.

The second section, which is absent from the REB (but see the NRSV), because it is only found in a Hebrew text, resembles Ps. 136 in its use of the refrain 'for his mercy endures for ever'. These mercies include, appropriately, God's protection of Israel, Jerusalem and its temple, the priesthood, and, importantly, the continuing Davidic line (has this author or editor concluded that the priestly line is threatened and the Davidic must have a future?).

The third part, an alphabetical or acrostic poem (like Prov. 31.10–31) known in three different recensions, is a final affirmation of the progressive, disciplined search for Wisdom (vv.13–14) *in the forecourt of the sanctuary*, and of Wisdom as God's gift (v.17), requiring scrupulous care in living, in penitence and in purity. The *reward* of *eloquence* (v.22), like much of this passage, recalls ben Sirach's emphases. 51.23 raises the interesting question whether *the house of instruction* is a metaphor or a description of an actual place of learning or of a particular group of scholars. The *yoke* of instruction makes possible *great refreshment* with little labour (see Matt. 11.28–30). Such a discovery belongs within the context of reflection and worship (v.29), and the reward for duty done in good time is given in God's good time (v.30).

Baruch

Today we are well used to the pooling of resources in order to meet crises or answer disturbing questions. Indeed, it can be said that today economic development itself depends not so much on the solitary individual of genius as upon the ability of a multitude of experts who are expected to pool their ideas and research. That is true of how we meet social, international and ecclesiastical crises; those who can contribute from the particular angle of their own experience or resources are called together to seek a common solution.

The Apocryphal book of Baruch seems to reflect that kind of process. True, the title would appear to suggest a single writer: Baruch was the name of Jeremiah's scribe (Jer. 36.4–32). However, Jeremiah's Baruch could hardly have been the author of this book since it claims to have been written in Babylon, whereas, according to Jer. 43.7, Baruch went into exile with Jeremiah to Egypt, not to Babylon. In any case the Apocryphal book of Baruch gives the impression of being the product of several people who worked at the same problem; and the name of Baruch was attached to the book as a kind of tribute to Baruch's memory. Since Baruch had been prominent in presenting Jeremiah's work to King Jehoiakim before the capture of Jerusalem by Nebuchadnezzar of Babylon, he was an appropriate person to be associated with a collection of insights recalling Jerusalem's capture and the subsequent exile (Bar. 1.2), events which provided an appropriate focus for the problem which the writers faced.

The narrative introduction establishes the problem: *to this day the Lord's anger and wrath have not been averted from us* (1.13). According to the narrative *this day* is the fifth year after the destruction of Jerusalem (i.e. 582 BCE). Baruch has assembled the leaders in Babylon to hear the book read (see Neh. 9.3; the opening reference to a book in 1.1 is very confusing and probably refers to the total composition rather than to the book mentioned in 1.3). With *tears and fasting* (1.5) they offer prayers, they contribute money to be sent with the temple vessels to Jerusalem, and they send an accompanying message, exhorting the Jews to work patiently under the foreign ruler (see Jer. 29.1–14) and to offer sacrifices with prayers for Nebuchadnezzar and his son Belshazzar in Jerusalem, and the attached prayer of corporate confession and petition that God's wrath be withdrawn.

There are various problems with that particular narrative setting and attached prayer. One is the close link between the prayer and Daniel ch. 9, which belongs to the period beginning with the Seleucid king Antiochus IV (about 167–163 BCE; see the commentary on 1 Maccabees). Some scholars suggest that the advice to work with the foreign rulers belongs therefore, not to 581 BCE, nor to the time of Antiochus IV, but to the time of Antiochus V, advising against the Hasmonean opposition to the Seleucids. Another problem concerns the language. The Greek text of 1.1–3.8 belongs almost certainly to a revision of the Septuagint of Jer. 29–52 (known at about 116 BCE), and although there are pointers to a Hebrew original of Baruch 1–3, almost certainly that would have been composed in Judaea, not in Babylon.

What the recipients of the message are to pray is set out in 1.15–3.8. The prayer proclaims God's righteousness, and Judah's and Jerusalem's shame (see Dan. 9.7; Ezra 9.7), since her history has been one of rebellion (1.19) from the Exodus onwards (see Jer. 7.25; Deut. 9.7). The prayer proclaiming God's righteousness and Israel's shame recurs in 2.6. The prophets, notably of course Jeremiah, whose warning was not to resist the foreign rulers, have been disobeyed (see Jer. 26.4–5). From Deuteronomy the author borrows the metaphor (not represented in the REB) that adversity and God's curse 'cling' to his people (1.20; see 3.6, and Deut. 29.19); the warnings of God have now been fulfilled (Bar. 2.1–2; Dan. 9.11–14). Bar. 2.3 sounds strange, but various references suggest that the horrors of a city under siege involved cases of cannibalism (Deut. 28.53; see Jer. 19.9). The sad fact is that Christians should ever have used this, as indeed they did, to support and deepen anti-Semitism. 2.11 marks a concern for God's name as does Dan. 9.15. The parallels with Daniel's prayer (Dan. 9.4–19) are very close, so close in fact that the translation of Bar. 2.12–13 could follow either Dan. 9.5 (as the REB does: *we have broken all your commandments by our sin*) or Dan. 9.15–16 (as the Greek of Bar. 2 might suggest: 'we have sinned. By your saving deeds *turn your anger away from us*). Baruch's petition includes one for favour before the foreign rulers (2.14; see 1 Kgs 8.50) and that all may *know* God, and know that his is *the name by which Israel . . . is called* (2.15; see Wisd. 12.27). The plea is to God in heaven to see the feebleness of *the living* (their state of near death), who alone (as distinct from the physically dead: Ps. 30.9) can praise his *justice* (2.18; see Deut. 28.65). The book of

Jeremiah provides the basis again for 2.21–23 and for the disasters that follow Israel's disobedience. So the sequence, associated with Jeremiah and the Deuteronomic tradition, becomes part of the prayer: sin (2.26) – punishment (2.29) – repentance (2.30–33) – restoration (2.34–35). In 3.1–8 the genuine pain and the dependence on God expressed in this address to God resemble the Psalms (see Ps. 61.2; 69.3–18). The sins are sins of the past and God's judgement (and curse) on the previous generation clings to this (*we are in the grip of adversity*, 3.4; see the note on 1.20). An exiled people promise their praise: *We shall praise you in our exile, for we have renounced all the wrongdoing of our forefathers* (3.7cd). The prayer is that those who praise God in exile, who have become *a byword and a curse*, may now be heard (3.8).

So the first writer offers the traditional pattern of repentance. The second explicitly links the cause of the exile with Israel's rejection of wisdom. Israel is in the *enemies' country, grown old* there, and *numbered among those that lie in the grave* (3.10–11) and the reason is that they have *forsaken the fountain of wisdom!* (3.12). To have followed God's way would have meant peace (3.13). They are urged to find understanding, strength and intelligence, so that they will have *length of days* (3.14). They are urged to find it as a nation, in response to a nation's departure from wisdom. The writer admits that it is not easy to discern where wisdom is to be found (3.15–23; see Job 28). Foreign rulers with their power and skills, the rich and the skilled craftsmen are dead, gone and replaced. Other generations and those with a reputation for their wisdom (for Canaanites see Zech. 9.2; Ezek. 28.4; moving south, for the Edomite Teman see Job's friend Eliphaz; Hagar's descendants are Arabs; add merchants, story-tellers and all seekers after understanding), *not one of them discovered the way of wisdom* (3.20–23). The giants of the ancient world *perished for lack of insight* and *in their folly* (3.24–28). Deuteronomy claimed that God's commandment, God's law, was neither to be fetched from heaven nor from across the seas; it was immediately accessible (Deut. 30.11). Bar. 3.29–31 uses the same pictures but switches from the Law to Wisdom, and asserts that no one can find her simply by seeking; *only the omniscient* Creator *God knows her* (3.32–35). *Every way of knowledge he found out and gave to Jacob his servant* (3.36). In a most remarkable phrase, one suggestive in both Jewish and Christian traditions, Baruch records that, *after that, wisdom appeared on earth and lived among men.* Wisdom is *the book of God's commandments, the law that endures for ever* (4.1a). In the study of ben Sirach we discovered a similar phrase, which the context interprets as a redefinition of law by means of the total piety of the individual's life. To know wisdom is to know the law in its total faith context. Baruch's context is different. Baruch is arguing that Israel must never yield up that which is its priceless and unique privilege: *Do not yield up your glory to another or your privileges to a foreign nation* (4.3). It is because they have made precisely that mistake that such disaster has befallen the nation. But why then has Baruch substituted Wisdom for Law? Perhaps for a similar reason to that of ben Sirach: because to know what is pleasing to God is to enjoy life: *All who hold fast to her will live* (4.1c; see 4.4). Wisdom is substituted for Law because what Israel must never yield up is the privilege of living by the commandments of God. Again, as in ben Sirach, it is in the divine commandments in their living context that wisdom is to be found. Here in Baruch, however, because the issue is the fate of the nation, the life which is offered by God is the life of the people of God (4.5), not primarily the life of the individual believer.

That second solution recalls the Wisdom traditions of the book of Job. It also points forward to Paul's solution: Paul, faced in the course of his Christian mission by the Gentile–Jewish question, brought together the puzzling aspects of divine wisdom at work in human history with the coming on earth of the divine deliverer from Zion. In Rom. 11.26, 33–36 wisdom is known in God's gift of the richness of life to the people of God.

The third contributor, in the same context of Israel's exile (4.6), offers a positive, coherent prophetic message similar to that of Isa. 40–66, but again with references to Jeremiah's prophecies and the Deuteronomic tradition: Israel *provoked* God by *sacrificing . . . to demons* (see Deut. 32.17) and forgot the eternal God; but Jerusalem (Isa. 66.7–14), having told of her suffering (Lam. 1.12–18), proclaims that *only the One who brought the disasters on you can deliver you* (4.17–19); and she is determined in her desolation (Jer. 6.26) to *call to the Eternal as long as I live* (4.20c; Ps. 116.2). She proclaims the imminent restoration in divine *glory* of a joyful people (4.21–26; see especially Jer. 30.10–31.40; Isa. 61.7), encouraging a *tenfold zeal* (a reversal of Num. 14.22) on the part of the people (4.27–29), and prophesying judgement on their oppressors. Jerusalem sees her children coming from east and west (Isa. 59.19; 49.18; 60.1–9); she is promised that, instead of mourner's clothing, she will be wrapped around in the gift of God, *his robe of righteousness* (4.36–5.4; the parallels with Psalms of Solomon 11.3–7 suggest a common devotional source rather than dependence of one on the other); the mountains will be brought low and every ravine filled and levelled (5.5–9). This is the section used by the

Canticle, The Song of Baruch. It is a royal procession to the royal throne (Isa. 66.20; 52.7), with the great high road prepared so that the people may *walk securely in the glory of God* (Isa. 35.8–10; 40.2–5). In its context in Baruch the text cannot be confined to a particular time; in its worship context it includes all the nations. God will lead his people with joy *by the light of his glory, in his mercy and his righteousness* (5.9).

All three responses are worth pondering with regard to the question of whether or not God will forgive. The first contributor presents the shame which humanity justifiably experiences in the face of the proven righteousness of God, and sees forgiveness as a restoration of the divine name through an everlasting covenant (2.15, 35). The second recognizes the privilege of welcoming Wisdom's appearance on earth and the corporate life which that encourages, centred on the divine will and purpose. The third offers the promise that in his mercy God will provide a means of renewed righteousness and homecoming.

All this is very interesting, but one of the major difficulties in reading the book of Baruch is that its language is set within the context of Israelite national expectations. Paul found that aspect of Israel's thought perplexing; and today we find such language controversial because of the recent histories of various forms of nationalism and nationalist aspirations. For us the very name 'Jerusalem', which is crucial for the book of Baruch, brings with it a host of apparently intractable issues, and has sadly become a symbol of the divisiveness seemingly inherent in religious and political groupings. That problem certainly requires a renewed pooling of resources and insights, and careful attention to many different traditions and stories, both Christian and non-Christian. If Baruch's discussion of whether forgiveness is possible makes any contribution in today's world, it does so only if we consider it against a very different social and political context from that in which it was written. Even the central question of the book of Baruch sounds very different today: Is it possible today that nations should repent and that nations should be forgiven? The resources, however, which the book of Baruch pooled do have an important contribution to make: the answer to the central question of forgiveness is rooted in the nature of God, and the nature and possibility of God's forgiveness has to be explored in many new and different ways.

A Letter of Jeremiah

Fear of the unknown is a common feature of today's world, as it has been over the generations. We do not know when the Letter of Jeremiah was written. It may be that 2 Macc. 2.1–3 is a reference to it, and there is a fragment of it in Greek among the materials from Qumran Cave 7 which is dated, on the basis of its script, around 100 BCE. But apart from those two references there are very few ways of giving a date to the Letter, except to say that it may have been written originally in a Semitic language. It is hardly likely to be a letter from the prophet Jeremiah warning those who were to be exiled to the Babylon of his day. Nor could it have been originally a part of the book of Baruch, despite the fact that the Letter of Jeremiah was designated chapter 6 of Baruch in the Vulgate and the King James' Version. The contents of the letter could apply to almost any generation up to and including the time of Jesus, and, of course, beyond. In the form in which we have the letter there is a hint that seven generations are to follow the exile (see the discussion in 1 Esdras); that could be an indication of a date about 300 BCE, but more than that is hard to say. Its comments on idolatry, not least its emphasis on idolatry and fear of the unknown, fit most eras.

In his recent discussion of 'Religion in English everyday life' (*Religion in English Everyday Life*, 1999), Tim Jenkins has a section on those 'sciences' which are a part of the attempt to understand and control the lot of human beings. He begins by noting that in most denominations there are those with unorthodox approaches to supernatural phenomena which fit uneasily with the particular denomination's declared position. The imponderable in human experience or, at least in one of its forms, the fear of the unknown, is not easily classified or explained; and Tim Jenkins' attempt to pioneer, admittedly on a limited scale, a fresh approach to establishing some critical ways of judgement about the supernatural is very welcome.

One way of understanding the Letter of Jeremiah is to recognize in it an attempt to challenge the fear of the unknown. It is basically, from beginning to end, about idols, and one of the many links between

Judaism and Christianity which we have been exploring in these studies in the Apocrypha has been the danger of idolatry. Long before and long after the separation of Judaism from Christianity, idolatry was understood as the basic form of blasphemy, to be avoided at all costs. In some of the previous studies on the Apocrypha we have considered how idolatry can attend all religions, not least Christian life and thought.

But, of course, idolatry can be interpreted in different ways. It is worth pointing out the interpretation of idolatry suggested by the translation of the Second Commandment in *The Methodist Worship Book* (p. 144), 'You shall not idolize anything God has made'. While that translation may not cover all the forms of idolatry relevant to today's world, it does cover some very important ones and, in particular, those which correspond very closely to what is attacked in the Apocryphal Letter of Jeremiah. Idolatry can be found in taking what God has made and making an idol of it, whatever that created element might be. The Letter of Jeremiah describes again and again how carpenters and goldsmiths take physical elements of God's created world (v. 45) and set them up as sham representations of power and control (vv. 51–56; see also the commentary on the Wisdom of Solomon).

But certainly the most significant emphasis in the Letter of Jeremiah is its constant reference to fear: *Clearly they are not gods; therefore have no fear of them* (v. 16, and see also vv. 23, 29, 69). It could be argued that fear in that context is interpreted by the REB as the same as awe (*Do not be* overawed *by the gods when you see* in front and behind them a crowd worshipping them; rather *say in your hearts, 'To you alone, O Lord, is worship due'* (vv. 5–6)). But that is not the full picture as the Letter of Jeremiah presents it. The Letter recounts the many and varied fearful features of human life: war, pillage, fire, distress and disgrace, death and disease; and it links the making of idols with a human attempt to provide some kind of explanation of and safeguard from such fearful features (v. 12, vv. 35–38). The warning not to worship idols in this letter implies not only 'Do not blaspheme', but also 'There is nothing to be afraid of' and 'There are right and wrong ways of trying to safeguard ourselves'. As the writer of the letter says of God, *My angel will be with you; your lives will be in his care* (v. 7).

A further interesting feature of the attack on idolatry here is the recurrent hint that the fear of the unknown can be taken advantage of and abused for profit by the unscrupulous, or even by the well-meaning but misguided possessors of a religious rite or secret (vv.

8–10, 28, 33, 43, 55). It would not be difficult to think of parallels to that kind of activity in today's contemporary headlines.

The Letter's answer to such fear may not be complete; it concentrates on satire, as do many other passages from the Old Testament, such as Jer. 10.1–16 and Isa. 44.9–20, not to mention the Psalms and Deuteronomy. (The reference to setting *an offering before them* as being *like setting it before the dead* resembles Wisd. 15.17.) But the Letter does offer by way of answer that the true God has power to command *the sun, moon and stars* (v. 60). His control of the universe and overwhelming appearance in fire and storm are signs of true deity, and indicate that the natural effects and appearances of the universe are not to be considered gods (vv. 60–65). The moral is then not difficult to trace: when disaster strikes it is because of human sinfulness (v. 2), and peace will only come when God himself brings deliverance (v. 3). Such an answer is, as we have seen from other parts of the Apocrypha, only one possible option and has its dangers. Certainly those who continue to find the world a fearful place today may well not be wholly impressed by it. But at least the Letter of Jeremiah registers the dangers inherent in such fears and warns that only in relation to the true God, and not in secret rites and rituals, is there a resolution of them.

The Additions to Daniel

Daniel and Susanna

The history of the detective story makes fascinating reading. As far as modern detective stories go, their recent history is, of course, closely tied in with television production and personalities, but the detective story has also become a medium for various kinds of social comment – sociological, feminist, technological and so on. Detective methods exercise a fascination on the modern mind. They have, however, a much earlier history. Roman legal brains used such methods to outwit and bring to justice ancient criminals, and some of their stories have recently provided material for genuinely Roman detective stories.

The book of Daniel has been amplified in various ways. Two (perhaps three) newly discovered pieces are from the Qumran material (4Q245.1.i, 4Q243–244, 4Q246), and, like Daniel chs 2, 4, 5, they describe Daniel as attached to a royal court and able to interpret dreams or visions. But our main interest is in the three Apocryphal additions to the biblical book of Daniel, two of which are in effect detective novels. The first of these is the story of Susanna, a story to which artists and dramatists have been attracted throughout the centuries. The names of the participants, Susanna, Hilkiah, Joakim, suggests all manner of backgrounds to the story. But, as we have it, the story has been linked to Daniel. It presents the young Daniel using skilful interrogation techniques to trap two lecherous old judges whom the beautiful Susanna has refused and who take their revenge by accusing her of having sex with an unnamed accomplice.

The additions to Daniel have Greek versions which involve the Old Greek text (found in Papyrus 967, Origen's Hexapla and MS 88) and also the text associated with Theodotion (second century CE, although it is undoubtedly earlier than that, and has some Semitic links). The Old Greek version leaves open the question of whether the story was Palestinian or Babylonian. The REB uses the version of Theodotion. This provides a literary opening and places Susanna before Dan. 1. The setting in the REB is the household of Joakim, an educated, leading upper class Jew in Babylon with a wife, Susanna, brought up strictly in the law of Moses (see Judith 8.7–8 and Esther 2.7). Joakim appears to belong to a politically powerful elite who gather in his house (see Jer. 29.5–6), but who make the mistake of electing two judges who operate from Joakim's house and misuse the authority given them (v. 5). This becomes evident when the two judges shamelessly take advantage of Susanna's walk in the garden: *they did not keep in mind the demands of justice* (v. 9c; see Deut. 4.8). At first the two do not confide in each other that each privately intends to seduce her. The two judges eventually catch each other out (vv. 13–14) and agree a time to find her alone. She enters the garden (called 'paradise' – is God's creative work at stake here? See Gen. 3) and *the garden doors are shut* (v. 20, a key point in the story); their plan is coercion, intimidation and, finally, rape. But when they accost Susanna, she follows the judgement of Deut. 22.22 and the warning from Deut. 22.24–27. In doing so she is aware that she risks the charge of adultery with an unnamed person, which she knows the judges will bring, and which if proven would carry the verdict of death. The court case begins; the judges' lust and Susanna's sense of decorum are evident from the beginning of the case; her law-abiding family is in distress. The case goes against her and in despair she declares to God her innocence (vv. 34–43). The Lord responds by means of *a devout young man named Daniel* who demands that the case be reopened. He insists that the two judges be interrogated separately; and the climax of Daniel's detection is the kind of 'roughing up' used in some court-room dramas today, and a violent pun. To the one old man who claims to have witnessed the couple *under a clove tree*, Daniel says: *This lie has cost you your life*; the angel of God *will cleave you in two*, and to the other who claims to have witnessed the couple *under a yew tree*, Daniel says: *This lie has cost you also your life*; the angel of God will *hew you in two* (vv. 50–59; note that both trees are found in Eden). The pun is a Greek one, although not untranslatable; probably the story was not originally told in Greek, but in an older Hebrew narrative, perhaps without the pun. The assembly praises God, *the Saviour of those who trust in him*. The two judges are condemned to death; Susanna's and Joakim's families give praise for her innocence; and *from that day forward Daniel was held in great esteem* (vv. 60–64).

Part of the fascination of the story is that it is told with different emphases in various versions, and these suggest all manner of interesting political issues. As indicated earlier, detective stories can be told with many motives and in many literary forms, and that would certainly appear to be true of Susanna's story. Elaborate reconstructions of the political and social battles behind the version have been attempted, and the description of the form which the detective story has taken has been given as novella, court legend, fable and parable; but so far no reconstruction has attracted a consensus. We have to content ourselves with the REB, which (v. 64) shows how a young man such as Daniel could become prominent in a foreign court (see the position of the story in Theodotion – and in the Old Latin version – before Dan. 1; see also the story in 1 Esdras 3–4); or perhaps we might take a hint from the Old Greek version that young pious men like Daniel bring with them a spirit of knowledge and understanding which is essential for the people's future. Shylock's 'A Daniel come to judgement' (*Merchant of Venice*, IV.i) fits that interpretation of the story excellently and shows Shakespeare's awareness of the Susanna story.

Daniel, Bel, and the Snake

The story of Daniel, Bel, and the Snake (or Dragon) shows Daniel outwitting the priests of the god Bel-Marduk (Bel means 'Lord', as in Baal). He shows the king, by means of a brilliantly executed trap, that it was not Bel's appetite that devoured so much food; it was the appetite of the priests and their families. The Dragon/Snake part is humorously told, as are other additions to Daniel, and as indeed are stories in the canonical Daniel. The reaction of the Babylonians is that *The king has turned Jew* and they threaten regicide (v. 28). They demand Daniel, whom they throw into the lion-pit (see Dan. 6). A miraculous ending involves the prophet Habakkuk, dragged by his hair (see Ezek. 8.3) to Babylon with a stew in order to sustain Daniel (is the name Habbakuk connected with an Akkadian word for a vegetarian soup?); and the king, discovering Daniel sitting in the pit unharmed, promptly feeds his enemies to the lions instead.

Once again there is the problem of different versions. The opening of the story raises questions about a connection with the canonical book of Daniel. The REB translates the Theodotion text, which begins, following on from Dan. 12.13: *When King Astyages was gathered to his forefathers, he was succeeded on the throne by Cyrus the Persian. Daniel was a companion of the king* (vv. 1–2a; see Dan. 10.1; Isa. 45.1); but the Old Greek text carries the heading: *From the prophecy of Habakkuk, son of Joshua, of the tribe of Levi* (see the REB v. 33) and introduces Daniel as if we had not met him before, describing him as 'There was a priest, whose name was Daniel, son of Abal, friend of the king of Babylon' (see Ezra 8.2; Neh. 10.6 as possible sources in a list of priests); the ensuing battle is then a priest against priests. It has been suggested that the origins of the Bel and Snake/Dragon story are connected with an ancient myth of a priestly killing of a dragon, but the translation 'dragon' may be misleading and the reference is rather to snakes, and perhaps to a hellenistic context where snakes were worshipped (see Wisd. 15.18–16.9). What was originally an older story than the book of Daniel had become an addition to Daniel's confrontation with Hellenism.

Like modern detective stories, these ancient additions to the book of Daniel engage our interest in key questions of the day by means of the plot, the comedy, the unexpected or the supernatural. For the raconteurs who developed these as Daniel stories the key question was: Who is the living God? As we found in the Wisdom of Solomon, here also the futility of idols is mocked and the major warning is the danger of substituting our own idols for the true God. The REB illustrates the theme of the 'living God': *I shall bow before the Lord my God, for he is a living God* (v. 25); and Daniel ensures that in the end both god and cult are dead.

The Prayer of Azariah and the Song of the Three

The third of the additions is found between Dan. 3.23 and 3.24 in both the Old Greek and Theodotion: the Prayer of Azariah, the prose narrative closedly related to canonical Dan. 3 which indicates how the three young men were saved from the heat of the furnace, and the Song of the Three. The Prayer of Azariah addresses the situation of those who, like himself and his two friends, are in danger because of an oppressive foreign ruler. Some Psalms of Suffering address situations caused by internal jealousy, arguments and disputes (see ben Sirach 40.1–11), but Azariah recognizes that God has *handed* his people *over to* their *enemies* (v. 9a), *detested rebels against your law, and to a wicked king, the vilest in all the world* (v. 9bcd). The result of this has been to strip Israel of her resources: *Now we have no ruler, no prophet, no leader; there is no whole-offering, no sacrifice, no oblation, no incense, no place to make an offering . . . and so find mercy* (v. 15). The descriptions fit well with the reign of Antiochus IV Epiphanes (see 1 Macc. 1.10) in the period from 167–164 BCE. As in other prayers which we have met, the appeal is to God's honour and the covenant promises to the forefathers (Bar. 1.15–3.8; Dan. 9.4–19; Esther 14.3–19; Deut. 4.30–31 includes the promise of mercy which will never forget the covenants). The appeal is made in recognition of the justice of God (see Ps. 111.7–10). It is also made as an offering, a sacrificial act of prayer by those with a *contrite heart and humbled spirit* reliant on the divine mercy (the Prayer of Azariah v. 16). In the past Israel's deliverance has come through signs and wonders; so Azariah addresses God: *Lord, Worker of wonders, deliver us, and let your name be glorified* (v. 20). This can mean, given the circumstances, that the enemy are *put to shame*; it can also mean that deliverance can come with the sacrificial obedience of martyrs.

Benjamin Britten's church parable, *The Burning Fiery Furnace*, creates the atmosphere for the Song of the Three Young Men. Against the background of pagan worship and culture they refuse to concede worship to any but the Creator God. The Song's reference to *fire and heat* (v. 43) blessing the Lord points to the rescue of Shadrach, Meshach and Abednego from the furnace by the Lord, who is blessed for all the elements of creation. (For the ability of fire to forget its functions at God's behest see Wisd. 19.19–21.) The Song is printed in various church documents as suitable (in longer or shorter form) for public worship and while it is an exhilarating and imaginative exaltation of God it raises the question: Is it true, or in what sense is it true, that what is animal or inanimate can bless God? One of the finest television productions of this century so far has been David Attenborough's *The History of Mammals*. Having seen the extraordinary history which that series of programme presents, it would be difficult, if you believe in a Creator God at all, to deny that the history of mammals is an incredible testimony to the amazing versatility and creativity of God. In that time-scale, the Song of the Three Young Men, 'Blessed are you, Lord' (the Benedicite), can make sense as an act of worship. It extends our thoughts and imagination towards the realities of God's creative work.

The Prayer of Manasseh

Forgiveness is a major contemporary concern. Political events, especially those in South Africa, have given the subject a fresh focus. Novels have centred on its individual aspects. John Grisham's best-seller, *The Testament*, focuses on a solicitor's confession of years of sin, the sincere desire for a new start and the discovery that God's forgiveness provides a way. The structure of forgiveness and absolution has been given fresh attention in Richard Briggs' *Words in Action* (T&T Clark, 2001), illustrating how to be forgiven and to forgive are integrally related. The Prayer of Manasseh has various insights to shed on the subject and does so in an intriguing way; it is a classic statement of contrition which might serve in any generation, and has so served in ancient, medieval, renaissance, reformation, modern and post-modern times. It was used by both Jews (apparently a Hebrew translation was made of the prayer) and by Christians in earlier days, and is still used today for the precise purpose of offering a shape for contrition and a form of words for the penitent.

The curious history of this prayer encourages its use in any time and place. We do not know its date or its origin. Its name, the Prayer of Manasseh, is only known to us from a late date. It comes from an association of the prayer with a narrative related to the Old Testament book of Chronicles, 2 Chron. 33. That particular chapter describes Manasseh (687–642 BCE) as leading Judah into ways more wicked than those of any other nation: idolatry, child sacrifice, sorcery and other evil practices – a picture almost identical with that of Manasseh's behaviour according to the account in 2 Kgs. 21. However, according to 2 Chron. 33.13 Manasseh repented of his evil ways and prayed to God, who accepted his petition and restored him to his throne in Jerusalem, whereas 2 Kgs. 21 implies that Manasseh died in his sins, and Jerusalem and Judah paid the penalty for their involvement in those sins. The Prayer of Manasseh is, according to a later author, what Manasseh might have prayed. But we have no evidence that it was ever used by Manasseh, or that it existed at so early a stage in Israel's history. It is, as it were, common property.

The language of the prayer also encourages its general use. The Prayer of Manasseh, as printed in the REB, is a translation from a Greek text of Ode 12 as printed in a modern LXX edition, and the Greek text sounds very traditional. Even where the English translation might sometimes give the impression that this really is Manasseh speaking, the English translator is in fact taking some liberties with the original. Verse 13 probably does not say *Destroy me not with my transgressions on my head* (that is, 'Do not let me die an abject sinner', as the English translator is presumably suggesting that the Manasseh of 2 Chron. 33 might have prayed). It simply says in the Greek, as the Syriac text of the Prayer also corroborates, 'Do not destroy me with my transgressions' (that is, the more general 'destroy the sin but save the sinner'). This very general character of the Prayer of Manasseh has been illustrated by some scholars through close comparison of it with Psalm 51. The shape of the Prayer, and the phrases used in it, make the parallel quite compelling; the Prayer fits the pattern of a general Psalm of Confession. The Prayer of Manasseh uses some important features which are not found in Psalm 51: a section at the beginning praising God's powers of creation, and a section at the end associating the one who prays with the songs of the angelic host. There are one or two parallels between 2 Chron. 33.6, 7, 11 and 12 and the Prayer of Manasseh vv. 9b–11; but even these are of a very general character. One translation of the Syriac version notes some thirty parallels in the Old Testament, Apocrypha (see especially 2 Esdras 8) and Pseudepigrapha (for example *Joseph and Asenath*, and the *Ascension of Isaiah*). All in all, we can say that the Prayer is ideally suited to the penitent in any generation and any time, and is probably intended as such.

General though its language may be, the Prayer nevertheless reflects the importance of genuine penitence before God. Genuine penitence begins in the presence of God and in acknowledgement of God's creative power, omnipotence, awesomeness, holiness and mercy. To speak of God as *relenting* (v. 7 REB; the Syriac has 'feel sorry over the evils of humanity') may be to accommodate God to the human framework of attitude and reaction. But Manasseh's prayer recognizes that the human experience of God can change, and it can change because we recognize God's involvement in the life of the world, in its disasters and tragedies, and that God has provided the priceless opportunity of *repentance as the way of salvation* (see the REB footnote on v. 7, although the REB omits the extraordinarily moving expression in the Syriac version, 'according to the sweetness of your grace'). From that starting point the penitent can begin to move into confession.

The major issue raised by the Prayer arises from the particularity of its title: the Prayer of Manasseh (found in the ninth-century CE Syriac version in Florence). Supposing that the one who prays the prayer has been responsible for a major crime, as Manasseh was, or has a position of public responsibility and, like Manasseh, has abused that position, causing mayhem in the community and untold damage to its innocent members; in such cases, are there conditions to be fulfilled before forgiveness can follow? Some early theologians judged that the Prayer of Manasseh did imply a condition, that of doing penance (perhaps a penance of the kind illustrated so powerfully in the film version of *The Mission*, where penance alone enabled a murderer to be led from the shackles of past action toward penitential tears; see Manasseh v. 10). Later theologians have emphasized the need for other actions, perhaps interrupting the progress of the prayer, actions involving some kind of reparation or reconciliation (as Jesus appears to have recommended according to Matt. 5.24), discipline or legal punishment short or long term (see Matt. 18.15–20, an adaptation of Jewish disciplinary patterns).

The translation of the Prayer of Manasseh, as we have it, does not directly answer the questions about forgiveness in the case of the abuse of authority or human beings. But it has a clear emphasis. As far as the Prayer of Manasseh itself is concerned, its major emphasis is on the mercy and grace of God. The possibility of divine forgiveness is where mercy meets human helplessness and misery. The declaration of that helplessness and misery needs the language of grief (v. 10b), and perhaps that is where written Psalms of Penitence such as this can assist, or indeed where a counsellor or confessor may help. A written form can be of help in channelling individual thought and prayer in positive directions, and a counsellor can perform a similar function. Nevertheless, the prayer needs to be not simply read, but spoken from the heart. Verse 11 confesses that *my heart submits to you*, or, as in the Syriac version, 'behold I am bending the knees of my heart before you'. The Prayer is suited only to the genuine penitent, and genuine penitence is both divine gift and personal struggle. The plea for forgiveness follows in the Syriac version (v. 12).

The Prayer of Manasseh concludes, as penitence should, with a note of confidence (*You will save me in your great mercy*) and even of joy, a joy shared with all heaven and earth (*I shall praise you continually all the days of my life. The whole host of heaven sings your praise*; see Luke 15.7).

As sinful human beings, we can know forgiveness; but the conditions which attend the full experience of that forgiveness are matters needing much greater attention and action. That is particularly true where abuse and the abuse of authority are involved. True contrition needs careful definition and the prayer for forgiveness needs to be accompanied by, and belong within, a new framework of living.

The First Book of the Maccabees

Few parts of the Apocrypha relate quite so closely to today's world as does 1 Maccabees. The relationship can be formulated as a series of questions: How can we deal with tensions between distinctive religious traditions and a world culture, between national identity and international law and order, between a minority revolt and the political will of the majority? For each of these questions we could name half a dozen contemporary situations which each cry out for a modern answer; and for each question 1 Maccabees provides a poignant area of exploration.

Central to 1 Maccabees is the political, social and religious collision in the second century BCE between Hellenism (the Greek culture given an international significance by Alexander the Great) and Judaism. 2 Maccabees (a book quite different in style, purpose and outlook from 1 Maccabees, but covering a similar chronological area) actually uses those terms – Hellenism and Judaism (2 Macc. 4.13; in 2.21 the REB avoids the term Judaism, replacing it with *the Jewish religion*. Since the term was probably coined in contrast to Hellenism and Hellenism needs to be very broadly described, Judaism is not likely to be the equivalent of Jewish religion only). Hellenism grasped the vision of Alexander the Great and his Syrian (Seleucid) and Egyptian (Ptolemaic) successors – one world, one language, one religion – whereas Judaism represented a challenge to that vision in the particularity of a divinely ordained Temple, priesthood, Law and people (1 Macc. 14.29).

Such collisions, as in Ireland, can never be described in simple terms. They are complex, often bewilderingly so; which is why solutions to them are so difficult to find. Although 1 Maccabees represents a Jewish tradition in line with the historical writings of the Old Testament, it presents Judaism as anything but united. The first major section of 1 Maccabees reveals many divisions. It attacks upwardly mobile Jewish families whose ambitions turn Jerusalem into a Greek-style city (1.11–15); it seems critical of groups who withdrew from the arena of conflict by going into the wilderness and refusing to fight on the Sabbath (2.29–38); and it applauds the heroism of those who, in confrontation with Hellenism, risked guerilla and then all-out warfare.

Within such a context a written history is bound to reflect a particular standpoint and one longs to hear a clear factual account of events. Often, as in the case of 1 Maccabees, that is just not possible. On the other hand we shall find that the anonymous author of 1 Maccabees is by no means careless as a historian, and we shall use his account to sketch out some of the important moments and movements which a modern, critically assessed historical account can value. There is also too a growing recognition that our anonymous author took some literary pride in what he was producing. On the one hand this, as is usually the case with a literary work, raises questions about the author's priorities: do literary shapes and linguistic skills take precedence over chronological precision? On the other hand literary skills can give a shape to history in a way which provokes thought and reflection by the juxtaposition of events and movements, and by the values and attitudes inherent in the choice of the language used. Alongside our attempt to see our author as a useful guide to what happened, we shall also try to assess his literary skills.

A guide to the shape of the book is given by the struggle between Judaism and the Seleucid successors of Alexander (Antiochus III, IV and V, Seleucus IV, Demetrius I and II with their respective administrations). The first part holds together for our attention Alexander the Great's death and the death of Antiochus IV (1.1–6.17). The second part holds together the events concerning a vital factor in the Seleucid administration, the Citadel in Jerusalem, and its eventual capture by the Jews (6.18–13.53). The third marks the decline in Seleucid power to the re-establishing of the Jewish high priesthood (14.1–16.24). So the whole book is about the establishing of Seleucid control over Judaism and Judaism's progressive dismemberment of the Seleucid administration. That overall picture in itself tells us a great deal about the interests and concerns of the author: it plots the rise of the main opposition to Seleucid authority, the Hasmonean dynasty.

For the text we are dependent on the LXX tradition once again. Behind that text was an earlier Greek version which was translated, for example, into Latin; and the Old Latin translation gives us evidence of the form of the earlier Greek version before the Greek text was revised in about 300 CE. That earlier Greek text seems itself to have been a translation of a Hebrew original. The Jewish historian contemporary with the Fall of Jerusalem in 70 CE, Josephus, made considerable use of 1 Maccabees in its Greek form in his *Jewish Antiquities*.

The deaths of Alexander the Great and Antiochus IV
1.1–6.17

The first major section of 1 Maccabees begins with one of the decisive moments in the history of the Western world: the death of Alexander the Great in 323 BCE. Alexander built on his father's conquests (Philip II of Macedon had conquered Greece: 1.1c) and his progress is sketched in geographically and strategically, until *the world lay quiet under his sway* (1.3). The Eastern Mediterranean world had been given a degree of uniformity in terms of overall rule, language and communication. The historian adds, however, a crucial comment, one which he will make again very shortly: *his* (Alexander's) *pride knew no limits* (1.3d). Pride here signifies the challenge to divine limitations on human ambition, the kind of ambition which ventures beyond divine law and judgement (see 1.21, and Mattathias' reaction to events subsequent to Alexander's death: 2.49). In political terms Alexander's pride involved gathering plunder and *an extremely powerful army* (1.4) together with much tribute money. 1 Maccabees is therefore a history in the Jewish historical tradition, where pride is mocked by God (Isa. 14.4–27), powerful armies can be overcome by the few warriors (Judg. 7.1–14), and God's hand can be evident in their overthrow (3.18–24). It is a history which places Jews among the nations and establishes the Jewish God as their deliverer (12.15; 16.3), and as the one who raises up his champions. The sequel to Alexander's death was the division of his empire among his generals (1.5–8), with the Northern Mediterranean passing to Seleucus and the Seleucids after him, and the Southern Mediterranean to the Ptolemies. The history of the succeeding years is well described from Israel's point of view, caught as she was between those two power blocks, as a story of *untold miseries* (1.9). One of the most significant of these miseries, for the story of 1 Maccabees, was the emergence of a Seleucid, *an offshoot of this stock*, Antiochus IV (Epiphanes) in 175 BCE (the dating of events used here follows a growing consensus; see on 6.16 below). As we saw in the discussion of ben Sirach, the Seleucid king Antiochus III could act positively towards the Jewish high priesthood, and allowed the Jews a form of government compatible with their laws. When Seleucus IV was murdered and his son Demetrius was held as a hostage in Rome, the throne was usurped by Antiochus IV. At the latter's accession one of the priestly and family divisions which had been in existence since Ezra's time reached a critical point of growth; *a group of renegade Jews* (1.11; see 1.34), with a strongly pro-Gentile bias and important external trade links, pressed the case that the isolationist policies inherited from Nehemiah and Ezra had been destructive of the Jewish economy and culture (see 2 Macc. 4.7–10, and the commentary there, p. 174). It is to this group that Antiochus Epiphanes gives fresh authority (1.13). 1 Maccabees summarizes their programme (see 2 Macc. 4.7–17) as turning Jerusalem into a hellenistic city, removing from its constitution Mosaic requirements, and opening it to the influences of Syrian life and society (1.14–15). In line with that programme Antiochus takes up the issue of Egyptian claims to Palestine and attacks, with partial success, the Ptolemaic empire (1.16–19; see Dan. 11.25–31); and on his return *marched up with a strong force against Israel and Jerusalem* (1.20; 169 BCE). This mark of supreme arrogance (1.21; see 2.49) leads to the pillaging of the Temple and the removal of all the valuable treasures there (1.21–24), no doubt to help the finances of the state and meet the costs of his campaigns. Not inappropriately these initial campaigns begin the section of 1 Maccabees which concludes with Antiochus IV *engulfed in a sea of troubles*, repenting of the *wrong he did in Jerusalem* in carrying off the silver and gold vessels and decimating the population of Judaea and, recognizing that this is why *misfortunes have come upon him*, dying *in a foreign land* (6.11–13; he died in Persia in Nov–Dec 164 BCE. This dating, based on the second-century BCE Babylonian tablet list of Seleucid kings, differs from the REB marginal note at 6.16). As Alexander's death marked the beginning of untold miseries for the Jews so Antiochus IV's death finds him in bitter grief for his significant share in their cause. At that point the bitter grief is his; at the desecration of the Temple the bitter grief is Israel's (1.25–28) and is echoed in 1.37–40, 2.7–14 and, in the aftermath of the Sabbath massacre, 2.38–41. At the desecration of the Temple Antiochus is arrogantly boastful (1.24); at his final grief he is bitterly disappointed by his failure to plunder Elymais (6.1–4; Elymais contained the plunder of Alexander the Great) and by the news that Judas Maccabaeus and his brothers have *pulled down the abomination built by him on the altar in Jerusalem* and also *fortified Bethsura, his city*. Much, although not all, of Antiochus's campaign was unravelled by the time of his demise. The literary balancing of events is thus effective and evocative.

We are now at the start of Antiochus's campaign against Jerusalem. As punishment for what he took to be a pro-Egyptian move in

Jerusalem, Antiochus sent Apollonius (see 2 Macc. 5.24) to establish the ascendancy of the hellenistic party and to garrison the city (1.33) with the Citadel (the Akra), which was to be a thorn in the side of the Jews for a long time to come (1.34–36). The deaths in the city and the Temple precincts are marked by a lament (1.37–40, reminiscent of Ps. 79). Finally *the king issued an edict* (1.41) requiring the abandonment of Jewish *customs* (1.42) to secure the uniformity of religion. As the story later requires, it was an edict to his entire *empire* (l.41b). Jerusalem is to be a gentile sanctuary (1.45–47), circumcision is no longer to be practised (1.48), and provision is made for officers to superintend offerings of pagan sacrifices at local altars (1.51). Effectively the faithful were driven into hiding (1.53). Then there was the ultimate blasphemy, still remembered in the text of the New Testament by the same horrific description, *the abomination of desolation* (1.54). Also horrific, to modern ears particularly, was the burning of *every scroll of the law*; its regulations were proscribed, and possession of the law or conforming to it was to be punished by death (1.56–57). Many stood firm against the use of unclean food (1.62), and *died rather than defile themselves . . . Israel lay under a reign of terror* (1.63–64). (There is a debate about the REB translation 'terror'. Literally the word translated means 'wrath'; see 2.44, 49; 3.8. Terror makes good sense in the context of 1.61–63, and could be inclusive of Antiochus's wrath or general anger; but it is also possible that, since the situation was to a degree a result of Israel's failures and disobedience, the divine wrath lay on Israel and expiation had to follow.)

The stages by which Antiochus's programme was reversed make clear the character and significance of that reversal, as the author of 1 Maccabees envisaged it. The first stage was the local revolt by the priest Mattathias and his family in Modin, some seventeen miles north of Jerusalem (see 1 Chron. 9.10 for the priestly *family*: there the Hebrew name is given as Jehoiarib; the Greek form of the name, as quoted in 1 Macc. 2.1 is *Joarib*). All five sons are named since each played a part in the subsequent events (2.3–5). The revolt specifically addresses *the sacrilegious acts* (2.6) in Judaea and Jerusalem. It will become evident that not all parts of *Judaea* and *Jerusalem* (2.6) were affected in the same way, and not all saw the necessity for a revolt (2.18, 46). 1 Maccabees sees it as enforced *apostasy* (2.15), and this is signalled by Mattathias's initial speech; he laments the crushing of Judah and Jerusalem, her abandonment to the enemy, and the giving up of *the holy place* to *foreigners* (2.7). Robbed of her glorious vessels, she has been robbed of her honour; *she is no longer free, she is a slave*

(2.9–11). 1 Maccabees is full of correspondences between the events described and past events, and full of reversals and contrasts. In Mattathias's lament the correspondence is with the destruction of Jerusalem and the Temple in 587 BCE, and with the literature evoked by those events (see 2.12, 18); and the contrasts involved are those of freedom and slavery.

Mattathias's refusal to commit *apostasy* (2.15) and his declaration, 'Though every nation *within the king's dominions obeys and forsakes its ancestral worship . . . yet I and my sons and my brothers will follow the covenant made with our forefathers*' (2.19–20), leads to his cutting down an apostate and the king's officer who supervised the sacrifices. The parallel drawn here is with the grandson of Aaron, Phinehas the priest, and his zeal for the law (see Num. 25.8; ben Sirach 45.23–24, where Phinehas is said explicitly to make expiation for Israel; 1 Macc. 2.54). By his action and words Mattathias challenges the people to follow him, *all who are zealous for the law and stand by the covenant* (2.27).

Another feature of 1 Maccabees is the use of particular pieces of vocabulary to give piquancy or depth of focus to particular events. In 2.28 Mattathias and his sons take to the hills. This means *leaving behind* all they possessed. Whatever the strategy involved, 1 Maccabees is drawing attention to the very many others who had 'left behind' their ancestral traditions, thus adding to the pressure on the faithful to choose the way of the *desert* (2.29). The penalty for such faithfulness is underlined by reference to another group. These took all their family and livestock into hiding; but such was their adherence to the law that they obeyed the commandment to honour the Sabbath day by refusing to fight on the Sabbath. Hence when they were attacked on the Sabbath by Seleucid soldiers they refused to defend themselves and they, their families and livestock were slaughtered (2.29–38; see 2 Macc. 6.11).

For Mattathias this was a turning point. 1 Maccabees draws out the significance of his decision: trust in God has in the past been honoured for its single-minded determination and rewarded by some divine act of deliverance (see Daniel and the Three Young Men in 2.59–60); however, Mattathias took this moment as a signal to draw *strength* of purpose *from the law* (2.61–64) and to fight; if on the Sabbath, then so be it.

A group of Hasideans or Hasidim is now mentioned as joining Mattathias; they adhered rigorously to the law and had a reputation as warriors (see 1 Macc. 7.12–16, where they allowed themselves to be deceived by Alcimus). Their role seems to be deliberately undervalued. But they express the wrath of the faithful towards sinners and renegades (2.44), a wrath from which those who escaped sought *refuge* among the *Gentiles. Mattathias and his friends swept through the country* (2.45), destroying altars, *forcibly circumcising . . . boys*, and hunting down enemies. Again the enemies are described as *arrogant* (2.46–47).

Mattathias gives his final address: *Arrogance now stands secure . . . these are days of calamity and raging fury* (2.49). His appeal is for zeal and the readiness for self-sacrifice in the name of the covenant (2.50). Like ben Sirach 44.19–49.16 (see also Wisd. 10–11), Mattathias recalls heroes from the past and promises to the faithful *great glory and everlasting fame*. Abraham, Joseph, Phinehas (who received *the covenant of an everlasting priesthood*: (2.54); Joshua, Caleb, and David (who was granted *an everlasting kingdom*: 2.57); Elijah, for his zeal for the law, was translated (2.58); the three young men and Daniel had faith and were saved (2.59–60; see Dan. 3 and the Additions to Daniel). So history shows that *trust in Heaven* gives strength. As if anticipating Antiochus's fate, Mattathias's judgement is: *Today he may be high in honour, but tomorrow not a trace of him will be found* (2.63). The roles of Symeon and Judas are defined. Having given his final testimony he blesses them and dies, to great sorrow and grief *throughout Israel* (2.70).

A fresh stage begins (3.1–2) with the guerilla campaigns of Judas Maccabaeus – local raids and harassment by insurgents working from well-protected hideouts in the Gophna mountains. These are carried out *with zest* (almost Robin and his merry men!). Elsewhere the word translated 'zest' can mean 'rejoicing', and in 1 Maccabees it is associated with festival celebrations (4.56–59; 7.48), success (10.66), or restoration and rehabilitation (5.23–24; 14.11). At the very least 3.1 demarcates a time of renewed hope (see 3.9b), dispersing the mood of frustration from Israel, generating cheerfulness; or perhaps the reference to Phinehas indicates that the anger or zeal of the rebels anticipates or turns away the divine anger, encouraging confidence and enthusiasm (Num 25.11; Ps. 106.28–31). 3.3–9 has been described as an acrostic poem (the opening letter of each line adding up to a recognizable pattern), originally composed in Hebrew and building the name 'Jehudah the Maccabee'. The poem has three functions: it emphasizes Judas's role as a soldier creating a fighting force (3.55), eventually restoring the cult (4.36–59) and (despite 6.28–50) militarily successful; second, it marks him out as significant well beyond his lifetime (3.7); third, it points to his ferocity before *renegades*, delivering Diaspora Jews (3.6c), confronting Seleucid kings and turning *wrath away from*

Israel (3.8). These three selected areas depict Judas as a Davidic figure, securing the land, restoring the Diaspora Jews and turning away divine wrath (see Isa. 11.12–12.6; 1 Chron. 14.17; on 1 Macc. 3.12 see 1 Sam. 17.51; Judas takes a sword from Apollonius, as David did from the dead Goliath). The contrasts too are interesting: renegades fear – freedom prospers; kings are angered – Jacob is cheered.

The first pair of Judas's campaigns listed here concern Apollonius, now, according to Josephus' *Antiquities* XII.7.1(287) a governor of Samaria. The record of Judas's victory over Apollonius is brief and to the point. Next, Seron, a low-ranking Syrian army commander wishing to make a name for himself, was caught in an ambush at Beth-horon (not the only army to be ambushed there – the Romans also fell foul of it). 1 Maccabees contrasts the attitudes of the two forces: Seron's soldiers show *insolence*, desire for prestige, greed, *lawlessness*, eagerness for revenge, apostasy; Judas's were fighting for their lives, few in number and hungry. But, says Judas, *Heaven can save just as well by few as by many . . . strength is from Heaven alone* (3.18c, 19b).

The focus now returns to Antiochus Epiphanes at the turning point in his affairs (3.27–37). News of Judas's reputation angers him. He mobilizes a powerful response (see 1 Chron. 19.16–18) with a year's subventions from his treasury. His *resources* run *low* (3.29a) due to low income from disaffected clients who object to his *abolishing* of *traditional laws and customs* (3.29b). Danger threatens; he resolves to collect tribute from the provinces on his way to Persia. He entrusts Lysias with the care of his son (later Antiochus V), and orders him, with half his army and his elephants, to crush Judaea and Jerusalem, resettle the area with foreigners and redistribute the land (at every stage in the ancient world, as now, a contentious policy). He himself sets off from Antioch for Persia.

Lysias chooses three of the king's friends, Ptolemaeus (see 2 Macc. 4.46), and, presumably under the latter's charge, Nicanor and Gorgias, and orders them to *devastate Judaea* (3.39). They occupy a position near Emmaus, and local traders move in with *a very large quantity of silver and gold* to buy Israelites taken captive in the coming battle. Judas and his brothers, recognizing the extreme danger, gather in full assembly to *pray and seek divine mercy*, using a Psalm of Lament for the devastation of Jerusalem (3.45). At Mizpah (for Samuel's intercession with fasting at Mizpah see 1 Sam. 7.5–7) their traditional mourning leads them to seek guidance from the law scroll (rather than other alternatives such as the decision-making process of the casting of lots, as in Esther 3.7, or of offering sacrifices such as Gentiles might perform before an idol); in the absence of the desecrated Temple they fulfil what they can of the ceremonies of the holy place and declare their helplessness before God unless he comes to their *aid* (3.46–53). The war *trumpets* sound for battle; Judas organizes his fighters, acting as Gideon did (Judg. 7.3) and as the law required (Deut. 20.1–9). The evidence we have of Seleucid armies gives an impressive picture of well-trained men, well versed in tactics. With guides from the Citadel Gorgias attempts to surprise Judas (4.1–2); but Judas has already left his own camp, giving the impression that they were in flight, and moves to attack Gorgias's base camp at Emmaus. Finding Emmaus well organized Judas encourages his poorly equipped troops to attack, awakening memories of the pursuit of Pharaoh's army at the Exodus, so that *all the Gentiles will know there is One who liberates and saves Israel* (4.8–11; see 2 Macc. 8). Those in the camp move out to meet Judas but the Syrian soldiers break ranks and rush into the plain, and are initially pursued northward and eastward. But Judas breaks off the pursuit and orders that no plunder be taken. Gorgias's troops are still in the hills. A Seleucid patrol sees what has happened (4.19) and that *their army* has *been routed*; panic-stricken, all flee to Philistia (4.20), whereupon Judas plunders the camp: *large quantities of gold and silver, violet and purple stuffs, and great riches were seized* (4.23). All the emphasis is on the glorious occasion (presumably also on enjoyment of what the traders left); the practicalities of collecting arms are unimportant! The celebration of the heavenly deliverance follows, using the response of Ps. 136: *because his mercy endures for ever* (see also the Prayer of Azariah vv. 67–68).

Lysis is *stunned at the news* (4.27), especially since he is committed to Antiochus for the wiping out of the rebellion. Late in 165 BCE with a much larger force he approaches from the Idumaean area (4.29a; see 5.3 for the animosity between Judaea and Idumaea, i.e. the ancient Edom). This time Judas's prayer recalls the exploits of David and Jonathan against the Philistines, and he prays that the enemies' *troops and mounted men may be humbled* (4.31). Again the contrast is made between the cowardly enemy and the faithful who love God and *praise* him *with songs of thanksgiving* (4.33; see Ps. 9.11–12). In the battle at Bethsura Lysias must have favoured his chances but his loss of so many men, perhaps with others beginning to drift away, made engaging with Judas's *army in fighting spirit* too treacherous a prospect. There may have been attempts at negotiation (2 Macc. 11.16–33). Whatever the precise circumstances, Lysias withdrew and no further attempt was made until the spring of 163 BCE.

Judas and his brother now move in to *cleanse and rededicate the temple* (4.36), one of their main objectives, as the author of 1 Maccabees would see it. They visit Mount Zion and record its state of devastation and desecration (4.38). The *Citadel*, the Akra, was besieged but not taken (4.41). *Priests* were *selected*, with the implication that the currently available priests were not reliable (4.42a). The *stones which defiled* the place were removed (were these the 'abomination of deso-lation'?) and, although the Temple was purified by their removal, the problem of the *desecrated altar* remained without any immediate solu-tion (4.44). The temporary solution was to take the altar stones and store them *until there should arise a prophet to give a decision about them* (4.46). The altar was then rebuilt from *unhewn stones* following the instructions of Exod. 20.25 and Deut. 27.5–6. *The temple courts were consecrated*, and new vessels made. The *altar of incense, the lampstand, the table, the Bread of the Presence* and *the curtains* were introduced (4.48–51). So on the 14th December, 165 BCE (the REB suggests 164, but if Antiochus IV heard of this before his death, 165 is the more likely), three years after the first heathen sacrifice there, *sacrifice was offered* (4.52–53). The author assumes the musical traditions from Neh. 12.27–28 and the Chronicler, and that the offerings associated with the purification of the Temple in 2 Chron. 29 were made (4.56). A festival is inaugurated; 4.59 calls it *the dedication of the altar*, although the word used here suggests renewal or restoration, rather than dedication (see John's gospel 10.22). The name 'dedication' may have been related to its first-century CE name, Hanukkah. The history of the festival involves different features (see 2 Macc. 2.18 and the commentary there). Josephus knows the feast as 'Lights' (*Antiquities* XII.7.7 (325)), explaining the name as the appearance of the right to worship when that could hardly have been hoped for. As well as decreeing the festi-val, Judas fortified Jerusalem against gentile incursions with a sur-rounding wall and towers (see 6.7b), and turned Bethsura into a Judaean fortress (see 6.7c).

A section follows demonstrating Judas's prowess as a military leader, showing how the surrounding areas were 'cleansed' (see 5.68) and preparing the way for the fatal message to be sent to Antiochus Epiphanes. The section is neatly organized. The opening verse (5.1) records a hostile gentile response to what Judas has done in Jerusalem. Then an opening and a concluding passage show how Judas deals with ancient enemies, the Edomites, the Ammonites and the Philistines (5.65–68; see their involvement in the earlier battles, particularly acting as refuges for pursued Seleucids). Between these there is a plea for help from Jews in Gilead and Galilee. Arrangements are made for Simon to go to Galilee, Judas and Jonathan to go to Gilead, and Joseph(us) and Azarias to defend Judaea. The Jews are safely brought back by Simon and Judas to Mount Zion (5.23; 5.45); Azarias and Josephus on the other hand unwisely and against orders take on Gorgias and are heavily defeated (5.55–62). So *Judas and his brothers won a great reputation throughout Israel and among all the Gentiles* (5.63). Throughout the descriptions of Judas's campaigns 1 Maccabees attaches parallels from the scriptures, deepening the impression that Judas stands in the long traditions of Israel's saviours.

The major intention of Antiochus to destroy the rebels has failed and his armies have suffered major defeats; his initial project of desecrating the Temple has been as far as possible reversed, the Temple has been secured by high walls, and Bethsura turned into a Judaean fortress; his plans to cleanse the area and resettle non-Jews has been foiled; and Judas is acclaimed everywhere as a great leader. Antiochus by contrast fails to take Elymais; in *bitter disappointment* he withdraws (6.4). The news of events in Judaea reach him in Persia (6.5). *Shaken* by the report, and *ill with grief*, on his death bed he acknowledges that he brought all these disasters upon himself. He summons Philip, *one of* the king's *friends*, gives him authority to bring up his son (Antiochus V) and makes Philip co-regent. He dies at Tabae between Persia and Media and his death was reported in Babylon November/December 164 BCE. Lysias, on hearing that the king has died, places Antiochus V on the throne (6.17).

The Citadel of Jerusalem
6.18–13.53

The second major section of 1 Maccabees begins with Judas's determination to make an end of the garrison of the Citadel, the Akra, and it ends many battles later with Simon finally capturing the Citadel (13.43–53), decreeing an annual festival, strengthening the fortifications of the Temple hill opposite the Citadel, and appointing his son John commander of all the forces. As an illustration of the jurisdiction which Israel gained, 9.23–11.74 tells how Jonathan, Judas's brother, gained jurisdiction over Samaria but still remained, like Onias before him, a Seleucid regent. On either side of that major central feature Rome emerges as part of the total picture, first as a result of Judas's initiative (8.1–32) and secondly as a result of Jonathan's initiative

(12.1–23). Following the first, Judas is killed in battle, and following the second, Jonathan is put to death by Trypho. The balancing of events is again skilfully done. The emergence of Judas, Jonathan and Simon during this section as a tradition of Israelite leadership serves 1 Maccabees as evidence of the strength of the Maccabean family, which through Simon will found the Hasmonean dynasty.

Precisely what the Seleucid Citadel looked like and even exactly where it stood is a matter of debate. The evidence for its appearance in 169–142 BCE is found in the *Letter of Aristeas* written possibly about 160 BCE:

> It is situated on a lofty site, fortified with a number of towers, which in their turn are built of sizable stones right up to the top, according to our information, for the protection of the area around the Temple ... There were catapults in position upon the towers of the citadel and a variety of engines; the place dominated the aforementioned precincts. (*EpArist* 100–101)

The letter goes on to describe its sentries, who were only permitted to leave at festivals, and could not under oath grant permission for access, except that Aristeas himself was admitted unarmed with one other, and the sentries could allow only five visitors at any time. The Citadel overlooked the Temple sanctuary; the height of the Citadel caused problems later and its height was reduced by Hasmoneans, although not by Simon. Simon expelled the garrison, strengthened the Temple's position alongside the Citadel and settled Jews in it. Precisely where the Citadel stood is still uncertain; it may well have been built to the south-east of the pre-Herodian Temple area but within the later Herodian precincts. It could then be cut off by a wall from the lower city (1 Macc. 12.36). These brief indications of the possible character and position of the Citadel illustrate why it was of such importance to the Seleucids and why the ejection of the Seleucid garrison was essential if Jerusalem was to regain its freedom. *The garrison of the citadel was confining the Israelites to the neighbourhood of the temple, and, by harassing tactics, giving continual support to the Gentiles* (6.18).

Judas laid siege to the Citadel. Some of the garrison escaped to link up with the pro-Gentile Israelites. Together they reported to the Seleucid king the various stages of the rebellion. King Antiochus V was still a small boy, so the actions would have been taken by Lysias. Advancing from the south through Idumaea, Lysias laid siege to Bethsura. Judas withdrew from the Citadel and at Bethzacharia faced

the royal forces. The description of the royal forces with their elephants, cavalry, gleaming equipment and shields, and their clashing
arms, paints a stirring and not improbable picture. Six hundred of the
king's men were killed and Eleazar Avaran, in true Maccabean fash-
ion, succeeded in felling an elephant carrying royal armour but was
crushed to death as it fell (6.46). But it is clear that Judas's forces were
no match for such a well-organized army, and he had to fall back to
Jerusalem. One of the problems for Judas's campaign was that this
was a Sabbatical Year (6.49). No crops had been sown or reaped in the
previous spring and summer, and so in the autumn there was no food
left in storage. Bethsura had to be abandoned, and Jerusalem was
home to refugees from gentile oppression. They *had consumed all that
remained of the provisions* (6.53). What came to Judas's rescue was
Antiochus V's co-regent, Philip. Returning to Antioch along with the
former king's army he claimed control of affairs. Lysias had to return
immediately. Under the terms of the peace settlement Judas and his
supporters were forced to leave their *stronghold* (6.61). Lysias took
over Mount Zion and, realizing the strength of the surrounding wall,
countermanded the settlement and ordered the wall's demolition
(6.62). He reached Antioch, which the royal army took by storm.

Antiochus Epiphanes became king by usurping the Seleucid throne
after the murder of Seleucus IV. Seleucus's son Demetrius was kept in
Rome as a hostage during his uncle's reign, but now Demetrius
escapes from Rome and returns with *a handful of men* to declare himself king (7.1). The army places Antiochus V and Lysias under arrest
but Demetrius wants them out of the way altogether. One of the consequences of Demetrius's chequered history was that from the beginning of his reign relations between Rome and Antioch were strained.
1 Maccabees turns to Roman affairs later in this second section.

The constitutional position of Demetrius with regard to Judaea is
illustrated by the fact that when Alcimus wishes to be high priest and
gathers support for blackening the name of Judas before the king,
Alcimus returns from Demetrius not only with one of the king's
friends Bacchides, but also as Demetrius's appointee to the high-
priesthood and with his authority to *wreak vengeance on Israel* (7.9). He
is described as an *apostate* (7.8) and leader of *all the apostates and renegades from Israel* (7.5). The opportunity for peace is there, but according to 1 Maccabees Alcimus causes havoc in Israel. As *a priest of the
family of Aaron* he is trusted by the Hasideans (7.14) but having gained
their confidence Alcimus turns against them, arrests sixty of them and
puts them *to death all on one day* (7.16; on 7.17 see Ps. 79.2-3).

Judas responds to Alcimus's damaging control over Israel by work-ing in the country areas where he could prevent Seleucid landowners from reaping any advantage from their recently acquired possessions. Alcimus has no alternative but to go back to the king for help. The king dispatches Nicanor (7.26) with a large army. Nicanor, having attempted to befriend and then to kidnap Judas, engages Judas at Capharsalama and loses five hundred men; the rest escape to Jeru-salem. Nicanor's reaction to the friendly pro-Demetrius attitude on Mount Zion causes great offence (7.34) and the priests pray for divine revenge on him. Reinforcements reach Nicanor. This time Judas's prayer before the battle recalls the fate of the Assyrian king Sennacherib (Isa. 37.36); he also reflects on the offence Nicanor caused: *Nicanor has reviled your holy place; judge him as his wickedness deserves* (7.42). After his death and the rout of his troops, not only is his head cut off but also the *right hand he had stretched out so arrogantly* (7.47). Judaea entered *a short period of peace* (7.50).

Judas is given a pro-Roman lesson in ancient history. The main theme is that to oppose the Romans is to court disaster and a brutal end. *With their friends, however,* and those who look to their protection, *they maintain firm friendship* (8.12). Romans avoided some of the trap-pings of royalty, especially through their senatorial constitution. That was to their credit. With a view to freeing themselves from slavery to the Seleucids, Judas, his brother and his people entered into a treaty of mutual protection with Rome. Again 1 Maccabees shows Israel stak-ing out its place among the nations.

Judas's death results from a heavy defeat at Alasa. He had been warned that the odds were too heavily against them, but Judas was determined, if necessary, to die bravely for his people (9.10; see the martyrs in 2 Maccabees). There was great grief (see 2 Sam. 1.19) throughout Israel (as in the case of Jonathan's death; see 13.26).

The *Jonathan* episodes are set in a time of oppression. Bacchides used the time of famine to control the whole area, established his sym-pathizers in key posts and took his revenge on Judas's followers (9.24–31). A new leadership was essential and Jonathan was chosen to take Judas's place. The position of Judas's followers was precarious, so much so that when their refuge in the wilderness was discovered by Bacchides, Jonathan entrusted his brother John and their baggage train to local Nabataeans, a people basically opposed to the Syrian government. The Jambrites, however, proved unreliable (9.36). In revenge Jonathan ambushed a Jambrite wedding; as the bridegroom with friends and kinsmen, fully armed, came to meet the bride and a *train of baggage* (9.39), Jonathan's men *leapt from their ambush, and cut them down*. Making off with all the goods they returned to their marshy retreat (9.42). Perhaps aware that, in the past, groups like the Hasideans had refused to fight on the Sabbath, Bacchides moves into position on the west bank of the Jordan. Jonathan and his followers crossed over to find Bacchides waiting for them. In the skirmish Bacchides just escapes Jonathan's sword but loses *a thousand men*. Jonathan and his men escape by swimming the river back to the relative safety of the east bank (9.43–49).

Bacchides now takes the precaution of fortifying and placing garrisons in various Judaean towns and cities, and imprisoning in the Citadel as hostages *sons of the leading men of the country* (9.50–53). Alcimus attempts to open up the sanctuary to gentile eyes by demolishing *the wall of the inner court of the temple* (9.54), but has a stroke, and dies in agony (9.55–56). With Alcimus dead Bacchides returns home, *and for two years Judaea had peace* (9.57). The opposition to Jonathan which Bacchides had fostered was by no means finished, but without Syrian help they were stymied. So once again they appealed for Bacchides' return. The strategy misfires, partly because their plans are leaked to Jonathan. There is evidence beginning to appear of divisions among the Seleucid supporters which Jonathan can exploit. Bacchides lays siege to Bethbasi. Strategically, Jonathan engages nomadic groups until he can approach Bacchides with advantage on his side (9.66–67). Simon with his group uses guerilla tactics and manages to set fire to the siege engines. In the end Bacchides loses patience with the siege and with the people who had asked his help, and decides to return home. This was the opportunity for Jonathan *to secure peace terms* (9.70); he secures also the release of some Judaean prisoners, and effectively *the war in Israel* comes *to an end* (9.73). Jonathan also governs from Michmash and starts to root out *the apostates* (9.73) – for whom the writer has obvious contempt.

Jonathan is now in a position of strength. Demetrius writes to him asking for his help against Alexander Epiphanes, the name Epiphanes betraying his possibly genuine claim to be a son of Antiochus Epiphanes and his evident pretensions to the kingdom (10.1). The price for help is *authority to raise and equip an army*, the status of an *ally*, and freedom for *the hostages* still *in the Citadel* (10.6–8). Jonathan moves from Michmash to Jerusalem. Mount Zion's fortification wall is repaired with squared stones. Alexander Epiphanes also writes to Jonathan, in his case offering him a purple robe and crown. Demetrius has no choice but to make further offers, this time to the nation. The offers now include exemptions from various *tribute* monies, levies, taxes, *tithes, tolls*, and transit fees (see also 10.38), the surrendering of *authority over the Citadel* and *the right to garrison it*, freedom without a ransom payment for *all Jewish prisoners of war*, provisions for Jewish mercenaries and more acceptable terms of service, the handing over to Jerusalem of Alexander's residence, *Ptolemais and adjoining land*, various regulatory provisions, grants and donations for the benefit of the Temple and its priests, asylum remissions, and, from the *royal revenue*, contributions to the *renovation of the temple*, the repair of the walls, their *fortifications* and other Judaean *fortresses*. But *Jonathan and the people put no faith in those proposals* (10.46; see Demetrius II's letter in 11.30–37). He favoured Alexander since the latter had made the first move. It was a wise choice and probably sensible in view of the support Alexander had from other rulers and nations. Demetrius was killed in the ensuing battle.

Alexander proposes a marriage alliance with Egypt (10.51–54) to which Ptolemy responds favourably, and Jonathan is invited to the coastal city of Ptolemais in state to meet the two kings. Jonathan is honoured, enrolled as a king's friend and appointed *a general and a provincial governor* (10.65, presumably of Judaea). Now Demetrius II appears on the scene. Following the death in battle of his father, Demetrius II takes up the rivalry between the Seleucid claimants to the kingdom. He appoints an Apollonius *governor of Coele-Syria* (the area between Tyre and Sidon and the River Orontes), who encamps at Jamnia with a force drawn from the hellenistic cities (10.69), and challenges Jonathan to a battle on the plain (10.71–73). The Jewish military capabilities have by now been considerably improved. Jonathan takes up the challenge, and that fact alone indicates the new stage which the Hasmonean dynasty has reached. Joined by his brother and reinforcements they terrify nearby Joppa, Apollonius's supply port, which submits to them (10.76). Apollonius now resorts to an ambush. He leaves a third of his cavalry in concealment and leads Jonathan into the trap. Jonathan and Simon are *surrounded* (10.80). The historian Josephus, himself a military strategist, tells us that Jonathan formed his troops into a square, then he and his troops fended off javelins from the cavalry with rows of shields until the cavalry tired (10.81; Josephus, *Antiquities* XIII.4.4 (94–97)), while Simon and his troops engaged the infantry. Simon *routed* the *enemy phalanx* (10.82), who fled to Azotus, which was burnt to the ground together with its heathen temple to the corn god, Dagon (see 11.4). It was a vitally important victory for which Alexander Epiphanes was particularly grateful. The

161

latter gave Jonathan *Accaron* (or Ekron) *and all its environs*, thus for the first time enlarging Judaea by a territorial annexation.

Ptolemy VI's mother was the daughter of the Seleucid Antiochus III and had no high opinion of Alexander's abilities – an opinion that was perhaps shared by many of Alexander's subjects. While Alexander was occupied with an uprising in Cilicia, Ptolemy began a campaign to take over Alexander's territories. It started innocently enough with a *progress from town to town* (11.3). In each place he left a garrison. The people of Azotus showed him the debris and corpses from Jonathan's vengeance on the city but Ptolemy greeted Jonathan favourably in Joppa (11.6) and Jonathan accompanied Ptolemy northwards towards Ptolemy's initial destination at *Seleucia* (the key port for Syrian Antioch). Next, Ptolemy offers Demetrius II Alexander's wife and Demetrius's father's old kingdom (11.9–11) and enters Syrian Antioch claiming *the crown of Asia*. The campaign ended with Alexander being beheaded by an *Arab chieftain* and Ptolemy's death from a battle wound. The chief beneficiary was Demetrius II. Another was Jonathan, who laid siege to the Citadel. His renegade opponents again sought the king's aid. The phrase in 11.23, *elders of Israel and priests*, could suggest that Jonathan was working with a fresh constitution involving a council. However that may be, when Demetrius II reacted sharply by moving to Ptolemais and ordering Jonathan to stop the siege and meet him at Ptolemais, Jonathan took selected *elders* and *priests* with him and a treasury of gifts, and went to see the king (11.22–24). Despite the renegades' slanders, Jonathan was well received, confirmed as high priest and in the role of king's friend, and took the opportunity to make a request (11.25–28). As if assuming responsibility for *Judaea*, and for *Apherema, Lydda and Ramathaim*, three southern districts in Samaria (see the REB footnote to 11.28), he raised the issue of exemptions from tribute for those areas, adding crucially a gift of *three hundred talents* (11.28; by way of recompense). Demetrius's response conceded the exemptions from tribute, salt-tax and crown levies, grain and fruit collections and Jerusalem tithes and revenues, confirmed *possession of the lands of Judaea* and of the three Samarian districts as belonging to Judaea under the high-priest, and made the concessions *irrevocable for all future time* (11.33–37). Jonathan is in a powerful position, but holds his position as granted by the authority of the Seleucid ruler, and the Citadel is still intact in Jerusalem.

A peaceful period was broken when Trypho (or Diodotus) took advantage of Syrian *disaffection* in the army. Demetrius II had *dis-*

banded all but the *mercenaries* from Crete, and pressed Imalcue – a son of the Arab chief who killed Alexander yet had brought up Alexander's son Antiochus – to let Antiochus take his father's place (with Trypho of course as regent: 11.38–40). Other historians fill in the details of Demetrius's difficulties, but 1 Maccabees gives most of the credit for his survival to Jonathan's experienced soldiers. Jonathan had asked for the Citadel guard to be withdrawn and Demetrius had agreed to this, providing Jonathan sent troops to Antioch to replace those who had defected (11.41–43). The citizens of Antioch took to the streets, forcing the king to take *refuge in the palace*. Demetrius summoned the Jewish forces (and other mercenaries, although 1 Maccabees has no interest in recording their role) and the Jewish soldiers are so effective that the citizens plead with Demetrius to call them off (11.41–43). The unfortunate sequel was that, once peace returned, Demetrius reneged on his promises about the Citadel and revoked some of the previous exemptions too (11.52–53). Trypho, on the other hand, had by no means finished. He returned to Antioch with Alexander's son, now crowned as Antiochus VI. The disaffected soldiers rallied to Trypho and Demetrius was defeated and fled, leaving *Trypho master of Antioch* (11.54–56). Jonathan now renewed his alliance with Antiochus VI's branch of the Seleucids. His role as *high-priest*, his *authority over the four districts* and his status as king's friend were confirmed by Antiochus. Moreover *Simon*, Jonathan's brother, was given *command* of the coastal strip (t*he Ladder of Tyre to the Egyptian frontier* formed a Syrian southern district with its own governor: 11.59). 11.60–74 is far more than a mere factual report; it shows both Jonathan and Simon operating outside of their precise territorial responsibilities. Jonathan tours the province Beyond-Euphrates (see 7.8) gathering Syrian troops. On the coastal plain Ascalon receives him *with great honour* (11.60c) and Gaza is plundered and hostages from there held in Jerusalem (11.62). Simon secures Bethsura as a garrison. Jonathan travels north to Damascus to meet Trypho and discovers that Demetrius is trying to intercept him (11.63). The record of the battle of *Hazor*, where Jonathan engaged with Demetrius's forces, is unusual (11.67–74). The result of the encounter turned on the bravery of *Mattathias son of Absalom and Judas son of Chalphi* and on Jonathan's courage in rallying his troops. The Hasmonean leadership is being presented as the divine means to conquest.

The main central section of 1 Maccabees, 9.23–11.74, has secured a wide jurisdiction for Jonathan and for Simon. Balancing the embassy to Rome in 8.1–32 and Judas's battle at Alas and grief at his death

(9.1–22), there is the further embassy to Rome and the letter to the Spartans (12.1–23), and the despicable treachery of Trypho which ends in grief at Jonathan's murder (12.24–13.30) – another neat balancing of material. The second mission to Rome by Numenius and Antipater was to confirm the friendship formed in 161 BCE (see also 14.16–19) and was apparently successful. The envoys were given letters of *safe conduct* back to Judaea (12.4). 12.2 also signals contact with Sparta (12.5–23; see also 14.16–24). Why Jonathan (and the Jewish Council or *Senate*) should have seen that as a useful strategy is unclear, and the letter seems excessively self-centred and inappropriate for the situation in 144 BCE; perhaps it was the author of 1 Maccabees who wished to impress the reader, valuing the association of the Hasmoneans with such a brave people as the Spartans, famous for their laws and their military discipline, relatively uninfluential though they were at this stage of Rome's ascendancy. Such associations in the ancient world were established and fostered by genealogical lists, and 12.21 cites a letter from Arius to Onias (presumably Arius I addressing Onias I about 300 BCE) referring to their common descent from Abraham. We know of only the most general arguments for a common Abrahamic link and no just cause for the correspondence in 300 BCE. 12.1–23 has structural and ideological functions, and these explain its presence rather than any historical basis in fact.

Jonathan's travels continue on Trypho's behalf. The stand-off at Hamath seems to have been the result of espionage from both sides, with Demetrius's troops lacking the confidence to take on Jonathan's men, who plunder yet another Arab tribe. Jonathan, returning to Jerusalem, convenes the *senate* who agree to *build fortresses* in Judaea and divide off the Citadel from the lower city markets with a wall (12.35–36). Various repair works on the city are begun and also within strategic villages.

Trypho now has his eye on the crown of Asia and, according to 1 Maccabees, recognizes Jonathan as a main hindrance. He determines to capture and kill him (12.39–40). Jonathan is no easy target and arrives with an uncomfortably large army. What Jonathan did not anticipate (although he might have done, see 5.15) was that the citizens of Ptolemais would close the gates on him and slaughter his bodyguard (12.48). Jonathan is now a prisoner. His troops retain their discipline so that Trypho cannot prevent their return to Judaea (12.49–53).

Simon assumes control in the face of gentile threats and local panic

(13.2), and presents the credentials of the Maccabees: *we have fought for the laws and the holy place . . . All my brothers have fallen . . . fighting for Israel* (13.3–4). The leadership is affirmed by the assembly in 13.9, and Jonathan, the brother of Mattathias son of Absalom (see 11.71), is sent to replace the gentile population of Joppa with a Jewish one. All this enables Judaea to respond to Trypho's military offensive. Trypho changes direction: Jonathan, he claims, owes the *royal treasury* money and for this reason has been detained; to ensure against a further rebellion Trypho demands *two of his sons as hostages* and a hundred silver talents as a ransom. Simon has no wish to be remembered as signing Jonathan's death warrant, and despite his misgiving pays the ransom. As Simon suspected, *Trypho* breaks *his word* (13.12–19). The Citadel begs Trypho for supplies, but Trypho cannot find a way to reach them; *a severe* (snow?)*storm* descends, and Trypho has to withdraw. At Bascama he murders Jonathan and buries him there (13.23). Simon continues to handle the matter circumspectly and honourably, erecting a monumental tomb to the family at Modin, which at the writer's time (104/103 BCE?) could still be seen at sea – a reminder of the Hasmonean aspiration to emulate Solomon's maritime achievements. Simon's own death will be marked rather differently (14.27–45).

13.31 reflects the writer's sympathy with the line of Alexander and contracts the events of several years into a single statement: Trypho deposed Antiochus VI in 142 BCE, acted tyrannically through the few years of his reign (see 13.34) and murdered Antiochus in 139/8. Simon has continued the work which he and Jonathan began in Jerusalem (12.35–38) and approaches Demetrius II for a remission of heavy taxes with a generous gift. The reply not only grants exemptions from the *crown-levy* and cancels previous debts but confirms the agreements regarding *strongholds*, Judaea and the three Samaria districts and encourages service in the Seleucid royal guard (13.39). More important still, 1 Maccabees implies that the document marks the beginning of the new Hasmonean era. Simon takes Gazara, preparing the way for it to serve as a strategically placed military base, with Simon's son John (Hyrcanus) as commander (and successor in waiting), and starves out the Citadel (13.49). Simon decrees an annual festival (28th May, 141 BCE) in celebration and the festivities are similar to those in 4.54.

The re-establishment of the high-priesthood
14.1–16.24

The third section of 1 Maccabees begins with the defeat and arrest of Demetrius (140 BCE). The text credits Arsakes king of Persia and Media with this crucially important sequence. The likelihood is that the victor was Mithridates, the Parthian king, in a westward movement which was to begin a new stage in the history of the Mediterranean world. For Judaea a golden age began. The writer gives an up-beat resumé of this new situation. Her borders are extended, internally she is at peace and prosperous; the Temple and the Law are honoured; prisoners are repatriated; and from the Seleucid strongholds *all pollution* is *removed* (14.4–7). Agriculture in this period of peace thrives and the social consequence is that the poor are the major beneficiaries. All this is described in a prophetic style (14.8–13; see Mic. 4.4–8). Simon's accession is treated as an international event, with a renewal of the friendship treaty with Sparta and a confirmation of the alliance with Rome (14.16–24). The whole truth was undoubtedly somewhat different (15.10, 25; 16.13–22), but the message from 1 Maccabees could not be clearer: the Hasmonean era has begun, and despite reservations about the future behaviour of the leadership, the era of freedom is welcomed.

The inscription in 14.24–49 is recorded on *bronze tablets* and *placed on a monument on Mount Zion* (14.27). As a text it reads unevenly, not altogether in the regular pattern of such decrees. Some parts may well be an accurate citation (major sections of 14.35–40, for example). Other parts are sufficiently close to the author's narrative and sufficiently out of place in the sequence of the inscription to be his work of editing (see 14.30). It is primarily a decree to honour Simon, and to set on record his constitutional position: as *leader and high-priest in perpetuity until a true prophet should appear . . . their general . . . to have full charge of the temple* and *of the work of reconstruction* with *supervision of the country*, of arms and fortifications (14.41–42; later in 14.47 he is called *ethnarch of the Jews and the priests*; is this parallel to ben Sirach 50.1, 13?); he is *to be obeyed*; all documents are *to be drawn up in his name*; he is *entitled to wear the purple robe and gold clasp*. The context of the inscription deserves three further comments: Simon is not proclaimed king, as some later successors will claim to be; his sons are to hold copies of the document, so the dynastic element is present; the decree is proposed by the Jews and their priests (14.41), not by the council or senate who carried the resolution, which is an indication of the importance of the high-priestly role within Simon's position. As Josephus the historian would indicate later, Second Temple Judaism remains essentially a matter of high-priest, Law and Temple.

Antiochus VII, the son of Demetrius I and brother to Demetrius II, enlists Simon's support against Trypho (15.1), affirming the remissions previously given, authorizing the minting of *coinage*, confirming the freedom of the Temple and of Jerusalem, the occupation of *fortresses*, the cancelling of *debts* to the royal treasury and *future liabilities*, and promising to *confer honours on you and on your nation and temple* (15.2–9). Antiochus pursues Trypho to Dor and raises a blockade, encircling Trypho there (15.10–14). As previously in 1 Maccabees (see chs 8 and 12), a passage dealing with a letter interrupts the narrative. This time it is a circular letter from Rome dealing with extradition, in its format as delivered to Egypt, naming all the addressees in order to indicate the extent of Roman influence (15.16–21). When the siege of Dor is resumed (15.25), Simon's offer of assistance is spurned and the agreements made with him by Antiochus *repudiated* (15.26–27). Athenobius is commissioned to inform Simon that he has occupied Joppa, Gazara and the Citadel (referred to as cities) and has assumed control of or authority over various part of Antiochus's kingdom *beyond the frontiers of Judaea*; he is to return the cities and the tribute exacted from those outside Judaea to Antiochus, or pay a massive fine or, in the last resort, face war (15.28–31). This amounts primarily to a strategy to secure money and resources for Antiochus to ward off the Parthians, since if Simon so wished he could pay for the privilege of holding on to cities outside Judaea. More significantly it is also a claim to sovereignty over a vassal. When Athenobius reaches Jerusalem, he is staggered by the *magnificence of Simon's establishment*. Simon denies all the charges, arguing that *we have taken only our ancestral heritage, unjustly seized for a time by our enemies* (15.33), an important approach which replaces the case for possession by conquest with the case for possession by inheritance. Not surprisingly, Athenobius's report infuriates the king. The king then decides to concentrate his attention on Trypho, who has escaped, and to send his commander-in-chief Kendebaeus to replace Simon in charge of the coastal zone and take control of the area to the west of Jerusalem, where John was stationed. Simon is by now too old to withstand a military campaign so he commits the safety of Judaea to his eldest sons, *Judas* and *John* (16.1–3). Using the ancestral centre of Modin the two sons gather their forces, including now a cavalry element, and move beyond Gazara to the Kedron valley. John's bravery is highlighted by his courage in leading the troops across the valley, where they defeat Kendebaeus and, despite wounds to Judas, hunt down the fugitives to Kedron, which Kendebaeus had rebuilt (16.4–10; see 15.41).

Simon's death is the result of treachery. *Ptolemaeus,* a *son-in-law* to the *high priest,* and an *over-ambitious commander for the plain of Jericho,* perhaps with the connivance of Antiochus (see 16.18), invited Simon and his two sons Mattathias and Judas to a *small fort called Dok,* where concealed men waited for the visitors to be drunk and then murdered them. Ptolemy requested the king to give him *authority over the country and its towns* (16.19) and planned to murder John (Hyrcanus) in Gazara. However, the report of the murders and the information of the plot were brought to John, who *arrested and put to death* the men sent to kill him (16.22).

There is no further tribute to Simon, and the record of John Hyrcanus's high-priesthood is left to the annals, without any reference to the length of his time as Simon's successor and without mention of any of his successors. One inference from that could be that 1 Maccabees was written towards the end of John Hyrcanus's regime, about 104 BCE. The stage was set for the Hasmoneans to behave as hellenistic kings.

The Second Book of the Maccabees

It is significant that one of the most memorable results of the writing of 2 Maccabees is to be found in the Vatican Museum. No one who has visited the Raphael rooms there will ever forget the fresco commissioned by Pope Julius II in 1508 and painted by Raphael between 1512 and 1514 which gives its name to one of the rooms: 'The Expulsion of Heliodorus'. It captures the moment when the Syrian chief minister Heliodorus has entered the Temple treasury in Jerusalem: *there appeared to them a horse, splendidly caparisoned, with a rider of terrifying aspect who was clad all in golden armour; it rushed fiercely at Heliodorus and, rearing up, attacked him with its hooves* (3.25). Raphael is at his most expressive and electrifying, and captures the drama and fearsomeness of the moment: what the writer calls a divine 'epiphany' (see 2.20–21, 3.24, 14.15, and probably 15.27. The REB uses various translations for the term, such as 'apparitions', 'manifest', 'divine care'; but the author's repetition of the term 'epiphany' and the association of the word with miraculous divine intervention probably merits attention; our use of the translation 'epiphany' in each case will suggest this).

It is significant that Raphael's work should have captured the drama of the moment because that passage is, typically for the writer of 2 Maccabees, virtually a parable for the whole book. The book is about the danger of interfering with the Temple when its patron deity is too powerful for words. Some of the finest preachers have a gift for an initial evocative parable to capture the intent of the whole sermon and the imagination and interest of the hearer. In terms of his method of presentation, the writer of 2 Maccabees, so different from the measured, organized discernment of 1 Maccabees, has precisely that gift. Like Raphael's fresco, the image burns itself into the memory, leaving a kind of after-image that remains with the reader throughout the reading of the entire book. The writer of 2 Maccabees is also a narrator to match his method. He is, as has been argued at length and with stimulating examples, a writer of 'history with feeling'. The psychological make-up and inner reflections of some of the key characters such as Antiochus Epiphanes attract the readers' attention in such a way as to make the character live. That does not of course mean that the history which the author writes is closer to the facts. It probably means that it is closer to fiction. But fiction has the capacity to engage and stimulate the reader's reflective attention, and so influence the whole person through the enterprise of reading.

The shape of 2 Maccabees is not therefore the cleverly built presentation of Hasmonean development which is to be found in 1 Maccabees. It opens intriguingly with two letters. The first is a letter of 'invitation', dated 124 BCE, from the Jews in Jerusalem addressed to the Jews in Egypt, inviting them to a joint celebration of the new feast of Tabernacles which is also a feast of the purification of the Temple. Contained in it is a reminder of a previous invitation given in 143 BCE with a similar message. The second letter (this time from Judas Maccabaeus, his 'senate' and people, to Aristobulus and the Jews in Egypt) is also an invitation to a joint celebration of the same feast, indicating that it is to celebrate God's rescuing of his people *from great evils*, and the purifying of the Temple. Obviously the writer will have to spell out later what those great evils were (see 4.7–9.28; 10.10–13.26; 14.1–15.35, with 4.7ff. and 14.1ff. having a common pattern), how the Temple came to need purification, and indeed (see 10.1–8) how the festival purification took place.

After the two letters comes what is virtually an overture (3.1–4.6), opening with the Heliodorus story, and returning at the end of the book with the death of Nicanor (15.28–37), proclaiming the greatness of the one who is patron of the Temple and noting a festival celebrating the death of Nicanor which happily fell alongside Mordecai's day (see the commentary on Esther).

Punctuating these historical narratives are a series of generalizing comments (4.17: *To act profanely against God's laws is no light matter, as will in due course become clear;* 5.19: *the Lord did not choose the nation for the sake of the sanctuary; he chose the sanctuary for the sake of the nation;* 6.31: *by his* (Eleazar's) *death he left a noble example and a memorial of virtue, not only to the young but also to the great mass of his countrymen;* 7.42: this concludes the grotesque happenings and *our account of . . . monstrous tortures*). These four comments act as a focus for the narrative sections. That is particularly true of 5.17–20, 6.31 and 7.42. These bring together the reason for the sanctuary being abandoned (it *had its part in the misfortunes that befell the nation,* 5.20a; and the rivalries of the élite and the duplicity of its high-priests were part of those misfortunes, 3.1–5; 4.23–29; 14.3–36), and the reason why it was *restored again* in all its splendour (since *the great Master was reconciled with his people* through the loyalty, prayers and self-sacrifice of the martyrs: 5.20c; 6.19, 28; 7.2–41; 8.27–30; 14.37–46, and the recognition of the people's dependence on divine help: 13.13–17; 14.35–36).

This outline should not give the impression that the organization of the book is without its muddles and contradictions. A clear case of this is that the second of the opening letters gives a different picture of Antiochus's death from that in 2 Macc. 9. Also various narratives fall out of the schemes which are announced early on. But the writer is fully aware of the infelicities. His epilogue comments: *If it is found to be well written and aptly composed, that is what I myself aimed at; if superficial and mediocre, it was the best I could do*. As mixing wine and water produces a delightful taste, *so too variety of style in a literary work charms the ear of the reader* (15.38–39). This corresponds to the ending of the overture (2.19–32), for there he explains that he is summarizing five books of Jason with their *mass of statistics* (almost certainly an incorrect translation; 'the massive number of lines' would be better) and the *sheer bulk of material*. To his credit he aims at *entertainment for those who peruse for pleasure, aid for students* who have to struggle with memorizing, and assistance for casual readers – a costly and time-consuming task like that of preparing a banquet. His aim is to provide an *abridgement* (an epitome) whose headlines take precedence over detail, like a painter concerned with highlighting important features rather than an architect planning the whole structure. *Here then . . . I begin my narrative, for it would be absurd to give a lengthy introduction to the history* while abridging the history itself. The author, it would appear, thus has available to him the work of a Greek-speaking Jew, Jason of Cyrene; but a Judaean base for the author himself, certainly in the light of the material which follows, cannot entirely be ruled out.

Chapters 1–2

The first letter (1.2–10) from Jerusalem to Egypt (no more exact definition is possible) begins as 1 Esdras does with a festival reference which sanctifies the restoration of the Temple. It has five prayers or blessings, each of which has God as the subject of the action: *may he keep in mind the covenant . . . may he give . . . hearts to worship him . . . may he make your minds open to his law . . . may he bring you peace . . . may he be reconciled to you* (an idea repeated in the context of the martyrs and the divinely given victory over Nicanor (7.33; 8.29), suggesting a close

171

link between this letter and the highlights of the book). The second letter is probably not authentic, even if, as seems likely, the author of the book did not compose it (1.10–2.18; see the discrepancies with ch. 9). It celebrates the divine order which is the concern of the whole book. God authorizes the cult, as the death of Antiochus in God's purpose shows (1.17). This sanctioning of the cult continued as the fire hidden at the time of the exile, transmuted to nephthar (1.19, 36; 2.1), was used by Nehemiah after the exile so that the sun could rekindle the altar fire for sacrifice. Accompanying the sacrifice would be prayers for God to liberate his people from oppressors and gather together the Diaspora (1.18–29). Nephthar is interpreted as 'purification', one of the themes of 2 Maccabees (see 2.16–18; 10.3–7). The divine sanctioning included Jeremiah, Moses, Solomon, and the records of these, claims the author, had been gathered by Judas Maccabaeus. These records and the narratives which constitute the bulk of the book create a link between the rescue of the Temple and celebratory narratives such as were common in the hellenistic period as 'salvation feasts'. The letters of invitation belong to the same hellenistic pattern. It was God's clemency and favour which Jason of Cyrene set out in his five books: the epiphanies (REB 'apparitions'), the martyrs, the victors, the recovery of the *world-renowned temple*, the liberation of *the city of Jerusalem,* and the reaffirmation of *the laws* (2.19–22). The author's famous description of his abridgement follows (2.23–32).

Chapter 3

In 2 Maccabees the story of God's defence of his Temple begins in the time of Seleucus IV (and so at an earlier point than 1 Maccabees). Seleucus's father, Antiochus III (see the commentary on ben Sirach), had favoured a federal constitution for the Seleucid kingdom, and had been engaged in negotiations with the young Ptolemy V to secure from Ptolemy the control of Coele-Syria (for the importance of this area see the commentary on 1 Maccabees). His plans were challenged and finally shattered by the growing power of Rome and his defeat by Rome at Magnesia in 190 BCE. The Treaty of Apamea which followed that defeat (188 BCE) only succeeded in triggering further unrest concerning Coele-Syria, and piling war reparations payable to Rome on all Seleucid subjects, including the populace of Judaea. When Antiochus III died attempting to plunder a temple of Bel, Seleucus IV initiated less aggressive policies and Jerusalem enjoyed *unbroken peace and prosperity*. Seleucus even paid for the Temple sacrifices *from his own revenues* (v. 3), more generous even than Antiochus III. But the Seleucid financial crisis caused by the Treaty of Apamea was acute; hence Heliodorus's attempt to take money from the Jerusalem Temple. It may be that the event which disrupted the peace was part of a power struggle between influential families. Simon was the brother of Menelaus, a future high-priest of some notoriety (4.3,24) and would no doubt have found any number of issues regarding what could and could not be sold in the city market, or who had authority to supervise, to constitute grounds for an argument with the high priest Onias III. He alleges before the Seleucid governor Apollonius that treasures had been lodged in the Jerusalem treasury not related to the Temple sacrifices. Apollonius passes the question to the Seleucus, who, much in need of extra finance, sends *Heliodorus, his chief minister*, to investigate. The high-priest argues that the deposits are *held in trust for widows and orphans*, apart from those of an otherwise unknown Hyrcanus. These relied on the *sanctity, dignity* and *inviolability* of a temple (v. 12). Insisting that these deposits be confiscated for the royal treasury, Heliodorus, a gentile, enters the inner court of the Temple with his bodyguard. This entry, and the well-founded fear of what else might be taken from the Temple, causes a scene of high drama, confusion, deep apprehension, and *solemn entreaty to Heaven* (vv. 16–21). As we have already seen, *the Ruler of spirits and of all power* sends a mighty epiphany, and Heliodorus is attacked by the terrifying *horse* and *rider* and beaten by *two young men* of strength and beauty. He is carried out on a stretcher, though not quite dead, since he was *compelled*, like his bodyguard and the onlookers, *to acknowledge the sovereignty of God* (v. 28; see Wisd. 18.18). The Temple meanwhile is filled with *joy and gladness* at the epiphany of the Pantocrator (*the Lord Almighty*). Onias III, fearful that the king might suspect *foul play* (v. 32), offers a sacrifice for the dying Heliodorus, who revives and, *as the expiation* is *being made*, is visited by the same two men who had beaten him, giving him this assurance: for Onias's sake God has spared you. *You have been scourged by God . . . proclaim his mighty power to all*. He offers a sacrifice and a free-will offering (vv. 31–36). On his return the king asks whom he might send on any other occasion to Jerusalem, and Heliodorus quips: send an enemy and he'll return, if he does return, soundly beaten. *A divine power* surrounds and watches over *the place* (vv. 37–39). A powerful opening narrative.

Chapter 4

4.1–6 records Simon's response, which was to lay the blame for events at Onias's door and to deepen rivalries to the point where murder was committed. Onias was obliged to bring Simon's case before the king, since otherwise he could see that Simon would never rest from his folly. Thus the passage transfers us to the reign of Antiochus IV. Here comparisons can be made between 1 Maccabees and 2 Maccabees, since from this point they are covering the same area of time.

2 Maccabees 4.1–10.8 and 14.1–15.36 have basically the same sequence.

1. Betrayal of Judaism by leading Jews (4.7–5.10; 14.1–10).
2. An attack on the Temple, city and people by the king or his general (5.11–6.11; 14.11–36).
3. Loyalty to God by martyrs (6.18–7.42; 14.37–46).
4. Deliverance under the guidance of Judas Maccabaeus with divine help (8.1–36; 15.1–27).
5. Vengeance on their enemies (9.1–18; 15.28–35,37).
6. The feast to commemorate the deliverance, and thanksgiving to God (10.5–8; 15.36).

With 4.7–10 the betrayal begins. Seleucus IV had been murdered in September 175 BCE and Antiochus Epiphanes succeeded to the throne almost immediately; Onias III was deposed and his brother Jason *procured the office of high-priest* at a cost and offered extra if he could establish *a gymnasium* and set up in Jerusalem those *to be known as* 'Antiochenes'. Jason forces *the Greek way of life* on his fellow-Jews. 1 Macc. 1.14–15 is similar, but there are differences which point to the varying emphases of the two books. 1 Maccabees mentions circumcision, the covenant and marriage; 2 Maccabees mentions the gymnasium built at the foot of the Citadel and (loosely translated by the REB) an *ephebeion* (an exclusive male finishing school for future aristocrats). The precise extent of the changes which Jason made is not entirely clear. It may be that the major overall change was to style Jerusalem a Greek polis called Antioch-in-Jerusalem, with its citizens called therefore Antiochenes (and of course the ordinary inhabitants automatically so called, too). What 2 Maccabees implies is that the changes were such as to denigrate the Temple worship in favour of work towards *hellenic honours* and to devalue the traditions of Jewish ancestors in favour of those who would turn out to be *vindictive enemies* (vv. 14–16); his comment (v. 17) is that *to act profanely against God's laws is*, as will be seen, *no light matter*. Two examples of Jason's policies are given: he sent representatives from Jerusalem to the quinquennial games in Tyre with money for a sacrifice in honour of the god Hercules. The bearers used the money instead for the fitting out of triremes; and when it appeared that the new Egyptian Ptolemy, now come of age and enthroned, was *hostile* to the Seleucids, for the sake of security Antiochus visited his southern borders, including Joppa and then Jerusalem, where Jason welcomed him with lavish hospitality (vv. 18–22).

Jason in turn was outbid for the office of high-priest by Menelaus, Simon's brother. Menelaus is described as having *the passions of a cruel tyrant and the temper of a savage beast* (v. 25). Menelaus seems not to have paid the king the bribes he had promised, even though Sostratus, the Seleucid commander of the Citadel with responsibilities for collecting revenues, continually demanded them. The king summons them both and both leave deputies behind them (vv. 23–29). Antiochus himself is called away to deal with a revolt caused by his concubine, and he too leaves a deputy, Andronicus – probably the Andronicus who murdered Seleucus IV's son. Menelaus has *appropriated gold plate from the temple* (see the Heliodorus episode and 3.12), selling some of it and using some to bribe Andronicus. Onias III goes to a haven of safety and denounces Menelaus, but Andronicus lures him out of the sanctuary and murders him (vv. 30–34) – a crime, deplored and *detested* by Jews and gentiles alike, for which Andronicus pays with his life on the very spot where the outrage was committed – *repaid by the Lord* once Antiochus returns and learns of it. Antiochus in 1 Maccabees is a villain from the beginning. In 2 Maccabees he makes a reasonable start. He is *deeply grieved . . . moved to pity and tears as he thought of the high character and disciplined conduct of* Onias (vv. 35–38).

Menelaus's plunder and sacrilege continue, drawing in Lysimachus, commander of the Cypriot mercenaries, who, alarmed by the furious reaction of the crowds, has to engage Auranus and an army to deal with them. Lysimachus's hand is recognized in their treatment, and some of the crowd pelt him and his men with anything available, wounding some and killing others, including Lysimachus himself (vv. 39–42), on a spot near the treasury. In Tyre the three-man Jewish senate argue before the king the involvement of Menelaus in all this, but Ptolemaeus is bribed by Menelaus to turn the king's judgement against the three. The three are condemned to death for their temerity, to the disgust of even the Tyrians. Antiochus is beginning to lose credit! Menelaus, *thanks to the cupidity of those in power*, goes *from bad to worse* (vv. 43–50). The stage of attacks on temple and city (Stage 2) is well on the way and reaches its climax in Antiochus's own attack.

Chapter 5

5.1 is one of four particular cases where 1 Maccabees and 2 Maccabees differ on the order of the events they describe (The four are: Antiochus's two Egyptian campaigns; the Maccabees' flight to the hills; Lysias's first campaign; and Antiochus IV's death and the dedication of the Temple). 2 Maccabees seems to have coalesced the two Egyptian campaigns into a single occasion, following which Antiochus raids the Temple and makes off with 800 talents. He is now audacious, proud, murderous, savage, barbarous and villainous.

5.2–4 concerns a divine epiphany. Prodigies take many forms; here for forty days the *apparitions* seem to be of powerful armies involved in warfare. Perhaps the text means that everyone took the portents or epiphany favourably, albeit of course favourably according to the side you favoured. Jason makes the mistake of acting on rumour (vv. 5–10). False news of Antiochus's death on the Egyptian campaign leads him to attack Jerusalem. Menelaus takes refuge in the Citadel and Jason embarks on a massacre of his fellow-citizens (2 Maccabees' common-sense judgement is given in v. 6). All Jason reaps is dishonour and death: *he, who had driven so many into exile, himself died an exile. He who had cast out so many to lie unburied was himself unmourned; he had no obsequies . . . no resting-place* in an *ancestral grave* (vv. 9–10). This is a pattern of comment we shall encounter several times in 2 Maccabees.

Antiochus disengages himself from Egypt and returns, 'his inner self driven like that of a wild beast' (vv. 11–12). Jerusalem suffers yet another massacre; and, guided by Menelaus (*traitor to religion and country*, and so different from Onias), Antiochus enters the Temple (see again Heliodorus) and sweeps up the treasures given by other kings. But, unlike Heliodorus, Antiochus does not experience an epiphany. He would have done, *had they* (the people) *not been guilty of many sinful acts* (v. 18). The sanctuary is caught up in the nation's history; it was *abandoned when the Almighty was roused to anger* (v. 20) and restored *when the great Master was reconciled with his people*. Antiochus (see Isa. 10.5) is for the time being an instrument of divine judgement; he sees himself, like Xerxes, as able to bridge the Hellespont and cut a canal through Mt Athos. His subsequent action, the disposition of commissioners, makes good sense; but the sending of Apollonius (explained in 1 Maccabees) lacks any explanation here. There is simply the sabbath day massacre. But – the one ray of hope – Judas Maccabaeus escapes with nine companions into the desert, abiding by the law and eating only vegetation.

Chapter 6

The hellenization of Jerusalem and Mt Gerizim is now put into the hands of an elderly Athenian, and the desecration of the Temple, the altar and the festivals amounts to the suppression of Judaism. The horrific pictures of Jews being forced to eat entrails and women who had circumcised their sons being hurled from the ramparts leads the author to beg his readers *not to be disheartened by those tragic events* (see 7.42). Whereas the Lord withholds his hand from the judgement of other nations till the extent of their sins has been reached, with Israel in his mercy he inflicts retribution earlier, *to discipline* them *by disaster* (vv. 1–17; see the discussion in Wisd. 16).

2 Maccabees now turns to the next stage (Stage 3), where absolute loyalty is shown to God. Eleazar is force-fed with pork but spits it out. The officials, from long acquaintance with him, urge him to bring some meat he could eat, so that *he need only pretend to comply with the king's order to eat the sacrificial meat* (v. 21). Eleazar refuses on the grounds that young people might see his action and interpret it as apostasy. He could not be untrue to himself and *stain* his *old age with dishonour*, and *alive or dead* he could not escape the Almighty's hand (vv. 18–27). So he submits himself to torture by officials now become hostile, and with his dying breath acclaims the Almighty as all-knowing, who knows *that in my soul I suffer gladly, because I stand in awe of him* (vv. 28–31). Eleazar's virtue is affirmed, as indeed the four cardinal virtues will be affirmed by the martyrs, and the explanation which Eleazar gives for his actions is an honourable one (REB translates v. 23 as *made an honourable decision*, whereas a Greek reader, well aware of the parallel with those like Socrates who preferred death to a dishonourable life and who could argue their case, would surely understand the phrase to mean 'took up a noble line of reasoning'). That is true also in 2 Macc. 7, where the mother of the seven brothers and the seventh brother give well-founded reasons for what they do. It is not inappropriate for these martyrs to be called Jewish philosophers. It is by means of the martyrs (and as we shall see, by means of

the heroic figures in the Jewish story) that the laws and customs of the Jewish people can be restored and the power of the tyrant broken. They play their part in the restoration of the ideal state and polity of the Jewish people. They are turning points in the history of which they are a part and they initiate the crucial stage in the rescue of the Jews.

Chapter 7

This deeply moving story of the seven brothers and their mother has a number of parallels in Jewish literature (see the *Assumption of Moses*, ch. 9), and especially in the parallel document 4 Maccabees which bears some kind of relationship to 2 Maccabees. Particularly through 4 Maccabees the history of the Jewish martyrs became an important subject in Jewish and Christian writing and worship (see Hebrews 11.35–38 and the Martyr Festivals in Antioch), and in later times in art, music and drama also. In Daniel 7, and in the Additions to Daniel, martyrs are recognized as suffering for the people, as representatives of the nation who because of their faith and fortitude enable their countrymen to be delivered. That the martyrs in 4 Maccabees could be said to give their lives for many provides a parallel for the gospel testimony to Jesus' mission as expressed in Mark 10.45.

Verse 2 establishes in the presence of the king that the brothers are prepared to die *rather than break our ancestral laws*. The hideous nature of the torture and death of the sons is matched by the encouragement which the mother and her sons give to one another: *The Lord God is looking on, and we may be sure he has compassion on us* (v. 6). The second son makes explicit the martyr hope: *the King of the universe will raise us up to a life everlasting made new* (v. 9). The third son relates this to the physical feature of his tongue and his hands, which he will *receive again* (v. 10). The fourth denies that the king can know any *resurrection* (v. 13). The fifth promises that God's *mighty power* will *torment* the king and his descendants. The sixth recognizes that *we have ... brought these appalling events on ourselves*, and there will be no escape for the king from the *consequences* of his actions (v. 19). The mother, having watched her sons suffer, with *manly spirit* makes the point that since the Creator formed humanity, *devised the origin of all* (and therefore her sons in her womb), he can give them back life and breath, because they set the law above their concern for self (v. 23). The seventh son is offered rewards by the king if he recants, and the mother agrees to advise him; her advice is to have no fear of this *butcher*, and she confidently expects, by God's mercy, to *receive back* after their death all seven of *them together* (7.29). The seventh then accuses the king of having devised *all manner of atrocities for the Hebrews* and warns of God's judgement. He repeats the explanation that the king is God's way of disciplining the Jews for a brief time, whereas the king, an *impious creature, most villainous of the human race,* cannot escape the penalty of touching *Heaven's servants*. He and his brothers have, *under God's covenant, drunk of the waters of everlasting life*. His final prayer is: *May the Almighty's anger, which has justly fallen on all our race, end with me and my brothers!* (v. 38). The son dies, as later, without further comment, his mother does. The context of this chapter is that of an expanding interest in life following death to be found especially in the LXX. It is the arena in which God can deal with the injustices not rectified in this life (Ps. 72.23–26 LXX, as distinct from the REB translation of the Hebrew of Ps. 73; Job 19.26 LXX); there he can renew the life of God's people and punish their enemies (Isa. 26.19 LXX; Odes 1) and reward the faithful (Dan. 12.3 LXX). What is characteristic of 2 Macc. 7 is the theme of martyr death, which can be followed by revivification and physical restoration of the individual, a belief supported by the mother's reasoning that God's ability to organize the physical elements and breathe life into them (see Ps. 139.13) can reform those same elements in an identical way after death.

Chapter 8

The heroic warriors share the willingness of the martyrs to lay down their lives (v. 21). They share with the martyrs the virtue of noble courage (v. 16), the hope of life beyond death (see 12.43–45), and the prayer that their sacrifice will turn the divine anger from Israel. Judas gathers his troop of heroic warriors for battle. The troops include those who remain faithful to Judaism (as noted earlier the precise meaning of 'Judaism' is unclear but is wider than the REB's *Jewish religion*, 8.1). They plead for divine mercy (v. 2), adding a prayer that God will hear *the blood* of the massacred infants that cries to him *for vengeance* (v. 3). God's *hatred of wickedness* needs to be seen (v. 4). The story begins to move to Stage 4, and God's *mercy* now begins to be evident (v. 27) in the invincibility of Judas's *partisans* (vv. 5–7) and in *his heroism*. Part of the task is to defeat the enemy because of the *outrages* committed by the Gentiles against the *Temple*, against *Jerusalem* and the suppression of *Jewish institutions* (v. 17). It is to be God's hand of vengeance punishing *godless* individuals (vv. 32–33) and humiliating those who humiliated Israel; and part of the task is also the full *reconciliation* between God and his servants (v. 29). Interestingly, there is also an emphasis here on the charitable use of the war *spoils* (vv. 28, 30). To characterize Stage 4 in this way requires the author to choose a different order of events from those in 1 Maccabees. Hence Nicanor's defeat occurs here in 2 Macc. 8 (the conclusion of which in v. 36, in recollecting his sale of Jews as slaves, uses the same style of statements and antithesis found in 5.10 and 9.8). The defeat leads into Stage 5 with the death of Antiochus in 1 Macc. 9, and so into Stage 6 with the celebration of the cleansing of the Temple (2 Macc. 10).

Chapter 9

Antiochus suffers one reverse after another. The author hints at Daniel 11.44–45, so that the reader begins to anticipate the end of the Seleucid monarch. The description of his seizure (v. 5) is coloured by the recollection of how many victims he has disembowelled (see 7.42). But Antiochus's initial, characteristic response is described as a lordly superiority and an overweening arrogance (v. 7) that drives him relentlessly forward to his doom: *But riding with him was the divine judgement!* (v. 4c). His speed causes a fall from the chariot: the fall is coloured by pictures of his stupid pretensions to being superhuman (Job 38 mocks such royal pretensions) and like Heliodorus he is stretchered off. God's power is now evident. 8.9 offers an opportunity for secular parallels from the Greek historian Herodotus and prophetic passages such as Zech. 14.12 to build up the horrific picture of an impious human being rotting away. Antiochus's attitude begins to shift (v. 11); he sees things in a new light and, unable to bear the stench of his own body, acknowledges the wretched folly of claiming *equality with* God. He is now a polluted being (v. 13) and vows to declare Jerusalem free. Verses 14–17 highlight this with two extensive contrasts between what he had done to Jews and the Temple and the lavish future he plans for them. He will even become a Jew! There is no abatement of his pain. Despair sets in (v. 19), but what he writes hangs on a hope of recovery. He can still fan the embers of royal dignity (v. 22). He even concludes with the hope that his successor *will accommodate himself to* Jewish *wishes* (v. 27). But he remains *the murderer and blasphemer* and dies a tormented death such as he inflicted on others, and his death leads to the question of his son's future as king

(vv. 28–29). It is an extraordinary passage which cannot be reduced to simple moralistic comments. The issues it raises are in the form of a narrative of agony and horror.

Chapter 10

Stage 6 has been reached and the Temple can be *purified* (see 2 Macc. 2.19), the *altar* dedicated and the *incense, the lamps, and the Bread of the Presence* restored (v. 3). The climax of the first part of 2 Maccabees is the institution of an annual festival and it is balanced by the climax of the second part in 15.36. In 2 Macc. 10 the eight-day festival with sacrifices and music is celebrated *like the feast of Tabernacles* (1.6a) and with *garlanded wands and flowering branches*, perhaps as a reversal of pagan rites which were a feature of the Temple's desecration (v. 7). The festival, however, includes the prayer that such disaster should never happen again, or, if Israel were ever to sin, that God would discipline them himself rather than by the hand of gentiles (v. 4).

Lysias's activity has now been transferred by 2 Maccabees into the reign of Antiochus IV's successor. The accession of *Antiochus Eupator* forces Ptolemaeus, as one who had treated the Jews with justice, to commit suicide, and Gorgias and Timotheus initiate once more Seleucid attacks on the Jews (see 1 Macc. 5.3–5). Judas Maccabaeus' reliability is a theme of this section of 2 Maccabees (see v. 21), which is set out as narratives of his success (v. 23). In the rout of Timotheus an epiphany of five horsemen confronts the enemy, giving protection to Judas Maccabaeus and causing mayhem among Timotheus's troops. The wicked, blasphemous taunts of the remainder of Timotheus's troops who had fled to the Gazara stronghold incite twenty of Judas's followers to storm the wall, allowing their colleagues to burn the towers, occupy the city and kill Timotheus and his brother.

Chapter 11

Following Gorgias and Timotheus, Lysias too finds the Hebrews invincible. Again an epiphany, a horseman *arrayed in white and brandishing golden weapons*, leads the Jewish army, and Lysias escapes with his life (vv. 1–13). He therefore decides to make a settlement with the Jews, and Judas Maccabaeus even states the terms. Four letters concerning the negotiations follow, three of which, like Lysias's campaign belong to Antiochus IV's time. Verses 16–21 are Lysias's letter informing the Jewish community that Antiochus IV has accepted their terms. The date is between October 165 BCE and February 164; the month has an unknown name in the Greek text (11.21); presumably the month stated in the REB, *Dioscorus*, is an adaptation of the unknown name in the Greek text to make it similar to a known Cretan name. Verses 22–26 are the king's response to Lysias. *Now . . . our royal father has joined the company of the gods* implies that the sequence of letters represents Antiochus Eupator's concession (in fact, his acceptance of the *fait accompli*) of the restoration of the Temple and, furthermore, the self-regulation of the people according to their *ancestral customs*. Verses 27–33 are then the letter from the king to the Jewish senate, which includes a very tight timetable between the sending of the letter and the declaration of the amnesty. As for Menelaus, he has not hitherto played the role of a mediator and would hardly have been any reassurance to the people. The fourth letter, verses 34–38, is from Roman envoys, otherwise probably unknown to the Jewish people, and relates in date and contents to the first letter. It is therefore the earliest known contact between Rome and the Jews, deliberately referring to them as a *people*, to the discomfort of the Seleucids since the term implied an unwelcome semi-independence.

Chapter 12

The opening verses of the chapter tidy up the negotiations between Lysias and Judas Maccabaeus, and note that the Jewish agricultural work, central to their economy, was disrupted by some governors. The Joppa incident (vv. 3–12) shows Judas Maccabaeus as the divine arm of judgement on those who murder God's people despite the latter's peaceful intent. Outside Jamnia, after the attack on him by Arabs, we see his common sense in making peace and useful alliances even with those who had initially fought against him (vv. 10–12). 12.13–16 resembles 10.34–36: blasphemous provocation is a motivation for onslaughts by Judas's men. The campaign in Gilead moves to Charax in the Tubian area. Two Jewish generals, Dositheus and Sosipater, destroy the garrison there while Judas pursues Timotheus. Again aided by a divine epiphany of *the all-seeing One* Judas destroys many thousands of Timotheus's troops. Dositheus and Sosipater, when they finally take Timotheus, allow him to leave out of concern for Timotheus's Jewish hostages, whom Timotheus promises to set free unharmed (vv. 17–25). Still in Gilead, Judas moves victoriously via Carnaim to Ephron and Scythopolis and from thence to Jerusalem to celebrate Pentecost there (vv. 26–31).

The battle which follows Pentecost provides one of the most discussed events in 2 Maccabees. Gorgias is almost taken prisoner, but Dositheus loses an arm in the attempt. Gorgias's army is *put to flight*, so Judas and his force purify themselves (see Num. 31.13–30) in Adullam, keeping the sabbath there. When they gather the Jewish dead next day they discover that each of the dead had been wearing an amulet *sacred to the idols of Jamnia* (12.40, perhaps taken as spoil from the battlefield). God is praised as the one who sees and reveals what we hide (v. 41). The troops also turn to prayer, considering that the sin that had occurred had been fully *blotted out* (that is, by the self-offering of those who had died on behalf of God's cause). Judas points to the moral of the situation and levies a contribution for a sin-offering (that is, to make expiation for inadvertent sins on the assumption that those who died were part of, and remained a part of, God's people). Verse 44 indicates Judas's belief that the fallen rise again and therefore prayer for the dead is by no means superfluous. Since he also believes in a *splendid reward reserved for those who die a godly death*, what he conceived was holy and pious. That is why he offered a purificatory offering for those who were dead, so that they might be released from (an unwitting?) sin. The issue here concerns the appropriate activity of the people of God when one or more of their number have died having committed an unwitting sin. The answer given is that the purificatory offering, which would be made if they were still alive, is still an appropriate community act.

There are, of course, many facets to this passage in the light of ancient practices and literature, such as those involving travel among the dead (see the commentary on Wisd. 17). The LXX includes examples of the redeemed people of God entering the heavenly Jerusalem (Odes 1.13). There are frequently cited references to 1 Cor. 15.29, but these are unhelpful because of the theological assumptions which on the whole guide the conclusions made, and they may indeed be irrelevant to the 2 Maccabees passage if the 1 Corinthians passage refers to the desire of individuals to be united with other individuals after death. Within the Christian context the subject has been extremely divisive, providing for some Protestants sufficient cause in itself for rejecting the Apocrypha.

From a Christian point of view, however, it is entirely appropriate for the community of the faithful to continue celebrating the redeeming work of God in Christ as relevant to all the faithful whether alive or dead. The action of Judas and his followers is parallel to that. It could be argued that the offence which Judas gives to the believer today is the linking of action in relation to the dead with a view to their reward. But again, the requiem prayers offered in many Christian communities are for 'eternal light to shine upon them', once more stressing the plural rather than the individual case, as in 2 Maccabees. As a recent writer on the subject has said: a significant proportion of Christian prayer involves our asking God to do what we believe a loving God will do anyway. That it would be possible to link a quite different understanding of prayers for the dead with 2 Maccabees is not to be disputed. But to reject the Apocrypha because of a text which, when carefully read, by no means requires such additional interpretations, is a standard which would mean the rejection of much of the canon, including, as we have just seen, 1 Corinthians.

Chapter 13

13.1 gives one of the few absolute dates in 2 Maccabees. With barbaric intent to outdo his father, Antiochus V leads an enormous army, along with Lysias, against Judas in the autumn of 163 BCE, initially with Menelaus's prompting. Menelaus's disingenuous plotting finally reaps its reward and his death is a classic case of the character of a sin becoming the means of punishment (see Wisd. 11.16). He *had desecrated the sacred ashes of the altar-fire*, and by the ashes' tower in Beroea *he met his death* (v. 8; see Lev. 10.1–3).

Judas recognizes that *law, country*, city and *temple* are at stake in the forthcoming battle, so the preparation of the Jewish army includes three days of prayer, fasting, prostration and Judas's exhortations. He decides to move out to meet Antiochus's army, and commits *the outcome to the Lord of the universe*, associating their mission with Modin, his home town (according to 1 Maccabees the inspiration of the first Maccabean rebellion), and giving the troops the watchword *Victory with God!* (vv. 13–15). The outcome is indeed little short of a miracle, and there is nothing in 1 Maccabees' parallel materials (see 1 Macc. 6.46 on the stabbing of the elephant) to corroborate such a successful, speedy victory. In a night attack by a small force, 2000 enemy troops are killed, the camp is reduced to confusion, and Judas withdraws his men before daybreak without a casualty! The Bethsura siege and the attempt to supply the garrison have different outcomes too from what we find in 1 Maccabees, so one has the impression that 2 Maccabees cannot see Judas worsted while God is his support. However, 1 and 2 Maccabees agree that the story ended with a hurried treaty and Antiochus's departure for Antioch, following due sacrifices, since (as 2 Maccabees expresses it) *Philip had made a mad bid for power* (v. 23). Hegemonides was hardly the right choice for a governor who would be expected to bring peace to a region like Ptolemais with its anti-Jewish history, and Lysias too has to struggle to win the people over. Eventually he too departs for Antioch. Perhaps 2 Maccabees is making a point that, after all, Jews and gentiles, if given a chance and with suitable leadership, can get on together.

Chapter 14

With 14.1 the six-stage sequence begins afresh, albeit with briefer stages: in 162 BCE Demetrius I lands in Tripoli; Alcimus, formerly a high priest and probably appointed by Lysias, recognizes his dangerous position caused by the overthrow of Antiochus and Lysias. It is not clear precisely what Alcimus had done to submit to *defilement*, and the term defilement may not in his case refer to particular events. It may only mean that he did not leave Jerusalem during the hellenizing process and so was not acceptable when the Temple was purified. In 161 BCE Alcimus approaches Demetrius with symbols of allegiance, and when asked in the king's council about the Jews, Alcimus names Judas as the trouble-maker and the Hasideans as his supporters (vv. 1–11). Demetrius I assigns to Nicanor the task of dealing with Judas and his army and *installing Alcimus as high priest*. The Jews remain trustful that God will assist them with an epiphany, and the battle lines are drawn. Despite an initial skirmish in which Simon *suffered a slight reverse*, the battle was never in fact joined according to 2 Maccabees. Instead Nicanor negotiated a settlement and even began to warm to Judas; and on his advice Judas settled down to married life. Alcimus, now back in Jerusalem, disapproves of this turn of events, tells the king of the settlement and charges Nicanor with appointing as a deputy someone plotting against the kingdom. The king rises to the slander and orders Nicanor to arrest Judas and send him quickly to Antioch. Nicanor looks for a way out of the dilemma and Judas, sensing a coolness in Nicanor, goes into hiding (vv. 26–30). Nicanor has then to confront the *priests . . . offering the regular sacrifices*.

He threatens to destroy the sanctuary and build there a temple to Dionysus, if they do not surrender Judas. The priests call on God to protect from defilement the Temple *so recently purified* (vv. 31–36). The time has come for loyalty to God to be demonstrated once more. The demonstration is as bloody as it is memorable: Razis, *a member of the Jerusalem senate*, known as *Father of the Jews*, is to be arrested on Nicanor's orders. He prefers to *die nobly* but fails to deliver the fatal blow, *heroically* throws himself into the crowd and, *still breathing*, dashes to *a sheer rock* and disembowels himself over the crowd. *Thus invoking him who disposes of life and breath to give them back to him again, he died* (vv. 37–46). He shares the loyalty and self-offering of the martyrs, and their role in turning events toward the deliverance of God's people.

Chapter 15

Nicanor hears that Judas and his men are in the Gophna hills northeast of Modin and plans to attack them on the sabbath. The 'thrice-sinful villain', later *a bragging blasphemer*, mocks the observance of the sabbath *made holy by the all-seeing One . . . the living Lord* who is *ruler in the sky* by claiming himself to be *ruler on earth*. Without explanation as to the reason for the failure, the report is that his outrageous plan was not successful. Either sufficient of the Jews in his force refused to participate, or the actual attitude of the Maccabees to fighting on the sabbath was incorrectly assessed (vv. 1–5). Nicanor boasts haughtily that he will set up a victor's *trophy* from the armour of Judas's dead warriors. Judas, in addition to the speech required by the Law, charges Nicanor with breaking the treaty and cheers his troops with a *waking vision worthy of belief* (or, a trustworthy dream like a waking reality: vv. 6–11). The vision concerns Onias (see 2 Macc. 3) and Jeremiah (see Jer. 50.35–37) both offering prayer for the people and the Holy City. Jeremiah presents to Judas *a golden sword* as *a gift from God* to shatter the enemy (vv. 12–16). The symbolism is common to ancient preparations for battle; the associations of priestly prayer and prophetic action are distinctively Jewish. The reaction of the troops and, when they hear of it, of those shut up in Jerusalem (v. 19), is to recognize that this is the decisive moment (vv. 17–20). As the battle order is drawn up Judas prays for deliverance such as King Hezekiah experienced: *send a good angel once again* (v. 23; see 8.19–20). In the *hand-to-hand fighting* Nicanor's army is decimated and Nicanor himself is found *lying dead in full armour* (v. 28). Judas orders his head and arm to be cut off (see 14.33 for the action of Nicanor in swearing to destroy the Temple; see also Judith 14). The action in sending for the men in the Citadel and (v. 35) the hanging of Nicanor's head from the Citadel illustrate the fictional character of the narrative (see 1 Maccabees for the occupation of the Citadel by Seleucids until Judas's death). *The godless Nicanor's tongue* is cut out and the sky rings with *the praises of the Lord who had shown his power* (vv. 33–34). So the book ends in v. 36 as it began, and as the first sequence of events ended in 10.8, with a feast of celebration. In 1 Macc. 4.59 and 2 Macc. 10 it was to be a December feast of renewal or purification; in 2 Macc. 15 it is the March celebration of Nicanor's and then Mordecai's day, when the Jews gained relief from their enemies.

If the books of Maccabees do nothing else, they alert us to the deep hurts and tragedies when minorities are crushed by their persecutors. Today, when international law can play a larger part in the redress of such minorities, the books of the Maccabees remind us that such legal redress, while crucially important, is only the beginning for those who live with the agony of what they and their families and peoples experience and the wounds they will all carry for many decades to come. It is a frightening picture of the destructive powers which are at work and which need to be understood and recognized by us all.